The
Home
Insulation
Manual

Author

Ian Alistair Rock MRICS

Technical editor

Acknowledgements

SPECIAL THANKS TO

Andy Walker at SURE Insulation; David Pickles at English Heritage; Sam Hollis & team at Green Puzzle; Nigel Griffiths – author ofHaynes Eco House Manual,; Andy Blackwell – author of Haynes Home Plumbing Manual; Peter Morgan at Kingspan; Susan Sheehan @ Hyde Farm CAN; Basil Parylo at Leeds City Council; Tony Clelford, Architect; ECD Architects; Dr Jeremy Harrall @ SEArch Architects / Greening The Box;
Tom Cullingford @ rubber4roofs Ltd; Damian Haigh @ Structherm Ltd

PHOTOGRAPHY

Ian Rock and Andy Walker except where credited, with thanks also to Andy Blackwell and Nigel Griffiths.

Thanks also to

Harvey Fremlin, David Murphy & Verdi Taylor@ NSBRC; John McKay & Mike Baker; Steve Gapic and Sarah Wright @ British Gas; Andy Clewlow and Tony Pensom @ NBT; Catherine Macintosh @ Proctor Group; Robert Prewett, Architect; Tony Clelford, Architect; Matthew Clements; Meredith Childerstone @ Selectaglaze; Green Square Group; Wetherby EWI

Published in April 2013

British Library Cataloguing in Publication Data: A catalogue record for this book is available from the British Library

ISBN 978 0 85733 275 2

Published by Haynes Publishing,
Sparkford, Yeovil, Somerset BA22 7JJ, UK
Tel: 01963 442030 Fax: 01963 440001
Int. tel: +44 1963 442030 Int. fax: +44 1963 440001
E-mail: sales@haynes.co.uk
Website: www.haynes.co.uk

Haynes North America Inc.
861 Lawrence Drive, Newbury Park, California 91320, USA

Printed in the USA by Odcombe Press LP,
1299 Bridgestone Parkway, La Vergne, TN 37086

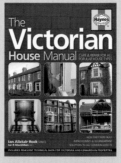

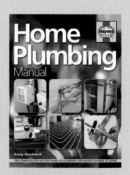

CONTENTS

1 BEFORE YOU START

Photo: Dow Insulation

KEY TO HAMMER RATINGS

Easy, suitable for novice with little experience

Fairly easy, suitable for beginner with some experience

Fairly difficult, suitable for competent DIY

Difficult, suitable for experienced DIY or professional installers

Very difficult, suitable for professional installers or expert DIY

The Victorian Terrace Project by BRE proved that old buildings can be retro-fitted to match or exceed newbuild thermal efficiency standards

The benefits of insulating

- ◼ A warmer home in the colder seasons.
- ◼ Reduced fuel bills (over 60% of domestic energy consumed is for space heating).
- ◼ Reduced condensation, damp and mould.
- ◼ Greater comfort with fewer draughts.
- ◼ A cooler home in hotter summer months.
- ◼ Improved EPC rating to qualify for grants and add value.
- ◼ A more eco-friendly building.

In chilly, overcast Britain, there are two major benefits to insulating our homes – lower energy bills and improved comfort. Paying to warm up the sky is an expensive luxury, so it makes sense to stem the leakage of all that valuable heat by wrapping your home in a giant 'tea cosy'.

But keeping warm in winter isn't the only problem. You only have to step into the average conservatory baking in the hot summer sun to witness the stifling effects of a lack of thermal insulation. In fact, the problem of how to keep cool in tropical climes was solved centuries ago. Plantation houses in the West Indies are notable for the coolness of their rooms even on the most sweltering days thanks to thick masonry walls combined with the intelligent exploitation of natural shading and breezes. This is the other side of the same coin that we face in colder countries when it comes to making our homes cosier and cheaper to run.

Why insulate?

Not so many years ago, when most of our current housing stock was built, there was little understanding of how buildings performed thermally. Houses merrily leaked heat and no one paid much attention to running costs. But the cost of heating an uninsulated home is nearly three times that of heating a modern well-insulated property of the same size. So today, all new dwellings have to meet increasingly ambitious energy-efficient standards. But to really make a difference at a national level we need to take action to insulate the existing housing stock of over 26 million homes. If only we could see clouds of £20 notes floating out of our walls, windows and roofs, we'd waste no time in plugging the gaps through which they're escaping.

As energy bills have rocketed in recent years, awareness has grown of the shocking extent of heat leakage. But there are other compelling reasons why investing time and money insulating your home is worthwhile. For one thing, properties are increasingly rated on the basis of their energy performance. There's also the comforting thought that with your carbon footprint reduced down to the size of a pea, you're doing your bit to beat climate change.

insulation is sexy

energysavvy.com

You could even go the extra eco-mile and invest in renewable energy. But before spending money on generating power, it's obviously sensible to take steps to ensure it doesn't all leak away.

By insulating your home to super-high levels, the heating may need to be turned on only in extreme cold spells, perhaps only for a few days a year – which may be why Barrack Obama famously declared 'Insulation is Sexy'!

Energy performance

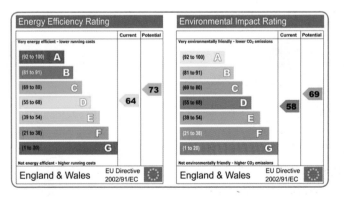

By law all residential properties being sold or rented must have an Energy Performance Certificate (EPC). These remain valid for ten years and measure the energy efficiency of buildings, from super-snug 'A' down to decidedly chilly 'G'. At the present time the average UK home only scores a less than impressive 'D'.

This is something that currently comes into play when selling

Heat loss

The heat loss attributed to different parts of a typical property's envelope is widely quoted as shown below, but in practice much will depend on the age, type and location of the property, and the extent to which it's already been insulated:

- Walls 35% (up to 45% in homes with solid walls).
- Roof 25%.
- Floor 15%.
- Doors and draughts 15%.
- Windows 10%.

or letting your home, but increasingly the government is gearing financial incentives towards properties with higher ratings. For example, to qualify for solar PV Feed-in Tariff payments, properties need to achieve a rating of 'D' or higher. In future Council Tax bills are likely to be geared to energy ratings, and these sort of targets will become increasingly stringent in the years ahead.

For landlords, tax allowances can already be claimed on a range of improvements under the LESA scheme (Landlords Energy Saving Allowance). From 2016 landlords will be legally obliged to give consent when tenants request energy efficiency improvements to their properties. Non-compliance will result in hefty fines. And from 2018 it will be unlawful to rent out any property scoring lower than an 'E' rating.

In the following chapters we flag up the correct approach for boosting the energy ratings for different types of property and highlight potential pitfalls.

Key questions

The right solution for your property will depend on a number of factors. So before setting about the task of insulating your home, there are ten important questions to consider:

1 CAN MY HOME BE MADE WARM AND COMFORTABLE?

For many homeowners banishing cold, draughty rooms and associated problems of damp and mould is probably more important than calculating longer-term financial payback. The good news is that nearly all existing homes can be upgraded to achieve significantly improved levels of heat retention and increased comfort. Importantly, this can often translate into improvements in health and general wellbeing.

2 HOW MUCH MONEY WILL I SAVE?

When it comes to forking out hard cash, insulating can sometimes seem like a less glamorous option than, say, refitting the kitchen. But stemming the flood of expensively generated heat seeping out of the house means this is one of the few home improvements that will actually reward you by paying money back with significant savings in your bills. This is just as well, because for most of us the noble aim of reducing our carbon footprint probably isn't by itself likely to provide sufficient incentive to spur us into action. Unless you're a deeply committed Greenie, the thought of gloating over minuscule future energy bills in a warm and comfortable home is probably a more persuasive call to arms than cutting carbon emissions.

Of course, not all insulation works immediately reward you with large financial savings. Some, such as loft and cavity wall insulation, are relatively inexpensive and pay back swiftly. These 'quick and easy' upgrades are the low-hanging fruit of the insulation world. But some improvements reward you in less obvious ways. For example, by lining your walls you should reap longer-term savings in maintenance, because they won't need decorating or re-plastering for many years. And done well, external insulation can transform the kerb appeal, and hence the value, of some blander-looking properties.

3 WILL I NEED PLANNING PERMISSION?

Most of the work described in this book isn't likely to bother the planners. Indeed they'd probably welcome your good intentions. Even insulating walls on the outside is now classed as 'Permitted Development' and in most cases shouldn't require planning permission, although major changes such as raising the height of the roof will still need approval.

However when it comes to Listed properties, even fairly minor alterations, both internally and externally, will need Listed building consent. And in Conservation Areas, anything visible to the 'principle elevation' (normally the front) will need consent, but other works that can't be spotted from the street are usually OK, subject to normal planning laws. But it's always best to check first.

4 WHAT ABOUT BUILDING REGULATIONS?

Part L1B of the Building Regulations deals with upgrading existing dwellings to conserve fuel and power. This covers more than you might imagine, including:

- Thermal elements: walls, roofs and floors.
- Controlled fittings: windows, roof windows and external doors.
- Controlled services: ventilation, heating, hot water and fixed lighting.

A 'thermal element' simply means any part of the building's external 'envelope' – ie the walls, roof and floors. Where these are due to be renovated or replaced, minimum insulation standards will apply. See page 18.

For example, when you're replacing a knackered old felt covering to a flat roof the Building Regs stipulate that you must also upgrade the insulation as part of the job.

Similarly, maximum permitted heat loss standards apply where windows and external doors are replaced. Approval for such 'controlled work' can either be obtained directly by making an application to Building Control, or, more often, the compliance of such 'controlled fittings' is 'self-certified' by the installers.

In the following chapters we explain whether you need to notify Building Control for each specific project, and the minimum targets that need to be achieved when 'retro-fitting' insulation.

5 CAN I STILL LIVE THERE?

Retro-insulating a property normally means having to plan things very carefully so that life can go on around the works, unless of course you temporarily vacate the building. One of the things that sometimes puts people off insulating their homes is the thought of having to move lots of heavy furniture and accumulated possessions.

It's essential to assess in advance how much disruption and disturbance the job is likely to cause, and how long it's likely to take to complete. With some improvements you'll hardly notice they're happening – such as insulating cavity walls. Others can be noisy or intrusive for a short time, and you may have to temporarily vacate the individual room being upgraded. But then a couple of weeks' disturbance is a price worth paying for a major 'once in a lifetime' improvement that, unlike fitted kitchens and bathrooms, won't need redoing in a few years simply because it's become unfashionable.

If you live in a flat, as a Leaseholder you'll need to notify the Freeholder (or managing agent) and in some cases obtain their prior consent. If you're a landlord, then carrying out all but the simplest works with tenants living there is obviously a recipe for trouble. Better to synchronise the works with void periods between lettings or to coincide with tenants' holidays.

6 HOW IMPORTANT IS THE CONDITION OF THE BUILDING?

It's sometimes said that 'a wet building is a cold building'. This is because some materials have a nasty habit of losing their power to insulate if they get damp. In terms of thermal performance, wet insulation is about as effective as a piece of limp lettuce stapled to the wall. So there's no point spending money lining lofts, floors and walls if there's any risk of damp. The first step should therefore always be to ensure that the existing building structure is performing as intended and keeping the weather at bay, which means carrying out a simple survey of the building's physical condition and rectifying any defects.

Assessing the building's level of exposure to wind-driven rain

Damp checks

Common defects that can allow damp to enter a building and make insulation soggy and useless are:

- Flashings at junctions to roofs and chimneys.
- Uncapped pots to open chimneys.
- Badly eroded mortar joints to brick or stonework in walls.
- Leaking gutters, downpipes and overflow pipes.
- Leaks around windows and door frames.
- Windowsills that don't project out from the wall sufficiently, or have eroded drip grooves underneath.
- Garden shrubs or mounds of earth banked up against walls.
- A lack of ventilation indoors allowing a build-up of condensation from steamy kitchens and bathrooms.

is important when planning your insulation strategy because some insulation materials are better suited to dealing with harsh environments. For example, some types of cavity wall insulation aren't permitted in severe weather zones.

7 WHAT SORT OF BUILDING IS IT?

There are numerous types of insulation and many methods of applying it. The right choice starts with identifying the age and type of property that you're dealing with. Although the majority of homes in Britain are of conventional cavity masonry construction, there's a wide variety of other construction types, so it's essential to know what you're dealing with before steaming ahead. Get this wrong and you could end up causing serious damage. See page 12.

8 IS DIY A REALISTIC OPTION?

Some tasks are relatively simple and should hold no great terrors for the average DIYer – for example, loft insulation, or lagging tanks and pipework. Draughtproofing is another project that most of us can tackle with a fair degree of confidence. But there's a right way and a wrong way to go about even these simpler tasks, as explained in the following chapters. In classic Haynes Manual style, each project is rated in terms of difficulty with the well known 'spanner rating' – or in this case 'hammer rating'.

Lining solid walls internally can be a more complex operation than it might first appear, because of the necessary disruption to skirtings, radiators, pipework, electric sockets, coving and window

Project management

Major refurbishment work often involves coordinating several jobs, such as external wall insulation combined with re-roofing or window replacement. In such cases it can be worth appointing an architect or building surveyor who can:

- Draw up a programme of works designed to minimise disturbance to occupants.
- Produce a budget and breakdown of costings.
- Organise planning applications and liaise with Building Control.
- Prepare drawings and specifications for builders to price from, and for the Building Regs application.
- Invite quotes or tender the work to an agreed list of contractors.
- Project manage and administer the contract, including site visits.

Insulating a flat roof

Photo: EcoTherm Insulation

joiners or plasterers who specialise in dry-lining. However, contractors are increasingly specialising in projects such as external wall cladding, cavity wall insulation and loft insulation. Firms providing internal wall lining and floor insulation services are a little harder to track down. But one thing all professional installers should have in common is that before doing anything they thoroughly assess the property to make sure it's suitable.

reveals. So unless you're a confident DIYer this may best be carried out by a specialist contractor. Similarly, insulating floors is likely to involve a lot of associated upheaval to doors and plumbing etc, and requires careful planning and not a little expertise.

DIY-ing for it?

The potential for undertaking a project yourself will depend on two main things – the complexity of the property and how accomplished and skilled a DIYer you are, but the following is a rough guide:

- **DIY-friendly**
Loft insulation, lagging tanks, pipework and hot water cylinders, draughtproofing.

- **Advanced DIY or specialist firms**
Floor insulation and internal wall lining.

- **Employ specialists**
External wall cladding and cavity wall insulation.

Cladding walls externally is best left to professional firms, as is cavity wall insulation, which requires specialist equipment. However, that doesn't mean that installers always get things right, as we shall see in the chapters ahead.

9 WHAT PROFESSIONALS MIGHT I NEED TO EMPLOY?

Traditionally there's no such trade as 'the Insulator'. So on newbuild construction sites this is a job that sometimes gets passed to anyone in possession of a functioning pair of hands. The trouble is that not everyone has the necessary skills or knowledge, so inevitably things sometimes get skimped. Similarly, when it comes to upgrading existing homes there are plenty of things to get wrong if you don't know what you're doing, even with simpler tasks like insulating lofts. More demanding projects, like lining walls, need to be done with precision because if any small gaps are left it can encourage hidden damp problems to develop.

So the trades best suited to fitting insulation are probably

10 HOW AM I GOING TO PAY FOR IT?

Of course, we'd all like homes that are snugger with lower running costs. But what's the best way to fund these improvements? Splashing your own cash is more appealing when the savings

Specialist Installers

- **Solid wall lining**
Contractors should be accredited by SWIGA (Solid Wall Insulation Guarantee Agency), who provide a warranty. Cladding walls externally usually involves specialist technologies, so look for firms who are members of INCA (the Insulated Render and Cladding Association).

- **Cavity wall insulation**
Specialist installers should be members of the Cavity Wall Guarantee Agency (CWGA) and provide a 25-year CIGA guarantee (*Cavity Insulation Guarantee Agency*).

- **Windows**
Replacement windows should be installed by a company registered with Fenestration Self-Assessment (FENSA), who will be able to 'self-certify' the compliance of the works for Building Regs (not required where only the glass is being replaced).

- **Competent persons**
Over the years the Building Regulations have extended their reach so that a surprisingly wide range of work now requires consent, including things like window installations, electrical work, gas installations and much roofing work. But because Building Control have limited resources, to make this manageable it's sub-contracted to 'competent persons', normally the same people carrying out the work. You can check whether a contractor holds the appropriate degree of competency by visiting **www.competent-person.co.uk**.

Left and right: To insulate successfully can require the skills of a joiner - accurate measuring and cutting to fine tolerances

directly generated by the insulation work will pay back the original outlay within the space of a few short years; then you can look forward to pure profit in the form of annual savings in running costs.

Payback

The payback period is the amount of time it takes for the cost of an energy-saving measure to repay the homeowner by means of reduced fuel bills. For example, if every £1,000 spent on internal wall insulation results in savings of £50 per year, the simple payback period would be 20 years, equivalent to 5% net return (better than most savings accounts). This, of course, doesn't factor in possible savings in future maintenance, or value added to the property, nor does it include interest that could otherwise have been earned on your money. Nonetheless, it can be a useful guide. It's also worth bearing in mind that as energy prices inexorably rise in future, payback periods should continue to shorten.

The Green Deal

The Green Deal allows homeowners or tenants to have energy efficiency improvements made to their homes with no upfront costs. Instead, energy suppliers fund the works and then claim back the costs from a surcharge levied on future bills over a period of years. As a result, your energy bills, which would otherwise be lower thanks to the insulation works, will remain at a higher level until the loan has eventually been repaid (the maximum loan term is 25 years). The loan is like a mini mortgage that stays with the property, not the homeowner, so you're free to sell your house and move on in the meantime should you wish to.

The fact that there are no upfront costs is very appealing, but it's important to calculate the total cost of finance over the years ahead. Should you wish to sell your beautifully insulated home before the loan has been paid back, potential buyers will need to accept the fact that it won't yet reap the reward of lower fuel bills.

Who runs it?

There are three main players in the Green Deal. The customer selects the provider and installer of their choice:

1 The provider

- Offers a plan to customers, including finance.
- Has a contract with the customer and maintains overall responsibility for the work.
- Is licensed under the Credit Agreement Act.

2 The adviser

- Carries out a physical assessment of the house.
- Draws up a Green Deal Plan outlining all recommended measures (must meet the 'golden rule' – see below).

3 The installer

- Carries out work in the Green Deal Plan.

The golden rule

To safeguard customers, the *expected* financial savings (from energy bills over a period of years) resulting from the improvement works must be greater than the costs attached to the energy bill (*ie* the cost of installation work and finance). However, this also means there's a downside – some very worthwhile works may not qualify, such as solid wall insulation. There's also a maximum total budget of £10,000 allocated per property, although this may not stretch very far once you include things like new boilers (but homeowners are free to contribute additional money). However, the projected savings resulting from the works is only a theoretical figure – there's no comeback if it actually turns out that you're not saving as much as was calculated.

On the plus side, a reduced VAT rate of only 5% should apply to all approved works, helping to lower the total cost. However, in order to qualify, the measures must be carried out by an accredited installer, which prevents DIY enthusiasts participating in the scheme – although the DIY route may still work out a lot cheaper in the long run.

Sales-driven advice?

One reason for writing this manual is because insulation is a more complex subject than it may at first seem. And as with all advice dispensed where there are associated sales incentives, it's as well to do your homework first. The optimum solution for one property isn't necessarily right for others. Advice based on computer-generated EPCs may not go into enough depth for some older or non-standard types of property, and there's a danger that less well-known natural insulation materials may get sidelined. The best advice should focus on 'fabric-first' improvements, rather than a bias towards things like renewable energy generation.

For updated information see **www.decc.gov.uk.**

The ideal improvement is something that's relatively cheap and easy to do, which makes an immediate difference to heating costs, the classic example being loft insulation. But that doesn't mean that projects with longer paybacks aren't worth doing. For example, double glazing is one of the most popular home improvements in the UK, but can take as long as 90 years to pay for itself simply in terms of direct savings in energy bills. The enduring appeal of some less cost-effective improvements may be down to the fact that they offer important benefits such as significantly boosting comfort levels, and making your home less prone to condensation.

Incentives

There's one thing that makes any sort of home improvement considerably more attractive – someone else offering to pay for it. And making your home more eco-friendly could, with a bit of luck, qualify for some large dollops of cash to help fund the work, courtesy of HM Government.

From time to time alternative sources of funding pop up, such as local authority grant schemes. But most 'strings-free' money tends to be targeted at qualifying households, perhaps contingent upon being within a specific age or income group.

As part of the Green Deal (see panel) the Energy Company Obligation (ECO) requires suppliers to provide assistance to low income households and hard-to-treat properties, so this may be worth investigating. Although government-funded loft and cavity wall insulation works have on occasion been provided free for senior citizens, sources of state funding are as fickle as MPs' election pledges, changing with the whims of capricious governments, so the best advice is to check the Energy Saving Trust's database at **Energysavingtrust.org.uk**.

DIY funding

If you want to build an extension, or refit your kitchen or bathroom, you'd normally expect to fund it yourself, perhaps adding a bit to the mortgage. Mortgages are by far the cheapest and best way to borrow money, so when you compare the cost of this with Green Deal funding it may work out considerably cheaper in the longer term. When you factor in future savings from lower fuel bills, plus the enhanced value of your home, self-funding will be the best option in some cases. And when you eventually decide to move house there'll be no awkward explanations to cynical buyers about them being stuck with higher fuel bills for years on end to pay back an old loan.

External wall insulation being installed to solid-walled terraced houses

Photo: British Gas

Planning your campaign

In an ideal world, the whole of your home would be refurbished all in one go. This would be the swiftest and most efficient approach, with impressive results evident in the space of a couple of weeks. But in reality few of us have the luxury of being able to vacate our homes or have access to piles of ready cash to pay for it all. The exception is perhaps where you're buying a house to 'do up' and can live elsewhere for a few weeks to avoid the dust and mess. Otherwise trying to refurbish the whole building whilst remaining in occupation probably isn't advisable – unless you don't mind making yourself deeply unpopular with your fellow residents.

Of course, there are some improvements that can be done one at a time whenever the fancy takes you, such as insulating the loft or having cavity walls injected. Others can be done on a room-by-room basis, such as internally insulating walls and timber floors. But other more disruptive improvements are best done as part of a major refurbishment.

The smart approach is therefore to plan your campaign by drawing up a master plan. This should identify where major insulation works can be 'piggy-backed' on other improvements that were due to be carried out anyway, helping to share the cost and minimise disruption. So, for example, when you're next planning to redecorate it can make sense to carry out wall insulation at the same time. Planning ahead can also help achieve a better quality result technically. For example, combining scheduled window replacement with wall insulation works can help integrate the two, eliminating the risk of gaps being left causing 'cold spots'. Some other improvements may require prior enabling work to be carried out, notably external wall cladding. So if the main roof is due to be re-clad any time soon, the opportunity should be taken to extend the overhang of the rafters in preparation for the later addition of wall insulation.

DRAWING UP A MASTER PLAN

As well as scheduling the less disruptive works, a master plan can help identify future opportunities likely to arise that could facilitate more complex projects.

Easy options

These are improvements that are relatively inexpensive and aren't too disruptive. They can be done on a one-off basis when it suits you, using materials that are readily available from DIY stores (eg draughtproofing).

Golden opportunities

To identify opportunities that are likely to arise for upgrading insulation, start by making a list of future improvements you plan to carry out to the house over a number of years. Then try to match these to major insulation projects, such as lining solid walls, and coordinate them with the availability of funding.

Opportunities for improving the thermal efficiency of our homes can arise for many reasons, for example when worn-out windows or boilers are due to be replaced or if you plan to extend the house or convert the loft.

It's also a good idea to draw a scale plan of the individual rooms to be insulated. This helps highlight any potential loss of room space due to lining internal walls, fitting new suspended ceilings or raising floor heights. It's particularly important that small spaces such as cloakrooms and bathrooms can still function once internal insulation is added.

A similar calculation can be done for walls to be clad externally, *eg* where a wall is close to a boundary there needs to be sufficient access to do the job. Where space is tight, you also need to consider how much room will be left after insulating once the walls are thicker and project further out – if a wall over-sails your boundary, it will have legal implications.

Narrow side access with complex external services can restrict options for insulating walls externally

Photo: ECD Architects

Exploiting opportunities

Planned works	Insulation projects
Internal decoration. Re-plastering walls. Refitting kitchens. Refitting bathrooms and cloakrooms etc.	Internal wall insulation.
Rendering external walls.	External wall insulation.
Re-roofing.	Roof or loft insulation. If external wall cladding is planned, prepare the way by extending the roof at eaves level.
Replacement windows.	Specify high-performance windows and combine with wall insulation works.
Replacing old hot water cylinder.	Specify a twin-coil (or triple-coil) cylinder ready for the later installation of solar water heating.
Replacing worn-out boiler.	Specify 'A'-rated high-efficiency replacement.

Other energy efficiency measures

This book focuses primarily on how to prevent heat leaking out of your house. But the full savings from improved insulation will only be realised if heating controls are sufficiently responsive to adjust and turn down the heating where necessary. So upgrading heating systems and controls will also help cut running costs, as will fitting more efficient lighting – see Chapter 9.

Lifestyles

As the people who use the building, we have a key role to play. You can have the most energy-efficient building in the world, but if the lights are left on 24/7, or the heating turned up to max

with the windows left open in winter, you may as well have saved your money, because your bills will remain high. So it's as well to get into the habit of not leaving windows and doors open and if possible keeping the heating turned down a little lower, and remembering to switch lights off.

Lining the walls externally can transform the appeal of a property – but is not always feasible.

Photos: SEArch Architects

Website

Useful links and updates can be found on the book's website: **www.homeinsulating.co.uk**

Left: Looks like a conventional Edwardian house – but walls are of early cavity construction

Right: Looks like concrete construction – but the walls are rendered masonry

Original walls of solid stone, with extensions in stone-faced cavity blockwork

Typical heat leakage in UK homes

The amount of energy lost through the walls of our homes depends to a large extent on their age. As a rule of thumb, the more modern your home, the less heat it should leak.

Typical U-values for walls

Victorian solid wall, one brick thick (229mm).
   2.1W/m²K

1930s cavity wall, both leaves 100mm brick + 50mm cavity.
   1.8W/m²K

1970s cavity wall, brick and lightweight block, both 100mm + 70mm cavity.
   1.00W/m²K

1990s cavity wall, 100mm brick outer leaf, 50mm cavity batts, 100mm aerated block inner leaf.
   0.45W/m²K

2010 – cavity wall 330mm thick comprising 100mm brick outer leaf, 100mm part-insulated cavity and 100mm aerated block inner leaf, plus dry-lined; insulated plasterboard will achieve lower U-values.
0.25W/m²K (0.15W/m²K is achievable)

What type of property have you got?

Correctly identifying the type of construction is fundamental to specifying the right sort of insulation that will work in harmony with the property. Get this wrong and your improvement works could actually be setting-up serious problems for the future. A good place to start is with a copy of the survey from the time you bought your home. This should give some idea of both the age and the type of construction.

Just to make things more interesting, the older a property is the more likely it is that it'll have sprouted all manner of extensions and additions over the years. Many period houses comprise a mix of older solid walls and more recent cavity construction, topped off with a combination of pitched and flat roofs. So you may need to design different solutions appropriate for different parts of the home.

A building's energy efficiency and potential for improvement will depend to a large extent on its age. Until the 1930s, most homes were built with solid masonry walls and single-glazed windows. Since then most domestic buildings have been constructed with cavity walls, which are generally easier to insulate.

Insulating new homes as part of the construction process is a comparatively recent idea. Although energy efficiency standards made an appearance in the Building Regulations in the early 1980s, targets for overall thermal performance for dwellings weren't introduced until 1995. Subsequently standards were raised in 2002, 2006, 2010 and 2013, with further changes planned for 2016.

Looks like modern cavity masonry – but is actually timber frame construction

Meanwhile, the levels of insulation in existing housing have steadily improved, with varying amounts of loft and cavity wall insulation installed and many old single-glazed windows replaced by double-glazing. Major strides have been made with boiler efficiencies, from 65% or less in the 1970s to around 90% for new condensing boilers today. But in the vast majority of homes there's considerable scope for improvement.

Today, a typical semi-detached house of 90m² floor area, with an average amount of insulation and gas-fired central heating, uses approximately 25,900 kWh of energy per year for heating, hot water, cooking, lighting and appliances. This translates in terms of fuel costs to approximately £1,400 per year (including 5% VAT). As we shall see, by carrying out the improvements illustrated in this book you can reduce this by 75% or more.

House spotting

SOLID BRICK WALLS

Traditional solid walls are found on older properties built prior to the 1930s when cavity wall construction started appearing in mainstream housing. They're typically about 230mm thick (doorways are the simplest place to measure wall thicknesses). Solid walls are identifiable from the pattern of brickwork – the most common style being 'Flemish bond' with one brick laid sideways ('stretcher') and the next brick laid across the wall with only its head visible ('header'). Traditional solid stone walls are generally far thicker, often half a metre or more.

CAVITY WALLS

Modern cavity walls comprise two single parallel walls or 'leaves' built in 'stretcher' bond, with all the bricks laid sideways to the outer leaf. The inner leaves are generally made from concrete blocks, although pre-1950 cavity walls often had brickwork inner leaves. Walls of cavity construction have slowly increased in thickness over time, from around 250mm to over 300mm.

SINGLE THICKNESS WALLS

Cheaply built additions of substandard construction are fairly common on some smaller Victorian terraced houses. There's a potential trap here, because being single leaf these can appear to be of modern cavity stretcher bond, but a closer inspection may reveal that they're only one brick thick – of a very meagre 115mm wall thickness. To make it harder to spot any clues, the brickwork's often concealed behind a coat of render. This is an inferior form of construction that can be structurally unstable if more than one storey high, and being very thin will be cold and extremely prone to condensation. Major insulation work will be necessary – or even complete rebuilding.

MODERN TIMBER FRAME

Identifying the type of construction can be especially tricky when it comes to modern timber-frame houses. Here the inner leaf of the cavity walls is made from load-bearing timber panels that are pre-insulated (hence these properties perform relatively well in retaining warmth). But because the outer leaf is of conventional construction (usually stretcher bond brickwork), to all intents and purposes they can appear to be standard masonry cavity walls. These present a potential risk because the walls in timber frame houses aren't meant to be injected with insulation, because they rely on clear, well-ventilated cavities to disperse moisture. See page 41.

Cut away of modern timber frame wall with pre-insulated panelled inner leaf visible

Above: BISF steel frame

PERIOD TIMBER FRAME

Traditional 'Shakespearian' houses built around a load-bearing timber skeleton sometimes adopt cunning disguises. Although most properties of this genre feature walls of oak posts and beams infilled with creamy wattle and daub or brickwork, many were re-fronted in the Georgian era with fashionable stone or brick facades. Others may have fully rendered walls that even surveyors sometimes mistake for solid masonry. Some are clad with timber weatherboarding, or are tile hung (some with special tiles designed to impersonate bricks!). Timber frame walls can be surprisingly slender, often as thin as 115mm. The best advice is to treat all period properties as needing to 'breathe'– which normally means using natural insulation materials. See page 23.

CONCRETE AND STEEL FRAME

The post-war period saw a wide range of unorthodox construction types spring up. Mostly were built by Local Authorities in the 1950s as the bigger brothers of temporary 'prefabs', although high-rise blocks with panel walls and concrete frames continued to be erected well into the 1970s. There are several weird and wonderful varieties of pre-reinforced concrete (PRC) construction, with names like Airey, Cornish, Woolwaway, Unity, Hawkesley, Howland and Reema Hollow Panel. The two main types of houses with walls made from poured concrete are 'Laing Easiform' and 'Wimpey No Fines'.

Below and below right: 'Laing Easiform' poured concrete construction – with distinctive wall vent pattern

Large numbers of steel-frame homes were also built. The most common type are known as 'BISF' (British Iron & Steel Federation), with thin walls clad with metal sheathing and render, and steel-frame roofs clad with asbestos cement sheeting. Many such homes have since been designated 'unmortgageable' unless professionally upgraded – which normally involves re-cladding them externally.

Traditional buildings

Britain has a wide variety of traditional house types built with a enormously diverse range of natural materials – from mud and thatch to timber and stone. These all tend to be lumped together under the term 'traditional construction' – *ie* buildings with solid walls, mostly constructed up until the early 20th century.

Contrary to popular opinion, many such older houses can perform very well in terms of energy use. Those built with thick stone walls and relatively small windows can stay warmer in winter and cooler in summer than many modern houses. And because a lot of period properties are terraced, it means they find it easier to keep warm as there are fewer exterior walls through which heat can be lost.

Traditional building materials also tend to be more durable, and considerably more sustainable, than their modern counterparts. For example, the quality of timber used in traditional windows was far superior to modern timber, and can have an almost indefinite life if regularly painted.

Above left: 'Airey' concrete construction (PRC)

Above: 'Cornish' PRC construction

Left: 'Unity' PRC terraces – mostly re-clad in brick

How old houses work

Before fitting insulation on old houses it's important to understand that they work in a totally different way from modern buildings.

Breathability

Before the days of cavity walls, houses had solid walls built of naturally porous materials, such as brick and stone, bonded together with relatively weak mortars. When it rained, moisture was absorbed into the external surface but was free to evaporate out again once the rain stopped, helped by the drying effects of the wind and sun. This natural cycle is known as 'breathing'.

On the inside there was a similar process in operation. The walls were coated with lime plaster and decorated with natural paints. Any excess humidity from activities such as cooking and washing was swiftly dispersed thanks to effective air circulation helped by draughts and fireplace flues, or else temporarily absorbed into porous wall surfaces.

Modern cavity wall buildings work very differently, by forming a rigid barrier against moisture, relying on impervious outer layers that block it out. The building is effectively sealed inside a skin of hard masonry, tough cement and plastic paints and renders. Impervious materials are designed to prevent moisture entering the building in the first place, rather than relying on a natural 'breathing' cycle of absorption and evaporation.

Flexibility

Old houses have relatively shallow foundations, which means they tend to move in tune with seasonal ground changes. Because traditional materials such as brick, stone and soft lime mortar are relatively flexible they can accommodate small amounts of movement without cracking.

In contrast, modern homes have deeper concrete foundations designed to inhibit even the slightest movement. This permits the use of strong modern bricks, hard inflexible cement and impervious paints which would otherwise crack with even small degrees of movement.

Conflict

Problems begin when these two very different philosophies get mixed up and modern materials are applied to old houses. Whereas traditional lime mortars and renders had sufficient flexibility to cope with natural movement, modern cement-based materials simply can't tolerate it. The resulting cracking in re-pointed or cement-rendered walls then allows rain to penetrate. But instead of letting it naturally escape by evaporation via lime mortar joints, the hard cement traps it. Modern paints

add to the problem by sealing in damp. Internally, moisture from condensation also needs to be allowed to disperse, something that well-ventilated old houses managed very ably.

Today, however, many old houses have suffered from well-intentioned repairs that have unwittingly destroyed their natural breathing cycle, resulting in damp problems, eroded masonry and decayed timber.

Fortunately, when it comes to improving thermal efficiency there are a number of compatible natural insulation materials that are well suited for use on traditional buildings.

The issue of maintaining breathability is of most importance to external wall surfaces, since they're fully exposed to the elements. With many Victorian and Edwardian houses, the original lime plaster has been replaced internally with modern non-breathable gypsum plasters or sealed with modern paints. By the same token, as long as walls are dry, it can be acceptable to line the indoor faces of the main walls using modern non-breathable materials such as PIR boards, which are one of the most effective insulators. If properly installed, this can actually have the beneficial effect of barring any airborne humidity from penetrating through the insulation into the wall. For pre-Victorian properties, however, or those with a history of dampness, natural breathable materials are preferable to both internal and external wall faces.

Victorian and Edwardian

Victorian and Edwardian solid-walled houses constitute a significant proportion of existing UK housing (21% of housing stock was built before 1919). Once fully insulated, such traditional houses can achieve at least 42% reduction in energy consumption. This involves making the improvements listed below. The best possible 83% reduction can be achieved by implementing a range of higher specification measures.

Thermal element	Possible solution
Roofs: pitched, slate-clad	300mm or deeper mineral wool quilt to loft.
Main walls: 230mm (9in) solid	100mm PIR insulation board to external or internal walls.
Floors: suspended timber	200mm depth of mineral wool between joists.
Windows: timber sliding sashes	Double or secondary glazing with low E coating and argon fill.
Heating and lighting	New condensing combi boiler (90% efficient). New programmer, thermostat and TRVs. Low energy light bulbs throughout.

2 HOW INSULATION WORKS

The job description for a piece of thermal insulation is pretty straightforward: it has to act as a barrier to the transfer of heat. By blocking warmth from passing, the amount of heat lost from your house in the winter months is reduced, thereby maintaining a warmer atmosphere indoors. In summer, the process swings into reverse, keeping rooms comfortably cool by reducing the amount of 'solar gain' getting into the building.

Thermal imaging: 'warm' colours – red, orange & yellow – depict loss at night. Note predominant 'cold' colours once insluated (below)

There are many different types of insulation, some natural, others highly processed – everything from recycled denim jeans and old bottles to blocks of *styrofoam* – a close relative of squeaky white polystyrene packaging material. Natural insulation materials are either plant based (*eg* hemp and cotton) or animal sourced (*eg* sheep's wool). Minerals are used to produce rock wool and stone wool, and metal is a key ingredient in 'radiant heat barriers'. But in terms of sheer performance, some of the most effective insulators, such as polyurethane, are those derived from petrochemical sources.

Most types of insulation work on the same principle – that still air is a poor conductor of heat – so trapping thousands of tiny

bubbles of air inside lightweight, bulky materials creates a very effective heat-barrier. Performance can be boosted further if gases known as 'blowing agents' are embedded in the material instead of air. Other products employ reflective materials to direct heat back into the building, or combine the benefits of both systems.

Optimum performance

Depending on the property, insulation can be used to line the inside or outside surfaces of walls and roofs or is sometimes pumped into voids inside the existing structure. But wherever it's placed, there are three key dangers to guard against during installation, otherwise performance of the insulating material can be seriously affected:

1 MINIMISE AIR MOVEMENT
If insulation is exposed to even small gusts of wind it can suffer from the effects of 'thermal bypass'. Like blowing on your hot cup of tea to cool it down, in effect this amounts to the theft of valuable heat by currents of air swirling across the surface of the insulation. Such problems typically occur where cold draughts are able to circulate between joints in poorly installed insulation.

2 KEEP IT DRY
As we saw earlier, once insulation becomes limp and soggy its effectiveness can be massively reduced. This is rather like exhaling warm breath through a woolly scarf in winter – the scarf becomes wet and cold as your breath condenses. Wool quilts and fluffy loose-fill types of insulation materials are generally most vulnerable, although even a film of moisture clinging to the surface of rigid boards etc will reduce their performance. Hence the importance of checking the building is fully weathertight before you start.

3 SEAL THE GAPS
Gaps left in the insulation will significantly compromise performance. Cracks and gaps tend to attract humid indoor air, and once this finds its way through it has a nasty habit of condensing, causing damp inside the structure of the building.

U-values
The Building Regulations set performance targets not just for new homes, but also for upgrading existing properties. Targets are expressed in 'U-values'. These describe the amount of heat leakage (measured in Watts) transmitted through one square metre of a wall or roof etc (taking into account air temperature differences between the inside and outside). The lower the figure, the less heat should escape. U-values are expressed in W/m^2K – that is Watts per square metre for each degree of difference between indoor and outdoor air temperatures. So if the walls have a stated U-value of $0.30W/m^2K$ it means that 0.30W of heat can pass through each square metre of wall for every degree of temperature difference. This is a useful way to compare performance: for example, a wall with a relatively poor U-value of 1.0 will lose heat twice as fast as a wall with a U-value of $0.5W/m^2K$.

Approximated U-values for typical domestic construction	
Construction	**U-value (W/m²K)**
Walls	
Solid brickwork (225mm uninsulated)	2.30
Cavity (brick + dense block, unfilled	1.60
Cavity (brick + lightweight block, unfilled)	1.00
Cavity (brick + dense block, filled)	0.52
Cavity (brick + lightweight block, filled)	0.30
Modern timber frame or masonry wall	0.25
Superinsulated wall	0.15
Roofs	
No insulation	2.30
100mm loft insulation	0.40
150mm loft insulation	0.29
200mm loft insulation	0.20
270mm loft insulation	0.16
Floors	
Solid ground floor (uninsulated)	1.00
Suspended timber ground floor (uninsulated)	1.30
Modern insulated ground floor	0.18

Insulation thicknesses required to achieve a U-value of 0.2W/m²k	
235mm	Cellulose fibre
220mm	Glass wool fibre
210mm	Rock wool fibre
190mm	Extruded polystyrene foam
185mm	Polyurethane foam with CO_2
180mm	Expanded polystyrene
150mm	Polyurethane foam with pentane
135mm	Phenolic foam
130mm	Polyisocyanurate foam
120mm	Phenolic foam with foil face
95mm	Polyisocyanurate foam with foil face
75mm	Aerogel blanket
25mm	Vacuum insulation

Source: Architects Journal

AIM HIGH

As this is a 'once in a lifetime' improvement, it makes sense to make the most of the opportunity and super-insulate your home, to achieve the lowest possible U-values. For each improvement undertaken you need to calculate the amount of insulation needed to meet – or preferably far exceed – Building Regulations U-value targets. So, for example, if you decide to lay some loft insulation, the aim should be to exceed the target of 0.18W/m²K. But the thickness of insulation needed will depend on the type of material used, as well as how and where it's installed. The best advice is to check with the insulation manufacturers as to what thickness of their material is required for a specific project.

Natural reedboard insulation

RENOVATION OF THERMAL ELEMENTS (WALLS, FLOORS, ROOFS)

As we saw earlier, you might simply be planning to do a spot of improvement work, but if this involves renovating at least half the surface area of an individual wall, roof or floor it could turn into a much bigger job. This is because the Building Regs require you to thermally upgrade the whole of it to achieve the U-vales in the following table.

The term 'renovation' means the provision of a new physical layer in the element or the replacement of an existing layer, but draws the line at decorative finishes. Renovation includes cladding, rendering, internal dry-lining, and replacement of existing layers by stripping down to expose basic structural components (*eg* stripping a flat roof). So, for example, if you want to re-plaster a bedroom wall the 'relevant area' is the total surface of the room's main external walls. Another example as we saw earlier would be where you need to replace the covering on a flat roof. Here the Building Regulations require you to upgrade the roof insulation while you're at it (to at least 0.18W/m²K).

If this all sounds rather 'nanny state', you'll be relieved to know there are some generous exemptions. This is most relevant for period properties where such works need to be compatible with conservation. Where the floor area of a room would be reduced by more than 5%, or where the work won't pay back financially within 15 years, Building Control may accept more limited improvements. And if the work isn't 'technically or practically feasible' then the 'best achievable' standard will be accepted instead (*ie* give it your best shot). Also, upgrading work needn't be undertaken where the U-value of the 'relevant area' already meets the 'threshold' figures (right column in table).

Thermal element	Building Regulations (Part L1B)		
	Typical existing U-value	*Target U-value*	*Threshold U-value*
	W/m²K	W/m²K	W/m²K
Floor	1.00	0.25	0.70
Solid wall	2.10	0.30	0.70
Cavity wall	1.50	0.55	0.70
Pitched roof (insulated with loft insulation over ceilings)	0.44	0.18	0.35
Pitched roof (insulated at rafter level)	1.90	0.18	0.35
Flat roof	1.00	0.18	0.35
External doors or windows with U-values worse than 3.3W/m²K should also be replaced to achieve at least 1.8 and 1.6W/m²K respectively (see Chapter 7).			

Overall heat loss and SAP ratings

You can quibble about the performance of different bits of a building all you like, but what really counts is the bigger picture – the overall heat loss and energy efficiency of the home. For a modern,

Super-insulated wall - cavity insulation + thermal blockwork inner leaf + insulated plasterboard

Comparing performance

There are three key measures that show how well insulation performs:

Lambda value (λ): thermal conductivity

The test of how effective a particular insulator is depends on its 'thermal conductivity' – the rate at which heat is transmitted through it. Obviously the slower the better. This measure of a material's ability to transmit heat can be a useful guide when buying insulation materials. The lower the value, the better the product's insulating capacity (for a given thickness). It's measured in Watts per square metre of surface area assuming a temperature difference of 1° per metre of thickness (W/m^2K). For example, a typical roll of glass mineral wool loft quilt conducts heat at a rate of $0.044W/m^2K$, whereas PIR board achieves a more impressive $0.022W/m^2K$.

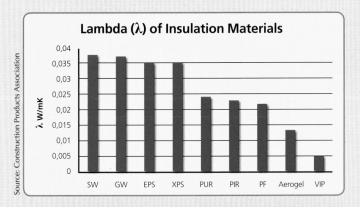

R-value: thermal resistance

This measures a material's ability to *resist* the transfer of heat, in relation to the amount actually used. To calculate thermal resistance you simply take the total thickness of the material and divide it by the conductivity – its lambda value (λ). This is a more useful figure because it tells you the overall resistance of the material based on the thickness you're actually installing. So the higher the R-value of any element (in W/m^2K) the better its ability to resist the transmission of heat and hence the more efficient it is at insulating. For example, to calculate the R-value of PIR Board that's 100mm thick = $0.1m \div 0.022$ (λ) = $4.54W/m^2K$. Or the same thickness of glass fibre = $0.1m \div 0.044 = 2.27W/m^2K$.

U-value: thermal transmittance

The best-known measure of heat loss, this is a 'warts and all' guide to the performance of the finished thermal element – *ie* the wall, roof or floor. It tells you the rate at which heat is transmitted through $1m^2$ of a structure, where the temperature difference between the inner and outer face is 1°C. U-values are measured in W/m^2K, and the lower the figure the better. They're calculated simply by adding together the R-values (thermal resistances) of all the materials in, say, a wall and then taking the reciprocal – dividing the total figure into the number 1. In other words it's $1 \div$ the total of all the R-Values (or $1/R$). So if R is large, U will be small, *ie* the greater the resistance the lower the U-value. But because in the real world thermal resistance is also created by things like fixings, surface finishes and air cavities, these must also be taken into account. Standard figures for these resistances are factored in when calculating U-values, together with the effect of any thermal bridges.

For example, to calculate the U-value for a wall containing 100mm of PIR board plus another 100mm of glass fibre, the combined total of their R-values is 6.81. Without an allowance for any thermal bridges, air gaps and fixings etc, the U-value is simply $1 \div 6.81 = 0.147W/m^2K$.

Element	Thickness	R-value
External resistance (Rse)		0.04
Brick outer leaf	100mm	0.14
Unventilated cavity	50mm	0.18
Blockwork inner leaf	100mm	0.16
Plasterwork	15mm	0.03
Internal resistance (Rsi)		0.13
Total		0.68

The combined U-value is $1/0.68 = 1.47$ W/m^2K.

(*Source: BRE*)

highly insulated house the amount of heat loss can be as low as 2kW. On the other hand, an older un-insulated house could be leaking around 20kW. Most homes fall somewhere between these two extremes, with an average semi typically scoring an overall heat loss of around 7.5kW.

As we saw earlier, Energy Performance Certificates (EPCs) are the preferred method of comparing homes in terms of the energy efficiency of the whole building (rather than just elements like the walls and roof, as with U-values). These are based on a cut-down version of SAP calculations ('Standard Assessment Procedure'). The EPC estimates the current and potential energy performance of a property expressed with a points score of 1 to 100 – the higher the number, the lower your home's energy consumption. This is translated into a chart showing seven bands ranging from A-G:

SAP band	Rating points
A	92–100 SAP points (most efficient)
B	81–91 SAP points
C	69–80 SAP points
D	55–68 SAP points
E	39–54 SAP points
F	21–38 SAP points
G	1–20 SAP points (least efficient)

An EPC provides an easy way to compare a property's running costs (for space heating and hot water) per sq metre of floor area, as well as its environmental impact. The EPC report concludes with a summary of each key element of your home – the walls, roofs, floors, windows, main heating system, heating controls, secondary heating, hot water, and lighting. Each is judged on a scale from

Heating by cat power?

Not a lot of people know this, but the average domestic cat gives off nearly 20W of heat. Why is this relevant? Because if your home was super-insulated so that it only lost 1kWh of heat a day, then the body heat of a couple of felines could be sufficient to keep the living space warm – at least until the temperature outside was 16° colder than inside.

The total heat loss of a building depends on two main factors – its average heat loss (*ie* how well insulated it is) and the temperature difference between inside and outside. Together these two factors tell you how much heat you need to generate to keep the interior cosy. So in this example with your living space set to a comfortable 20°C, only once the outdoor temperatures fell below 4° would you need to invite additional household pets into the home to boost the heating.

If the building is well insulated enough, the internal gains will be more than the total losses through the building. In other words the number of Watts of heat required would be less than the heat given off by occupants and from everyday activities, such as waste heat from appliances, cooking, hot water use, plus any solar gains received through windows.

laptop by an Energy Assessor. This is a particular concern with non-standard or more quirky buildings – for example, no allowance is made for the insulation benefits of thatched roofs. Consequently there's a risk that some buildings are wrongly assessed and homeowners provided with flawed reports, and if inappropriate advice is acted upon it can have damaging consequences. So this is no substitute for a bespoke assessment by a suitably qualified chartered surveyor or independent specialist.

WHAT CAN MAKE A DIFFERENCE TO THE SAP RATING?

Improvement	Rating can be improved by	Approx annual savings
Condensing boiler	47 points	£225 +
Cavity insulation	13 points	£100–£125
Roof insulation	10 points	£100–£125
Cylinder stat and insulation	8 points	£100–£125
Double glazing	4 points	£10–£15
Low-energy lighting	2 points	£10–£15
	NB: The extent of savings gained from these improvements will depend on how poorly the existing property performs, so this is only a very rough guide.	

(*Source: energykey.co.uk*)

very good to very poor, along with recommended measures to improve their efficiency, and approximate savings achievable.

However, EPC ratings aren't always as accurate as you might hope. Actual energy use may vary widely from that predicted, simply because people use buildings differently. More worryingly, the standardised advice churned out by computers can sometimes be inappropriate, being based on a few key facts tapped into a

Energy Performance Certificate SAP

1 Insulation Avenue, London W4 1UV

Dwelling type: End-terrace house
Date of assessment: 13 April 2012
Date of certificate: 10 April 2012

Reference number: 8009-8677-9829-3096-4423
Type of assessment: RdSAP, existing dwelling
Total floor area: 88 m²

Use this document to:
* Compare current ratings of properties to see which properties are more energy efficient
* Find out how you can save energy and money by installing improvement measures

Estimated energy costs of dwelling for 3 years:	£3,243
Over 3 years you could save	£1,521

Estimated energy costs of this home

	Current costs	Potential costs	Potential future savings
Lighting	£237 over 3 years	£141 over 3 years	
Heating	£2,712 over 3 years	£1,395 over 3 years	You could save £1,521 over 3 years
Hot Water	£294 over 3 years	£186 over 3 years	
Totals	£3,243	£1,722	

These figures show how much the average household would spend in this property for heating, lighting and hot water. This excludes energy use for running appliances like TVs, computers and cookers, and any electricity generated by microgeneration.

Energy Efficiency Rating

	Current	Potential
Very energy efficient - lower running costs		
(92 plus) A		
(81-91) B		
(69-80) C		
(55-68) D		83
(39-54) E	49	
(21-38) F		
(1-20) G		
Not energy efficient - higher running costs		

The graph shows the current energy efficiency of your home.
The higher the rating the lower your fuel bills are likely to be.
The potential rating shows the effect of undertaking the recommendations on page 4.
The average energy efficiency rating for a dwelling in England and Wales is band D (rating 60).

Top actions you can take to save money and make your home more efficient

Recommended measures	Indicative cost	Typical savings over 3 years	Available with Green Deal
1 Cavity wall insulation	£500 - £1,500	£69	✓
2 Internal or external wall insulation	£4,000 - £14,000	£576	✓
3 Floor insulation	£800 - £1,200	£129	✓

See page 4 for a full list of recommendations for this property.

To find out more about the recommended measures and other actions you could take today to save money, visit www.direct.gov.uk/savingenergy or call 0300 123 1234 (standard national rate). When the Green Deal launches, it may allow you to make your home warmer and cheaper to run at no up-front cost.

Types of insulation

Picking the optimum type of insulation for your property is fundamental to achieving a comfortable, energy-efficient home. But thermal performance isn't the only factor. For a start there's the question of cost – natural materials tend to be a little dearer. Then as we saw in the last chapter, the selected material will need to be compatible with your home's method of construction, as well as being able to withstand everything the local environment can throw at it for the foreseeable future. There's also the question of ease of installation – if it can't be installed reasonably easily it'll probably get fitted badly. So you need to consider what shape and form it's sold in and which type is more manageable – rigid boards, loose-fill, rolls or flexible semi-rigid batts. Last but not least, consideration should be given to the material's fire resistance, acoustic performance, moisture resistance and environmental credentials.

There are various ways of categorising materials, *eg* by source material, physical rigidity or performance:

Insulation types by physical form

■ Loose-fill

Loose materials are handy for reaching awkward spots in lofts and odd-shaped and hard-to-reach crevices. These can be laid by hand or blown-in using specialised machines. One of the best known is cellulose fibre (recycled newspaper). Cavity wall insulation

'Lambsulation' - soft & natural

is pumped through large hoses and therefore needs to comprise loose materials such as polystyrene beads (*eg* Perlite, Polypearl and Thermabead) or fibre materials like yellow and white mineral wools.

◼ Fluffy quilt

Soft, fluffy (and sometimes itchy) materials sold in quilt form include mineral wool, glass fibre wool, and sheep's wool.

◼ Rigid boards

Most rigid boards are made from petrochemicals, such as polyurethane (*eg* PUR) and polystyrene (*eg* EPS) although a number of natural materials like wood fibre are now also available.

◼ Semi-rigid batts

Semi rigid batts are a sort of halfway house – not entirely rigid, yet stiff enough to be squished between wall studs, joists and

rafters. The best-known materials are sheep's wool, hemp and mineral wool batts which are widely used in new construction. They can also be placed over ceilings or used to insulate timber floors.

Natural fibre insulation batts

Breathable or sealed?

Materials that are 'breathable' are especially well suited for use in older solid wall properties. Natural materials such as sheep's wool, wood fibre and hemp are able to absorb and release a certain mount of moisture, echoing the way old buildings work. Mineral wool also has a certain amount of breathability, but most mainstream manufactured materials are sealed, being neither vapour-permeable or air-permeable.

Insulation types by source material

◼ Foamed plastics

eg Polyurethane (PUR) and extruded polystyrene (XPS).

Polyurethane (PUR), phenolic foam (PF) and polyisocyanurate (PIR) are plastic-based, closed-cell products predominantly sold in rigid board form and widely used for insulating walls and roofs.

Styrofoam blue foamed polystyrene boards

Some types can also be used for floors. Facings are fibreglass-based or sometimes backed with aluminium foil. PUR, PIR and PF are very effective insulators with a high thermal resistance, being about twice as good as many EPS or mineral wools but up to three times as expensive.

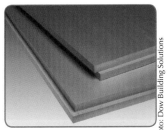

This extruded polystyrene (XPS) has reflecting particles within the foam for improved performance

High performance phenolic foam (PF) boards

Polystyrene is also a closed-cell product derived from oil and is expanded or extruded by the use of pentane gas. Its high compressive strength means it can bear loads, making it useful in floor screeds etc. It's cheaper than PUR and PIR but is a less effective insulator, although the latest 'grey' enhanced EPS products include graphite particles to improve performance. Polystyrene beads are widely used as cavity fill. In addition to EPS, it is available as Extruded Polystyrene (XPS) and Extruded Polyethylene (XPE).

None of these materials degrade when exposed to moisture, an important quality in a number of key areas in buildings. However petrochemical-based materials emit fine particles when cut, can be toxic when burned and don't biodegrade.

◼ Mineral based
Glass fibre, rock wool and vermiculite.

'SpaceRoll' mineral wool quilt

Vermiculite loose-fill

Mineral wool is a generic term that covers rock/stone wool, glass wool and slag wool, which are best known in the form of rolls of loft quilt. Rock wool is spun from volcanic rock, a plentiful resource, which is superheated and blown with gas. Glass wool and fibreglass are derived from silica, which is also abundant, although recycled bottles are increasingly used as a source material. Slag wool is made from the waste material from steel production mixed with basalt.

Although mineral wool is well known for causing unpleasant skin irritation during installation, many products have recently been reformulated with a soft 'cotton wool'-like texture, or else contained within protective plastic sheeting.

Another mineral-based material is Perlite beads. These small, white, lightweight balls, containing tiny air cells, are made from volcanic glass and are used to fill wall cavities. Vermiculite is an older form of loose-fill, although no longer widely used due to alleged health concerns.

■ Reflective foils
Foil-faced bubble wrap and multi-layered foils.

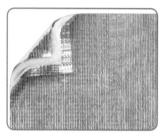

Multi-layered foil insulation comprises several thin layers of 'tissue'-like insulant material or plastic foam bonded and sandwiched between thin sheets of tough aluminium foil. Also known as 'radiant heat barriers', these work primarily by reflecting solar energy. The material is supplied in roll form, so the joins need to be lapped and taped when it's installed. It has the advantage of being very slim (about 25mm), so it's useful where space is at a premium, although it does require a clear air gap next to it to achieve optimal performance. It's relatively simple to install, but test results differ regarding its thermal performance, so it's best to check with local authority Building Control if a specific target U-value needs to be achieved. It's often used in combination with other materials such as mineral wool.

■ High-tech
Aerogel and vacuum panels.

Below: Vacuum panels
Right: Aerogel plasterboard & plywood laminate

Aerogel is an extremely effective insulator that was employed by NASA for Mars Rover technology. It's sourced from silica and is almost transparent, with a similar texture to jelly. The reason it's such a good insulator is its structure is full of millions of tiny holes – an almost invisible sponge-like glass foam that

Aerogel 'Spacetherm' blanket

soaks up air – typically comprising 97% air by volume. It has the lowest thermal conductivity of any solid and is highly porous.

Although aerogel is very light it has a very high compressive strength. Its incredible insulation properties can be demonstrated by taking a 1cm thick slice and applying a 1,300°C flame to one side: the opposite side barely even gets warm.

Just 20mm of this super-insulant has a thermal conductivity of only $0.013W/m^2K$. Thin strips of aerogel bonded to flexible, fibrous matting blanket, or sandwiched within lightweight PVC panels, are ideal for hard-to-treat areas. Strips can also be sandwiched between timber or metal stud wall framing and wall surfaces to prevent heat loss through the studwork. Aerogel blankets with high compressive strength and thin profile can be used for insulating areas where space is very limited, such as solid floors or window reveals. Inevitably the downside is its expense, although it should become cheaper in future with wider use.

Vacuum insulation panels (VIPs) are a recently developed super-thin, high-performance product, and are also ideal for use where space is restricted. VIPs comprise a micro-porous core (of silica or superfine fibreglass and phenolic foam) which is vacuum heat-sealed in a thin, gas-tight envelope comprising EPS-protected plates. Thermal conductivity is extremely low at around $0.008W/m^2K$, which means these high-tech panels can provide an insulating performance up to ten times better than most conventional materials. But once again the downside is cost.

■ Natural insulation materials
Natural materials are well suited for use in old buildings where breathability is important, but are also popular because of their low environmental impact and the fact that they're nicer to work with. These are some of the more popular alternatives:

Cellulose fibre
Recycled newspaper finely shredded and reprocessed back to its raw fibrous state is well suited for loft insulation. The product is available either as loose-fill or in compressed bales or batts. It's pre-treated with inorganic salts such as borax against fire, and to protect against fungal and rodent attack, in contrast to toxic fire retardants and pesticides found in many conventional insulation products. It isn't attractive to vermin and doesn't rot. UK-manufactured Warmcel 100 is supplied in bags

that are simply emptied into the loft space. It's non-toxic and non-irritant. As loose-fill it's effective at reaching gaps around pipes etc. Other types can be mechanically blown into position by specialist contractors. One downside is that it can't be used anywhere it might get damp. Recycled paper is also made into board form with the addition of jute sacking.

Proof that cellulose is fire-proof!

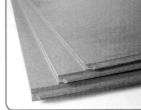

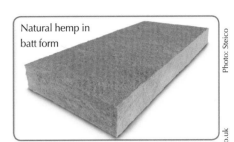
Natural wood-fibre board

Sheep's wool

Photo: Thermafleece

A natural fibre from a renewable resource, wool is very effective at absorbing and releasing water vapour rapidly, which helps its effectiveness as an insulant. It's simple to fit and doesn't irritate the eyes, skin and lungs like some mineral products, so can be installed without the need for protective clothing. An initial smell of lanolin quickly dissipates. It's normally supplied as batts or in quilt form in various widths and thicknesses with sufficient rigidity to adapt to the shape of rafters and joists etc. These contain a small amount of recycled polyester to give them rigidity and can be placed over ceilings, between rafters as loft insulation, built into walls, or used to insulate suspended timber floors. Wool is naturally fire-resistant, melting away from an ignition source rather than igniting. Untreated wool can become attractive to moths so it's normally pre-treated with inorganic salts (such as Borax) to make it insect-proof and improve fire-resistance. Brands like 'Thermafleece' are very effective at both thermal and acoustic insulation and can be installed as a sandwich between two sheets of laths.

Wood fibre

Wood fibre boards made from waste softwood can be used to line roofs, floors and walls (both internally and externally). It's also manufactured in the form of flexible batts and can be installed between studs and joists. Wood fibres have a relatively high capacity to retain moisture, which can help regulation of air humidity when installed on internal walls – a useful quality in traditional buildings.

Hemp

Hemp fibres combined with recycled cotton produce a highly efficient insulation material that's flexible and robust. It's sold in rolls or batts, and a small quantity of thermoplastic binder is added to improve stability. As well as being an effective insulator it offers good sound-deadening properties.

Natural hemp in batt form

Hemp can also be mixed with natural lime to make 'hempcrete' building blocks, ideal for use on many traditional buildings. Hemp in all its forms is easy to handle and install, plus it doesn't irritate the skin. Like wool it can absorb and release water vapour. Being cellulose-based makes it less attractive to rodents or insects, but it's treated with inorganic salts such as sodium bicarbonate for pest and fire resistance. It's claimed to smell like newly cut hay (in contrast to the chemical aroma of petrochemical-based products).

Reed

Natural reed formed into boards is sold as a base for lime-plastering internal walls and ceilings. It's an ideal way of adding a layer of wall or ceiling insulation, particularly for period timber frame or earth buildings. It's secured in place using screws set into nylon plugs with plastic washers, to prevent thermal bridging.

Cork

Sourced sustainably from the bark of cork oak trees, it's sold in the form of tiles of varying thicknesses that can be used for floors and flat roofs, with good sound-proofing qualities. It contains a natural wax that makes it impermeable to liquid and naturally resistant to fire, rot and insects.

Type of insulation		Insulation thickness (mm) to achieve a U-value of 0.2	Typical applications											
			ROOFS			WALLS						FLOORS		
			Rafters	Ceiling	Flat roofs	Internal	External	Cavity (full fill)	Timber frame	Steel frame	Panel	Solid concrete	Beam & block	Suspended timber
High tech	Vacuum Insulated Panels	30												
	Aerogel	50–55												
Polyurethane (PU)	Polyurethane with pentane up to 32kg/m³	105–115												
	Foil-faced "	75												
	Polyurethane soy-based	100–145												
	Polyurethane with CO_2	130												
	In-situ applied Polyurethane (sprayed or injected)	80–100												
Polyisocyanurate (PIR)	Polyisocyanurate up to 32kg/m³	95–105												
	Foil-faced "	80–85												
	In-situ applied polyisocyanurate (sprayed)	80–100												
Phenolic foam (PF)	Phenolic foam	80–95												
	Foil-faced "	75–85												
Expanded Polystyrene (EPS)	Expanded Polystyrene up to 30kg/m³	115–165												
	Expanded Polystyrene with graphite	115–120												
Extruded Polystyrene (XPS)	Extruded Polystyrene with CO_2	95–140												
	Extruded Polystyrene with HFC 35kg/m³	110–120												
Wool and fibre	Glass wool (up to 48kg/m³)	135–180												
	Glass wool (equal/greater than 48kg/m³)	155												
	Stone wool (less than 160kg/m³)	150–160												
	Stone wool (160kg/m³)	160–170												
	Sheep's wool (25kg/m³)	150–215												
	Cellulose fibre (dry blown 24kg/m³)	150–190												
	Hemp fibre	165												
	Polyester fibre	150–180												
	Wood fibre (WF)	154–225												
Alternative	Hemp lime (monolithic)	260												
	Cotton	165–171												
	Cork (120kg/m³)	155–200												
	Vermiculite	235												
	Perlite (expanded) board	190												
	Cellular glass (CG)	140–185												
	Strawboard (420kg/m³)	295												

Source: The Energy Saving Trust

How eco-friendly is insulation?

One important reason for insulating houses is to reduce damaging carbon emissions that contribute to global warming, so when you're choosing insulation materials it makes sense to compare how well they perform from a broader environmental perspective. This means taking into account more than just how good a material is at its primary job of preventing heat loss. You may come away with a different point of view when you weigh up the following factors:

- Thermal performance (R-value).
- The amount of energy consumed in manufacturing it.
- Whether the raw materials it utilises are sustainable (either recycled or renewable).

- Where it's manufactured (ie how many miles it has to be transported).
- Any potential health effects during installation.
- Whether toxins are released during manufacture, use or disposal.
- Can it be recycled at the end of its life?

As you might expect, natural products tend to score better in most of these categories, but in practice compromise is normally necessary. Key factors such as cost and performance (to achieve targets and comply with Building Regs) will sometimes trump longer-term concerns. A thin high-performance material may be the only solution in areas where space is limited, and in some situations a material may need to be versatile enough to perform more than one role, such as fire or soundproofing as well as thermal insulation. So, for example, mineral wool – which has good acoustic as well as thermal properties – could sometimes be the most effective solution in terms of overall performance.

It's also important to consider the impact of materials in terms of their 'embodied energy'. This is like an environmental price tag that totals all the energy consumed throughout the product's life-cycle – extraction of the raw materials, processing, transportation, installation and maintenance. In general materials that are used in a form as near as possible to their natural state will have the lowest embodied energy.

Insulation health risks

Probably the greatest health risk comes from attempting DIY work without the correct access, equipment or clothing. So in each step-by-step example in this book we highlight what protective clothing it's advisable to wear for each project.

Generally speaking, natural materials are more pleasant to work with, but it still makes sense to wear a dust mask to protect your throat and lungs. For example when cutting rigid insulation boards to size, fine particles are released into the air. Similarly, some forms of fibreglass insulation shed microscopic fibres into the air when disturbed. These tiny, sharp bits of fibreglass are easily inhaled, and can also irritate the eyes and skin, so cutting should be done outdoors. As well as donning a dust mask it's also a good idea to wear eye protection, and to kit yourself out with long sleeves and gloves when handling the stuff.

Questions have also been raised about petrochemical-based materials (such as urea formaldehyde foam) emitting small amounts of fumes over time, although there's currently no scientific evidence that suggests this is a valid concern.

Vermiculite is a naturally occurring silicate mineral that's an established form of loose-fill, but, as mentioned earlier, it's rarely used now due to mooted health concerns. Although the material itself hasn't been shown to be a health problem, some vermiculite insulation has been found to contain small amounts of asbestos fibres, which can potentially cause problems if inhaled. However, as long as it remains undisturbed (eg in attic spaces) and doesn't become airborne, it shouldn't be a concern. It's extremely rare for lofts to contain traces of asbestos (eg from old pipe insulation), and only where the material is disturbed could it become airborne with the risk of inhalation.

What can go wrong?

As with any home improvement, there are potential pitfalls if you don't prepare for the task with eyes wide open. So before wrapping your house in a thick coat of insulation, it's worth taking a few minutes to check that there's nothing that could inadvertently damage the existing structure.

Potential problems

Some insulated homes have suffered from the following problems as a result of poor workmanship or the wrong materials:

- Condensation.
- Blocked ventilation (to roofs and under-floor voids).
- Trapped damp.
- Floor joist-ends rotting.
- Reduction of indoor air quality.

In the following chapters we look at how such calamities can be avoided by taking a few simple precautions.

Breathable cellulose insulation used to insulate studwork wall

Photo: Excel

Condensation

The main risk from insulating your home is from dampness caused by condensation. This may seem counter-intuitive, because insulating the house is an important part of reducing condensation problems. This is because once surfaces are better insulated, and hence warmer, any indoor air that comes into contact with them will be less prone to condensing into water. But there's a flip side to this process. When you line a room with insulation, the wall that's now entombed behind it will become colder, because the insulation acts as a barrier between it and the warmer atmosphere of the room. The inner face of the wall is no longer exposed to warmth from the room, and hence its temperature drops.

All air contains a certain amount of water vapour, but warm air can hold considerably more moisture than cold air. So in a well-insulated room the amount of moisture invisibly swirling around can be deceptively high. And when this warm air reaches a lower temperature it can no longer hold as much vapour, and the excess water will condense out. This critical temperature is called the 'dew point'. So if warm air can leak through even tiny gaps in an internally insulated wall, floor or ceiling, as soon as it meets a cold surface it'll promptly cool below its dew point and condense into water.

This curious phenomenon, known as 'interstitial condensation', is particularly troubling because colder surfaces tend to be located nearer the outside of the building, hence damp is likely to accumulate in hidden recesses within the structure. And being out of sight it often goes unnoticed until serious damp or rot has taken hold. However, this is only likely to be a problem if there's a chink in your armour. Even small gaps of 1–2mm can dramatically reduce the effectiveness of the insulation. A 1mm gap that's a metre long is estimated to allow as much as 800g of water per square metre to enter into the structure every day. Condensation is also attracted to any areas where insulation is thin or absent (see 'Thermal bridging' below). And of course, the colder the weather is outside, the more powerful the effect will be. Hence the importance of making insulation continuous, without any gaps.

There are three ways this problem can be tackled:

1 Seal it 100%

Make everything vapour-tight and fully sealed so that it's physically impossible for moist air to penetrate the fabric from inside the house. It's easier to achieve a guaranteed 'no gaps' result with external wall insulation where the whole external envelope is evenly swathed to the full height of the building. Where walls are instead lined internally, the aim should be to achieve a continuous layer of insulation with as few interruptions as possible, all neatly sealed within an airtight vapour barrier. Inevitably, however, there'll be some areas that are harder to treat and seal, with potential for cold spots – see below.

2 Let it breathe

The opposite approach to sealing it means accepting that a certain amount of air may get into the fabric. But by using natural insulation materials, such as wood fibre, the moisture is free to escape again by evaporation because the surfaces are 'breathable'.

For older solid-walled houses the use of natural insulation materials separated from the internal wall with a cavity can be an appropriate solution – see Chapter 4.

This is a totally different approach to modern insulation systems that rely on airtight sealants, tapes and foams, particularly at joints between insulation boards. Critics point out that this is a relatively recent technology and any future deterioration in the materials used to fill and seal gaps could result in air infiltration, compromising the performance.

3 Extract moist air

In both cases it's important to address the root of the problem with mechanical extraction to remove water vapour and humidity in the indoor atmosphere caused by the activities of occupants – see next chapter.

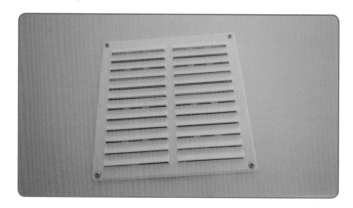

Thermal bridging

Making our homes warmer by insulating them can potentially lead to issues with damp and mould. This is because as room temperatures rise so too does the amount of water vapour held in

Window reveals should be insulated to prevent 'cold bridging' attracting condensation and mould

the air. So any areas where the insulation didn't fit properly, or is thin or missing won't be so well insulated and will remain relatively cold and can act as a 'thermal bridge'. The risk with such 'cold spots' is that they can attract damp from warm, humid air that condenses, because the other surfaces are now warmer and can no longer 'share the load'. Ultimately this can manifest itself in black mould growth or even localised decay to timbers. So special care needs to be taken, particularly when improvements are being made in stages.

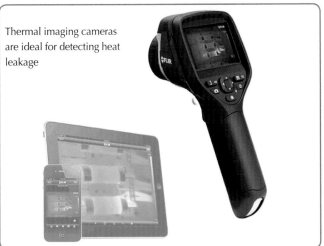

Thermal imaging cameras are ideal for detecting heat leakage

In reality however, total elimination of thermal bridging isn't usually possible; it's difficult to avoid some parts ending up a little less well insulated than the surrounding areas, unless you wrap your living accommodation inside a continuously insulated envelope. So cladding the walls and roof externally tends to be the best option since it largely overcomes this problem, but is often

Cold aluminium patio door frames attract condensation and mould

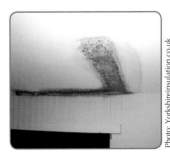

Gaps in loft insulation leave cold spots

impractical. The next best option is to identify high-risk areas and insulate them as best you can.

Classic locations for thermal bridging are found anywhere the main walls are connected to the internal structure, such as where floors/ceilings and internal partition walls or party walls meet the main outer walls. In theory this can be solved by inserting a thermal barrier to block the 'thermal path', but unless you virtually rebuild the inside of the house that's not normally realistic. In fact anywhere that the same depth of insulation ('thermal continuity') can't be easily achieved will be relatively cold. This tends to be more of an issue in certain awkward areas where there's not much space, such as at reveals to window and door openings and adjoining stairs, where the insulation has to be thinner. Fortunately, as we shall see in the following chapters, a lot can be done to minimise the risk of thermal bridging, for example by lapping internal wall insulation so it extends on to the partition walls etc.

Some properties are more at risk than others. For example, some terraced houses are built in a 'stepped and staggered' design, where one house projects forward of its neighbour or is stepped up a little higher. As a result the party wall is partially exposed, and therefore colder, and can act as a 'heat sink'. With solid wall properties (including some post-war houses made from poured concrete) this requires special attention to the continuity of insulation.

Internal partitions and party walls can act as a pathway or 'thermal bridge' conducting heat out of the building

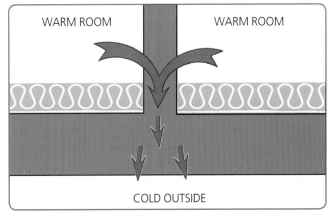

WARM ROOM   WARM ROOM

COLD OUTSIDE

3 AIRTIGHTNESS AND VENTILATION

Photo: ECD Architects

Blower door tests involve connecting a fan to an opening in the building envelope and pressurising it

British homes are notoriously leaky. Only in the last few years has airtightness been taken seriously in new construction, so in most properties a few simple draughtproofing measures should reap major benefits. The problem with draughts isn't just that they make our homes feel uncomfortable, it's the fact that they push up heating bills. This is because the natural response when you feel currents of cold air swirling around your ankles

Smoke pen in action

is to turn up the heating, and paying good money to heat cold incoming air is incredibly wasteful.

However, sealing up every nook and cranny in your home to make it perfectly airtight without providing compensating ventilation is a recipe for a stuffy, unhealthy indoor environment, with occupants left gasping. Air leakage and ventilation are twin issues that need to be tackled together. Ventilation is needed to maintain good air quality and to remove humid, stale air. The problem in most properties is that we rely on uncontrolled draughtiness for ventilation, and the amount of cold air getting in is far more than is necessary.

What's really required is a controllable supply of ventilation that directs fresh air to the right place when it's needed, rather than relying on haphazard gusts that occur even when the house is unoccupied. Once this has been achieved, all the gaps that allowed uncontrolled draughts into the house can be fully sealed. This approach is neatly summed up as 'insulate tight and ventilate right'.

Airtightness

Controlling the rate at which warm indoor air leaks out of the house and cold outdoor air gets in is essential not just for energy efficiency, but also for the comfort and health of the occupants. So the aim should be to provide just the right amount of fresh air, thereby wasting the bare minimum of energy.

Red-lining

Your first task is to walk around the house and take a look at all the inside surfaces of its 'thermal envelope', *ie* the parts that separate you from the outside world. This is your home's main line of defence

against the cold outdoors, and should ideally form a continuous 'red line' — an airtight sealed layer that excludes all draughts. It's normally fairly obvious where this barrier should be, such as the main walls, but it's usually more practical to exclude loft spaces and basement areas unless they're used as habitable space.

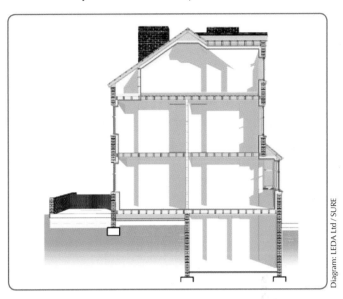

What causes air infiltration?

In a typical home the indoor air is replaced with colder air seeping in from outside as often as once every hour. This rate of air exchange is far more than is actually needed and results in excessive heat losses and general discomfort for occupants. It's caused by three things:

1 Gaps and cracks in the structure.
2 The wind setting up positive and negative pressures on the building, forcing cold air in through gaps (and warm air out).
3 The 'stack effect' inside the house, which causes warm air to rise and leak away through any gaps in ceilings and to be drawn up open chimneys. Open staircases also act like giant indoor chimneys drawing air up to the top of the house and straight out through uninsulated lofts etc, which is why you sometimes find doors or curtains at the bottom of the stairs in old cottages.

Common causes of draughts and heat loss – Ill-fitting windows and gaps around pipes & cables entering ceilings

How airtight is your home?

New homes have to meet stringent airtightness targets. Testing normally involves pressurising the building with a giant fan temporarily fitted into a main doorway, so that the rate of airflow out of the house can be measured.

Draughtproofing

Easy options

Draughtproofing is a simple measure that can be carried out at any time. Windows, doors and loft hatches can be draught-stripped and letterbox covers fitted. Suspended floors can be sealed and gaps around services pipes sealed with mastic or expanding foam – see Chapters 5, 6 and 7.

Golden opportunities

Draughtproofing alone is unlikely to completely nail the problem of air infiltration, because there are often lots of smaller unseen leaks that can be hard to trace, such as from floor voids. But when home improvements are being made there's usually an opportunity to upgrade airtightness. For example, it's a simple job to fill cracks with caulking when you're decorating and to seal gaps around pipes when carrying out plumbing work.

Common air leakage routes

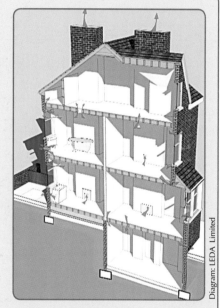

Diagram: LEDA Limited

Obvious air leakage paths, such as draughty windows, doors and letterboxes, can be dealt with fairly easily, but these only account for a small part of the infiltration in a typical dwelling. Other common ways that cold air gets into buildings include:

- Gaps between floorboards, around the edges of floors and to radiator pipes. This is more of an issue in traditional buildings with suspended timber ground floors which require air bricks to ventilate the under-floor voids to prevent damp and rot (so these need to be retained).
- Poorly pointed mortar joints in cavity brickwork, and around the ends of joists bedded in walls.
- Draughty windows and doors, and gaps between window/door frames and external walls.
- Gaps at the edges of ceilings beneath roof voids.
- Gaps around loft hatches.
- Open chimneys, and vents.
- Cable and pipe runs through ceilings and floors.
- Recessed light fittings in ceilings.
- Permanently open extractor vents to bathrooms and kitchens.
- Gaps around waste pipes to kitchens and bathrooms etc.

But when it comes to older properties, trying to pinpoint the source of draughts and where they enter can be surprisingly time-consuming. A fan pressurisation test is the most effective way to identify air leaks, with the aid of a smoke emitting device (eg smoke matches, smoke pencils or even joss sticks!). This helps locate draughts that may not immediately be evident (such as via cupboards, skirting and window boards). Smoke puffers can show how big draughts are and where they go. If the tests are repeated after draughtproofing this will highlight any areas missed.

Photo: Smokepencil.com

Smoke generators can be used to pinpoint draughts

Pressurisation tests measure the number of cubic metres of air leaking out of the house per hour (for each square metre of external envelope at a pressure of 50 Pascals). The maximum permitted figure for newbuild is $10m^3$, so if you can get your home somewhere near that it would be pretty good.

The airtightness figure for a typical existing house is about $18m^3$, but many homes are considerably leakier.

DRAUGHT-BUSTERS

The draughtiness of a building depends upon the amount of air that can pass through its external envelope – walls, windows, doors, floor and roof. This is known as 'air permeability'.

The aim should be to eliminate existing 'draught paths' as far as possible by sealing gaps and cracks to both indoor and external surfaces. Draughty gaps are commonly found where one element, such as a wall, meets an adjoining floor, window or roof. So when fitting new insulation it's important to ensure that each element is well sealed to the adjoining one. Wall insulation normally incorporates an airtight vapour barrier, which should overlap and be sealed to those in adjoining floors and roofs. Wherever possible cable and pipe runs should be kept within the vapour barrier envelope to minimise gaps.

DRAUGHT PATHS

A little time spent fitting draughtproofing strips, or applying frame sealant or a suitable mastic, can make a major difference. These are the key areas to target:

Walls

- Air leakage and air movement behind plasterboard dry-lining can be reduced by injecting continuous ribbons of expanding polyurethane foam or adhesive between the insulation boards and the inner face of the main walls.
- Any redundant air vents into rooms can be sealed by filling with mineral wool or expanding foam and boarding over the internal face. Don't block any vents supplying air for combustion to stoves, heaters or open fires. Also, don't block air bricks to ground floors and basements.
- Make good any eroded mortar joints and fill old redundant holes in external walls, especially around waste pipes. Ensure gaps are filled around extractor fan ducts.

Vapour control membranes

Achieving airtightness relies on the use of vapour control membranes (aka 'vapour barriers'). But there are two types – the ones that simply block everything from passing, and those that use discretion as to what they allow through.

Vapour control membranes are glorified polythene sheets designed to stop the passage of airborne water vapour. To work properly they must be completely airtight, so you need to be obsessive in your approach to sealing it all up – especially around the perimeter and at any points where pipes or cables pass through.

'Breather' membranes are a very different kettle of fish since, as the name suggests, they're vapour permeable and hence well suited for use in traditional buildings. There are also standard issue for lining new pitched roofs underneath the tiles, to provide a secondary defence against rain whilst allowing moist air in the loft to escape.

When placed next to a layer of insulation they have the effect of restricting airflow into and out of it. But because they contain millions of microscopic pores they allow moisture vapour levels on either side to stabilise, rather than build up to dangerous proportions.

When placed above insulation in a loft, for example, they help restrict air movement (and hence heat loss) into the ventilated space above the insulation. They also allow any moisture vapour within the insulation to evaporate harmlessly away. When placed underneath the insulation, despite being permeable, they limit the amount of air and moisture vapour entering from the room below. The performance of natural vapour permeable insulation materials used in older buildings can be enhanced by the addition of breather membranes.

Right: Breather membranes are fitted as standard on new roofs

Floors
- Seal gaps between floorboards, *eg* with silicone sealant (see page 104). Alternatively, timber floors can be improved by laying timber sheeting (*eg* hardboard) over the top. Sheets should be laid with very tight joints and sealed around the edges with mastic.
- Seal around the edges of the room and fill any gaps around pipes and cables. Seal to top and bottom edges of skirting boards with mastic.

Roofs
- Ensure the loft hatch fits snugly and apply draught-stripping between the hatch and the frame.

Services
- Seal gaps around any service pipes and cables passing through external walls, ceilings and floors.

Chimneys
- Disused flues are meant to be ventilated at the top with vented hoods over pots. Redundant flues should also be vented at lower levels, as a through-flow of air removes damp. To prevent draughts in rooms, vents fitted in boarded up former fireplaces can be sealed and replaced with an air brick fitted externally (which may require ducting to an external wall or via a floor void).
- Inflatable 'chimney balloons' are sometimes wedged in flues above fireplaces as a temporary measure to block draughts. These can be deflated and removed so the chimney can remain in use – just don't forget to take them out before lighting the fire! Recently arrived on the draught-busting scene are transparent Perspex fireplace shields that let you see your fireplace but seal it when not in use.

Windows and doors (see Chapter 7)
- Seal gaps around windows and doors (including any cellar doors) to prevent air leakage.
- Make sure letterboxes shut properly.
- Apply mastic externally around frames where they meet the walls.
- Seal internal gaps with mastic, *eg* at reveals and window ledges.
- Repair any damage to window frames and ensure that the casements, sashes and top-lights close firmly. Apply draught-stripping to any gaps.

Insulating gaps around pipes

A large gap is evident around pipework to kitchen floor

Cut a length of jointing tape (or similar material)

Fold tape and insert into the gap as support for foam filler

Inject polyurethane foam into and along the gap

Foam expands and can be cut back when cured.

Ventilation

We spend a great deal of time indoors, but rarely give much thought to the quality of the air that we breathe. Only when it comes to selling the house and showing prospective buyers around are we likely to focus on the value-adding qualities that the aroma of freshly ground coffee and baking bread are alleged to confer. But the fact is, on a day-to-day basis we often co-exist with a variety of odours (cooking, pets, nappies, tobacco

Airbricks provide essential ventilation to timber ground floors

Lack of ventilation contributes to condensation and mould

Ventilation

Easy options
Make sure that extractor fans and trickle vents are clear, and give them a periodic clean (a vacuum can be useful to suck out dust and cobwebs).

Golden opportunities
When an extractor fan needs replacing it's a good opportunity to fit low-wattage replacements with humidity sensors (humidistats), or swap them for heat recovery room ventilators (which typically need a wider 150mm diameter wall opening). If refurbishment work can achieve high levels of airtightness, then it might be worth fitting a whole-house heat recovery system.

Air changes

To ensure that the air stays fresh in rooms used for living and sleeping, about 0.5 air changes per hour should normally be sufficient. But for older traditional buildings between 0.5 and 1.0 air changes per hour are recommended to help them naturally release moisture. Since air infiltration rates in many older buildings are greater than this, draughtproofing is normally beneficial.

Most ventilation should be from controllable sources that can be closed when the rooms aren't in use.

However, special care should be taken in rooms with open fires or other combustion appliances, to avoid depriving them – and occupants – of sufficient air. Specialist advice should also be sought before sealing any rooms containing fires or heating appliances.

smoke, paint fumes etc), as well as a surprising amount of moisture generated from steamy bathrooms, kitchens, pot plants, dogs and clothes drying. If you could observe this indoor atmosphere through a microscope you'd discover a whole host of bacteria, mites, dust and pollen. Ventilation has a key role to play in diluting and removing these pollutants. So if a house is made airtight without an adequate ventilation system to provide a controllable supply of fresh air, it can be a very unhealthy place to live. On the other hand, installing ventilation systems in leaky houses will simply add to heat losses.

Extractor fans must be ducted to outside

A controlled supply of fresh incoming air is essential to:

■ Provide fresh air for the occupants to breathe.
■ Provide sufficient air for combustion in fires and appliances.
■ Draw stale air out of the rooms and remove unpleasant wafts, water vapour, airborne gases and pollutants such as ciggy smoke and paint fumes.
■ Help maintain cool conditions in warm weather.

Ventilation heat loss

As you improve the amount of insulation in a property and make it less leaky, it will hang on to a lot more of its heat. Paradoxically, this means that the *relative* amount of heat lost through any remaining air leaks and ventilation becomes much more significant.

For example, in a typical unimproved 3 bed semi, nearly 80% of heat loss is through the building fabric. Draughts and ventilation are a comparatively minor issue. But as you make further improvements to the insulation of the fabric, the losses from air infiltration and ventilation start to dominate, at nearly 60% of the total. So to make significant reductions in heat loss requires attention not just to the insulation but also to draughtproofing, and hence also the ventilation system. There comes a point when using an advanced heat recovery ventilation system can reduce ventilation losses to a fraction of the total.

Ventilation options

In most homes, background ventilation is provided by uncontrolled draughts. When the occasional blast of 'purge' ventilation is needed, windows are flung open.

But once airtightness issues have been addressed and draughts sealed, a more sophisticated regime to provide fresh air is required, with a controllable ventilation system. There are several possible weapons in the ventilation armoury:

TRICKLE VENTS
Replacement windows normally incorporate trickle vents, usually fitted to the head of the frame. Alternatively, it's often possible to retro-fit them to existing windows. Trickle vents provide a controllable background supply of fresh air and are easy to open or close as the fancy takes you. The standard arrangement of one vent above each casement head should normally be sufficient. Humidity-controlled trickle vents are the best option as they open and close in response to room humidity levels (and don't need an electrical connection).

Room ventilation

The Building Regs refer to 3 main types of ventilation – *background*, *rapid* and *extract*.

BACKGROUND VENTILATION

Habitable rooms require a free airflow of 8,000mm² (4,000mm² to kitchens, bathrooms, utilities, and WCs). This is normally provided by trickle vents in the form of slots at the heads of windows, or airbricks sleeved through the cavity wall to an internal grille. Additional permanent ventilation is required for rooms containing heat-producing appliances, such as open-flued gas fires of rated input over 7kW and most 'living flame' effect fires.

RAPID/PURGE VENTILATION

Rapid ventilation (aka 'purge' ventilation) is provided by openable windows that allow the occupants to rapidly clear the air of paint fumes, foul toilet stenches, cooking smells etc. So the windows in all habitable rooms must be openable with a clear opening area equivalent to at least 1/20th of the floor area unless an approved mechanical ventilation system is installed.

EXTRACT VENTILATION

The Building Regs require extractor fans fitted in kitchens to be capable of shifting 60 litres of air per second, and those in bathrooms and utility rooms 15 and 30 litres per second respectively. The best type to fit are the relatively quiet humidity-sensing fans that only come on when humidity rises to a preset level, or heat-recovery fans that recycle heat from extracted air.

Alternatively, PSV or continuous mechanical systems are an acceptable form of extract ventilation where certified by an approved body.

Note that solid-fuel appliances like Agas and wood-burning stoves aren't necessarily compatible with extractor fans. Open fires need to take their combustion air directly from inside the room. If this air supply is stolen by extractor fans, the consequential air starvation can leave occupants gasping. Hence the requirement for additional wall vents.

Single Room Heat Recovery units can be inserted through the wall to replace conventional extractor fans or as new installations to WCs, kitchens, bathrooms and utility rooms. They can recover up to 75% of heat from the air that would normally be lost through extraction.

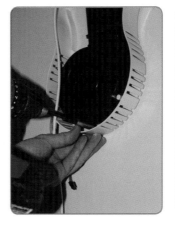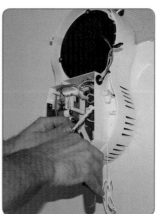

EXTRACTOR FANS

Extractor fans in bathrooms and kitchens are good at removing foul odours and moist, humid air. The trouble is, some older ones drone on for hours like an annoying moped stuck in your ceiling, and hence rarely get used. So be sure to fit the latest smooth operating semi-silent types. Units with DC motors consume considerably less electricity. It's essential to check that the ducting in the

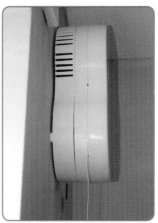

loft is properly connected to a suitable vent on the roof or eaves rather than just pumping lots of moist air straight into a cold loft, causing massive amounts of condensation. Be aware also that the longer the length of ducting, the greater the chance that the warm, moist air being channelled inside will cool, forming puddles of water that run back down – using specially lagged ducting can reduce this risk.

PASSIVE STACK VENTILATION (PSV)

The genius of passive stack ventilation is its simplicity. It can ventilate the house without the use of electric fans. Ducts link bathrooms and kitchens to terminals on the ridge of the roof. Humidity-controlled inlet vents control the extract rate, while humidity-controlled vents in living rooms and bedrooms control

AIRTIGHTNESS AND VENTILATION

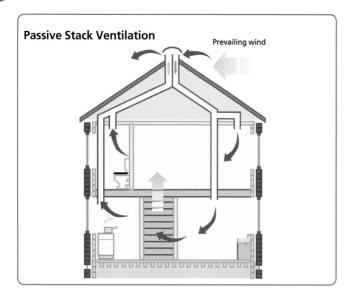

Passive Stack Ventilation

Prevailing wind

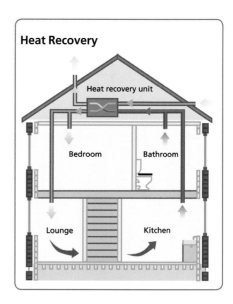

Heat Recovery

Heat recovery unit

Bedroom

Bathroom

Lounge

Kitchen

HEAT RECOVERY VENTILATION

All the above ventilation systems suffer from the same drawback – warmth is discarded along with the stale air. Heat recovery systems capture some of the heat in the exhaust air. This can be done on a room-by-room basis or with a whole-house system.

the incoming fresh air supply. But installing PSV requires careful planning to accommodate the stacks, and sometimes it may only be practical to serve upper floors.

MECHANICAL EXTRACT VENTILATION (MEV)

Continuous extract systems are ideal for improving air quality in airtight houses, so are often fitted to new homes. Moist air is sucked out of 'wet rooms' where water vapour is produced (ie bathrooms, cloakrooms, utilities and kitchens) and is extracted by a central fan and exhausted from the building. These work in tandem with trickle vents that allow fresh air to be drawn into living rooms and bedrooms. Extract rates can be boosted in different areas with passive infra-red moisture sensors (PIRs) and efficiency improved by using low wattage fans and humidity-controlled trickle vents.

The preferred option is a single centralised extractor fan unit with ducts to the wet rooms, but such 'whole-house' systems are more difficult to fit retrospectively to existing homes. Fortunately a new range of 'decentralised' fans has been developed that provide a simpler solution, more suited to retro-fitting. These can be installed in each wet room to run continuously. Referred to as 'decentralised whole-house extract' (or 'decentralised MEV') these

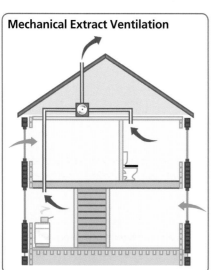

Mechanical Extract Ventilation

can be fitted as individual window or wall fans, or can be ducted so that the 'motor' isn't located in the room. It's unlikely that wall or window fans would be quiet enough to be left running continuously, so ducted systems with silencers might be the preferred solution.

ROOM VENTS WITH HEAT RECOVERY

These systems combine supply and extract ventilation with heat recovery in compact through-the-wall units. Heat recovery efficiency can be as high as 80% with fan power as low as 2W.

HEAT RECOVERY VENTILATION (HRV)

Whole-house mechanical HRV systems can recover up to 90% of the heat from the extract air. Typically, half an air change per hour is supplied, which is sufficient to provide good air quality. However, you need to select a system with high heat exchange efficiency, as some types only recover about 60%. The other essential consideration is fan power. If high wattage fans are used the cost of continuously running them can outweigh the heat recovery savings. Fan power is measured in total wattage per litre per second of extract air (W/(l/s)). Some systems use as much as 1.5 others as low as 0.5W/(l/s). But with low power fans, ducts need to be larger diameter (150mm), and of rigid construction with a smooth bore, with very few bends. Flexible ducts should only be used for the final terminations to air diffusers. The fan unit and all the ductwork must be located within the insulated airtight envelope of the house – ideally within a 'warm' roof space (ie one that's insulated at rafter level).

The downside is that retro-fitting HRV in existing homes is a major project, best carried out as part of a planned refurbishment of the house. To operate effectively, the whole house must be thoroughly sealed and tested for airtightness. No trickle vents are required to windows and if present should be removed, the holes sealed with foam and blanked over inside. Fireplaces also need to be sealed.

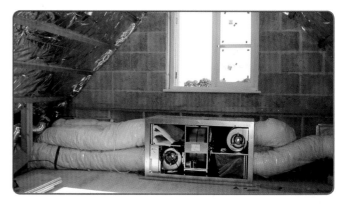

INSTALLING EXTRACTOR FANS

(Courtesy SURE Insulation)

Tools and materials
- Core drill with bit size to suit fan
- Extract fan and wall kit
- Mastic
- Sealant foam
- Electrical fan isolator switch

Health and safety
- Access equipment (indoor and outdoor)

Extractor fans should be provided to any rooms where water vapour is generated, such as bathrooms, shower rooms, kitchens, utility rooms and clothes-drying areas. It's also important that controllable trickle vents are fitted to windows in all rooms, and that if possible each room should have at least one opening window for summer ventilation.

There are two different types of fan suited to different rooms:

Type 1: Kitchens and bathrooms
These are designed to run continuously and shouldn't be turned off. They provide a controlled level of background ventilation once a reasonable level of airtightness has been achieved (*eg* EnviroVent Filterless Extract Fan). Note that cooker hoods are only needed to control excessive odours, and can be installed as an additional option – preferably an extracting type (with an external back-draught shutter) rather than the type that simply filters recirculated indoor air.

Type 2: Utility rooms and clothes-drying areas
These fans have timers and humidity sensors to switch them on and off automatically, but they can also be operated manually (*eg* EnviroVent Silent 100).

INSTALLATION
Power is normally provided from a lighting circuit (permanent live), or via a spur from the ring main. The fan isolator switch should be located somewhere reasonably accessible (so it can be turned off when the fan needs cleaning or maintenance), but out of reach of children, to prevent the fan being switched off by mistake. Key points include:

- Make sure that Type 1 fans are installed in a position where the pull cord is accessible. If necessary the cord can be extended using the eyelets on the cord.
- Ensure there's an airtight seal around the sleeving as it passes through the wall – both the internal and outdoor faces of the wall should be airtight. Use frame sealant or building mastic.
- Fill any voids between the sleeve and the wall with expanding foam to prevent cold air penetrating.
- Ensure that any electrical cables run to the fan are sealed to maintain airtightness. To achieve this seal use correct size grommets or small amounts of mastic.

Photos: LEDA Ltd

Above: Use drill with dust extractor to cut core in wall for vent sleeving.
Insert sleeving tube, fit exterior terminal and seal any gaps

Left: Screw fan body to wall and connect up

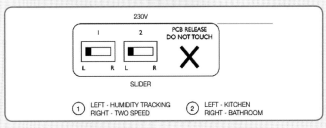

Setting the dip switches.

Programme the installed fans as follows:

Fan Type 1
Set the fan dip switches to the appropriate room, and set humidity tracking to 'run'. Set DP 1 to left; and DP 2 to left for kitchen, right for bathroom. (See diagram.)

Fan Type 2
These are wired with a dedicated switch (either wall-mounted or a pull-cord). Set the humidity level to 65% RH and timed run on to 30 minutes.

Home Insulation Manual

4 WALLS

Photos: Kingspan

When it comes to leaking heat, the walls of your home are top of the list – responsible for a whopping 35% of all heat loss from the home, or as much as 45% for older solid-wall houses. The good news is that most houses have cavity walls, which are relatively easy to insulate. But although older buildings with traditional solid walls can be more costly to treat, upgrading them can still reap generous rewards with improved comfort levels and significantly reduced energy consumption.

Natural wood-fibre insulation is suitable for use on walls of all types

And as you might expect, it's properties with large expanses of exposed un-insulated walls that stand to gain the most from being insulated – *ie* detached and semi-detached buildings.

What kind of walls have you got?

Before doing anything, it's essential to know what you're dealing with. As we saw in Chapter 1, clues to the type of construction are evident in the pattern of brickwork. Solid walls have some of their bricks laid across the wall, whereas cavity walls are built in 'stretcher' bond, with all the bricks laid lengthways. Particular care is needed to identify houses of modern timber frame construction, as the outer leaf can appear identical to a masonry cavity wall.

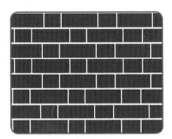

Opportunities

If you're planning major projects like refitting the kitchen or bathroom, or perhaps a spot of re-plastering, this can be an ideal opportunity to line the walls internally. Similarly, if your external rendering needs attention or extensive pointing of brickwork is required, it's worth exploring the possibility of insulating externally, as it could save you having to do some of this work.

Do I need planning permission?

Cavity wall insulation (CWI) isn't visible once completed, so you don't need to worry about planning consent. Internal wall insulation (IWI) can also be freely installed, except of course in Listed buildings. In Conservation Areas, external wall insulation (EWI) to the front of the property will definitely need consent (and sometimes also to the sides, if visible from the street).

Comparison of different wall insulation methods			
Insulation methods	*Internal IWI*	*Cavity CWI*	*External EWI*
Affects external appearance?	No	No	Yes
Potential for thermal improvement.	Good	Good	Good
Can you live there during installation?	Yes – subject to localised upheaval	Yes	Yes – subject to external upheaval
Does it give added protection to the wall structure?	No	Very little	Yes
Cost	££	£	£££

Targets

The Building Regulations set target U-values for insulating walls to existing dwellings. These are more demanding for solid walls than for more modern cavity construction (which is a little surprising given that solid walls are harder to treat).

Type of wall	*Target U-values for refurbishment (W/m^{2}K)*
Cavity insulated	0.55
Externally insulated	0.35
Internally insulated	0.35

Payback periods

When insulating solid-walled buildings, it's important to get the detailing right to avoid gaps and cold bridges and this can add to the cost. Payback periods are typically around 20 years. However, this still represents a relatively good return on your investment than putting money in savings accounts, and compares very favourably to double glazing payback times, which can be two or three times longer.

Period properties

Most older properties were built with solid walls, but as the buildings have evolved over time many have sprouted additions and by now comprise a variety of different types of construction – anything from perilously thin single-brick walls up to castle-like rubble-filled stone walls half a metre or more thick.

As well as containing bricks of varying age and hardness, old walls might comprise all manner of sandstone, limestone, granite or flint, not forgetting traditional materials such as timber or mud. Standardised computer programs can struggle to calculate the thermal performance of more complex properties, so the advice churned out in EPCs for older buildings may be misleading and should be treated with a large pinch of salt.

As we saw in Chapter 1, old houses work in a very different way to modern ones. Maintaining 'breathability' is important, so that moisture that's absorbed by the walls when it rains is free to

Heat loss through uninsulated solid walls is typically 50% greater than through uninsulated cavity walls

evaporate out in dry weather. Covering the outside of walls in non-breathable materials therefore risks trapping moisture within the wall, leading to damp and decay.

ORGANIC FABRIC

Masonry walls would traditionally be lime-plastered, and ceilings and stud walls lined with lath and plaster. This is thicker and lumpier than modern plasterboard, and is part of the history and character of the buildings. These naturally breathable materials allow moisture to escape from the walls and are worth preserving where possible. Where old plaster isn't sound enough to support new insulation, fixings may need to be driven a bit deeper into the masonry or timber posts behind. A better solution may be to build a new independent studwork inner wall (and suspended ceilings). This has the advantage of creating a separate ventilated airspace between the old wall and the new insulation, allowing retention of original features whilst assisting 'breathability'.

TIMBER FRAME HOUSES

One of the more difficult types of wall to insulate is the 'Olde Worlde' timber frame variety. Most properties of this age will be Listed, so consent is required for any works, inside or out. Because their walls are generally very thin – often not much more than 100mm – there's usually considerable scope for improving their thermal efficiency. But the real challenge is to achieve worthwhile gains without compromising the building's appearance.

Most timber frame houses were built with the frame exposed and the spaces between filled with wattle and daub (sticks and mud). Many such panels were later replaced in more robust brickwork – an early attempt at upgrading thermal efficiency.

Before embarking on insulation work, it's important to first check whether any repairs are needed. Piggybacking thermal improvements with any other works can be a useful way to spread the cost. A lot of old buildings suffer from self-inflicted damp problems thanks to the use of inappropriate modern materials, such as cement mortars, renders, gypsum plasters and paints. So the first job may be to replace these with traditional lime-based materials, which are breathable. Damp problems at lower levels can often be resolved by reducing external ground levels and installing a shallow gravel-filled ditch known as a 'French drain'.

WHAT TYPE OF INSULATION?

Natural breathable insulation materials compatible with historic timber frame walls include:

- Wood fibreboard
- Sheep's wool batts
- Hemp fibre insulation boards
- Wood wool boards
- Cellulose fibre
- Flax fibre batts

Sheepswool (Thermafleece)

Sheepswool (Thermafleece)

Hempcrete

Photo: Cat.org.uk

One material especially well suited for timber frame walls is 'hempcrete', which has long been used in France to repair traditional properties because it has the same stiffness, breathability and flexibility as wattle and daub and can accommodate a certain amount of movement in the timber frame. It's also a very effective insulation material containing a great deal of air, and has inherent 'thermal mass' (so when used internally can help moderate room temperatures). Insulation can be finished externally and internally with lime renders, tile or timber cladding or clay plasters.

IMPROVING THERMAL PERFORMANCE

Timber frame walls can either be insulated externally, internally or in between the frame. Each approach can present significant challenges, which are discussed in the following pages.

A less ambitious but very worthwhile and inexpensive solution is to tackle heat loss caused by draughts. It's very common for cracks and draughty gaps to have developed between the timber frame and the infill panels. These are sometimes so obvious that you can see chinks of light coming through. Traditional hair-lime mortars are a compatible filler. Don't use mastics, cement and other impermeable sealants, as they trap damp. For the same reason impervious vapour barrier membranes are best substituted with 'breather' membranes similar to those used on new roofs. These resist the passage of water into the wall but, crucially, allow moisture to escape.

Thermal mass

Thick solid masonry walls have a special quality known as 'thermal mass'. This means that in warm weather they act like giant storage heaters, absorbing heat and releasing it later when the surroundings have cooled down. So in summer the walls help cool the interior during the day by absorbing excess heat, which is then slowly released during the night. This has a beneficial stabilising effect on the indoor environment.

If you insulate the walls by lining them internally this has the effect of isolating the room from the masonry walls that have been treated. Hence you no longer get the full benefit of all that 'free warmth' embodied in these walls (although the other unlined walls in the room should still be functioning). This may be something of a loss on cold nights, but on a hot summer's night you might be glad that the walls aren't radiating heat and making the room even hotter.

CAVITY WALL INSULATION

Cavity wall insulation (CWI) is one of the most cost-effective of all energy saving measures, coming a close second to loft insulation. Filling the space inside your walls can reduce heat loss by a whopping 40%, with equally dramatic savings in heating bills.

Photo: British Gas

There are two further advantages: CWI requires zero maintenance and installing it causes very little disturbance. The insulation is pumped into the cavity through the outer masonry leaf, so the job can be done almost without the occupants knowing.

A typical installation costs around £300–£400, with the investment being recouped as savings in fuel bills in as little as two or three years. This may explain why more than half a million cavity wall installations are carried out each year in Britain.

The reason CWI is effective is because cold air circulating in unfilled cavities can seep into the house through lots of tiny gaps, such as old pipe holes or where floor joists are built into walls. Even in modern homes with dry-lined walls and joists supported on hangers, small gaps at mortar joints to the inner leaf blockwork can allow blasts of chilly air to swirl around behind the plasterboard. Filling your cavities reduces the movement of air, helping to banish draughts and reduce heat loss. This in turn makes the internal surface temperature of the walls warmer, reducing the potential for condensation and making the rooms feel more comfortable.

Detractors of CWI point to concerns about damp, and the fact that cavities are rarely wide enough to get sufficient thickness of insulation to achieve exceptionally good thermal improvements.

Photos: British Gas

Identifying a cavity wall

The first step is to check whether your home has walls that are suitable for filling. Cavity walls comprise two separate thin walls (known as 'leaves' or 'skins'), usually of brick or blockwork, with a gap in between. The inner and outer leaves are held together using metal wall ties. In theory, any moisture that manages to penetrate through the outer masonry wall should be able to trickle back out through small weep holes built into the outer walls; but these also allow cold air *into* the cavity.

As we saw earlier, the biggest clue to identifying brick cavity walls is that all the bricks are laid lengthways, end to end, so that only their sides are visible. An interesting exception to this rule is sometimes found in modern extensions to period properties where the planners required the brickwork to mimic traditional construction by using 'split headers' – so it looks like a solid wall (with alternate ends of half bricks visible).

Of course, many walls have outer leaves built from materials other than brick, such as natural stone, reconstituted stone blocks, or blockwork with a rendered finish or clad in tiles or timber boarding. Helpfully there's another clue in the thickness of the wall. Cavity walls are typically about 280mm thick (and rarely less than 250mm), which is significantly thicker than traditional 9in (229mm) solid brick walls. As a rule, the more modern the house, the thicker the walls and the wider the cavity. Some modern houses feature traditional-looking stonework or flint panelling set within a much thicker outer leaf, but are cavity walls nonetheless.

As we have seen, the age of the property can also assist with the diagnosis. It was known as far back as Victorian times that walls built from two single leaves tied together with a gap in the middle were very effective at preventing damp. But although a few such houses were built from the late 19th century, it wasn't until the 1930s that cavity wall construction started to become mainstream. Even then, many builders persisted with traditional solid walls, or hedged their bets with a mix of cavity walls to the ground floor and rendered solid masonry above.

As noted earlier, an important exception to watch out for is modern timber frame construction, fairly common in homes built from the late 1970s onwards. These buildings have a load-bearing inner leaf of insulated timber panel construction, and the cavities mustn't be insulated because ventilation is essential for removing moisture. Mistakenly filling such cavities can result in serious problems with rot to the load-bearing timber inner leaf. The trouble is, the outer masonry walls appear identical to conventional brick and block. Indoors, casually tapping the plasterboarded walls will merely illicit a hollow sound – which could equally indicate a conventional masonry wall dry-lined with plasterboard. To spot the difference you need to look in the loft, where the gable and party walls are made of timber panels rather than brick or blockwork. Another clue is that the walls are typically thinner than the equivalent cavity masonry variety (typically about 260mm compared to 280mm or wider). If in doubt consult an experienced chartered surveyor, architect or reputable specialist installer.

Hard-to-treat walls

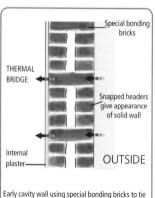

Photo: British Gas

1970s houses of cross wall construction – only the end walls are of cavity brickwork

THERMAL BRIDGE

Special bonding bricks

Snapped headers give appearance of solid wall

Internal plaster

OUTSIDE

Early cavity wall using special bonding bricks to tie leaves together. Looks like a solid wall, but overall thickness is a clue to cavity construction

Stone outer leaf

Iron cavity ties

OUTSIDE

Early cavity wall with stone outer leaf. Cavity widths vary and wall ties are of cast or wrought iron.

Just because a wall was built with a gap in the middle doesn't automatically make it suitable for filling retrospectively. For a start, any cavity that's less than 50mm wide isn't normally acceptable, because the narrower the space, the lower the exposure zone a filled wall can tolerate. The widths of cavities vary considerably, from less than 50mm in some early designs to 100mm or more in modern construction; but a typical cavity in houses built from the 1950s to the early 1990s would be around 60mm to 80mm. So this is rarely a problem except for some much older properties with impossibly narrow 'finger' cavities (because a finger is about all you can stick down them).

There are a number of other potential concerns to watch out for that could render a property unsuitable, with cavities deemed 'unfillable':

TALL WALLS
Wall height can be a limiting factor in buildings higher than 12m (about four storeys). The higher the wall, the more exposed to driving rain it's likely to be, hence there are certain restrictions on height. But in a conventional two-storey house with walls around 6m high (plus another 3m or so at any roof gables) this shouldn't be a problem.

POOR ACCESS
It's not unusual for conservatories, garages and lean-to extensions to obstruct access to upper walls. Scaffolding is one way round the problem but the additional expense could make the project uneconomic. Although in theory cavities could be injected from indoors through the inner leaf, in practice unless you have exposed 'feature brickwork' it's not normally an option – removing dry lining or drilling through plasterwork to reach the brick or blockwork will cause considerable upheaval and increased cost.

PANEL INSERTS
Many houses built in the 1960s and '70s feature large decorative wall panels. Various forms of tile hanging were popular, along

with timber weatherboarding (many subsequently replaced in UPVC) or thin sheets of painted plywood. Behind these facades there's usually a thin backing wall of breezeblock or timber studwork. Either way, these are about as thermally efficient as a tea towel. This rather spoils things for cavity wall insulators, because there's no cavity to inject. Hence these thin, leaky panelled areas commonly get overlooked. Some buildings from the same era are of 'cross wall' construction where the entire front and rear elevations are similarly constituted. Insulating means treating them as solid walls – ie lining the wall internally or externally, where possible reinstating the coverings over the insulation. Alternatively these (usually non-load-bearing) panelled areas can be rebuilt in matching cavity masonry with insulation installed during construction.

BAYS
Bay windows, very common on cavity wall houses built in the 1930s to 1950s, are often of similar tile-hung construction as described above. But since they're devoid of a cavity these can be the weakest link in a property's thermal defences.

PARTY WALLS
The wall that separates you from next door normally isn't, by definition, exposed to the elements. The exception is where terraced houses were built in a 'staggered' design with some projecting

a little further forward than their neighbours. Although in most cases insulating these 'dividing walls' tends to be less of a priority, research has shown that cold air flowing inside party wall cavities can be a significant source of cooling. Insulating them can also provide acoustic sound-deadening benefits.

However, many party walls are actually of solid construction. Even where they were built with cavities, the gap may sometimes be too narrow for filling. Drilling a discreet hole through a mortar joint in the 'firebreak' party wall in the loft will reveal any cavity – taking care not to penetrate right through! (If the drill hasn't located a void after about 100mm it's probably solid masonry).

Many older homes will have traditional fireplaces occupying a central position, only leaving alcoves either side to fill. More modern cavity party walls sometimes conceal hidden flues, pipes and electric cables. Be aware also that works to party walls legally require advanced notice to the neighbour under the terms of the Party Wall Act.

PRC AND STEEL FRAME

BISF steel frame construction

Houses of non-conventional construction such as concrete or steel frame are normally unsuited for CWI. One reason for this is a lack of mortar joints for drilling into. Some structures of this type are officially deemed 'defective', with potential corrosion issues to metal components. They also tend to have thin cavities with the risk that injected insulation can snag on the frame leaving cold unfilled gaps. External or internal wall lining is normally the best solution.

THICK STONE WALLS

Traditional 'solid' stone walls, typically half a metre or more thick, were commonly built with a space left in the middle between two thinner solid walls. This would be partially filled with rubble and mortar, but some contain voids. Pumping foam insulation into thick walls of this type isn't advisable because any cavities will be extremely uneven, plus the foam can interfere with breathability, risking damp problems. Lining such walls internally can be a better option.

MODERN TIMBER FRAME

As noted above, buildings of modern timber frame construction also fall into the 'difficult to treat' category, and shouldn't have their cavities filled. These buildings are generally 'warmer' than

those of conventional brick and block because the inner timber panels are pre-insulated to achieved better U-values. But there may still be scope for improvement. Older walls may only contain about 25mm of insulation (typically mineral wool quilt fitted to the inner leaf), and over the years this may have settled, leaving gaps. Frames are normally a minimum of 90mm deep with plenty of spare capacity for beefing up thermal performance. The simplest improvement is to draughtproof gaps at sockets and switches that penetrate into the structure.

When it comes to adding insulation, there are two main methods by which this can be done. Either strip off the inner surface layer of plasterboard and fit rigid or semi-rigid insulation between the studs, then line with a vapour control sheet and new plasterboard. Alternatively, holes can be drilled in the plasterboard and loose-fill insulation blown into the panel spaces (which look a little like bookshelves, separated from the cavity with timber sheathing board). Blowing requires specialist equipment but is less disruptive. Or you could line them internally or externally, as with solid walls.

How does filling the cavity affect the wall?

Houses with cavity walls were first constructed in exposed coastal areas as a method of preventing problems of dampness from wind-driven rain experienced by some solid-walled dwellings. The idea was that the cavity would act like a 'moat of air' that

Exposure zones and rain penetration

The Building Research Establishment states that 'in exposed locations, driving rain can penetrate the outer leaf of masonry leading to wetting of the cavity insulation and reduced thermal performance'.

It's important therefore to assess a property's location before specifying the appropriate insulation work. The UK is divided into four 'exposure zones'. Zones 1 and 2 are classified respectively as 'sheltered' and 'moderate'. Zones 3 and 4 are 'severe' and 'very severe'.

Buildings located in the more severe weather zones may be subject to restrictions, and walls may require additional protection with rendering or cladding. Mineral wool fibre and expanded polystyrene beads are certified for use in cavities up to 12m in height (from ground to apex) in all geographical areas within the UK. However, not all types of cavity fill are suitable for use in zones 3 and 4. For example, some types of foam insulation have certain restrictions.

Exposure zones	Approximate wind-driven rain (litres/m² per spell)
1. Sheltered	less than 33
2. Moderate	33 to less than 56.5
3. Severe	56.5 to less than 100
4. Very severe	100 or more

prevented moisture from passing across from the 'wet' outer leaf to the 'dry' inner leaf. So when cavities are filled it effectively bridges the gap between the two masonry leaves. Consequently concerns are sometimes raised about the risk of dampness affecting the insulation, or tracking across the cavity, resulting in reduced thermal performance.

The good news is that CWI has been a popular treatment for residential properties for many years, and statistically it doesn't appear that filling cavities has resulted in significantly greater incidences of damp problems than in houses where the walls have been left untouched. The insulation material is, after all, water-resistant. However, that doesn't mean that it's without risk.

Experts at the Building Research Establishment (BRE) confirm that 'there can be an increased risk of rain penetration if a cavity is fully filled with insulation, where moisture is able to transfer from the outer to the inner leaves resulting in areas of dampness on internal finishes'. But the risk of such problems largely depends on the severity of the weather in a particular location (see panel).

Today the most commonly used materials in new wall construction are rigid foam boards (which are intrinsically waterproof), semi-rigid mineral wool batts and, more recently, polystyrene beads. But the requirement to insulate new homes was only introduced in the Building Regulations from 1985, and was initially achieved simply by substituting an inner skin of thermally efficient blocks in lieu of dense concrete blockwork. Placing insulation inside cavities only became standard newbuild practice from the late 1990s and doubts are periodically raised about quality control, with gaps and poor joints between boards or batts.

What can go wrong?

As with all types of building work, there's always the possibility that workmanship could be less than perfect. For example, any unfilled pockets of air left inside the insulation can form 'cold spots' on the inside walls, which are likely to attract condensation patches and black mould. The wrong choice of insulation materials for the location can also lead to problems. Another potential concern is that, over time, some materials can be prone to compacting and settling, leaving large un-insulated areas at the tops of walls. Overenthusiastic installers have been known to block flues or airbricks and blow insulation out the tops of walls into lofts, or even into adjoining properties.

Foam insulation has squirted out the tops of the walls!

Probably the biggest worry is the risk of damp. Wet insulation can be worse than no insulation at all, in the same way that a wet vest will make you colder than wearing no vest. The key factors when it comes to avoiding damp penetration are the condition of the existing wall, especially the pointing to mortar joints, and the building's exposure to wild weather.

More of a concern is where the walls were poorly built in the first place, *eg* it's not unusual to find mortar

Thermal bridging

Cold corners can attract mould staining - cavities may be partially blocked at lower levels

Insulated cavity closers in new wall (but metal fixings bridge across)

By the nature of their construction cavity walls incorporate thermal bridges. Metal wall ties can potentially form localised 'cold spots' on inner walls, despite being surrounded by insulation. In fact anywhere something crosses a cavity is potentially at risk. In some very early properties bricks were used as ties, physically bridging across the cavity. Such walls are unsuitable for filling.

Other common weak points are found at window reveals and at the tops of walls where bricks were used to seal off the ends of cavities. In new construction today insulated cavity closers are fitted to prevent this. At the tops of walls, extending loft insulation over the wall head can help maintain consistent coverage, or installing coving to the upper walls to bedroom ceilings.

In some cases where condensation issues are reported after insulation, the problem can largely be due to poor ventilation and steamy lifestyles! So part of the solution is to install controlled ventilation – see Chapter 3.

droppings on the wall ties, which can sometimes allow damp to track across. In one recent case a damp problem was traced to a builder's donkey jacket bricked up at the base of the wall (complete with an original 1970s tobacco pouch of Golden Virginia!).

Where flooding or serious damp has occurred cavities can sometimes be cleared by sucking wet insulation out of the walls using injection pumps set in reverse.

WALL TIE CORROSION

Wall ties perform the vital task of holding the inner and outer leaves of a wall together, making the whole edifice structurally stable. In normal dry conditions they should last a good century or more. Many date back more than 70 years and are still doing fine, sitting quite happily in filled cavities. But being made of iron or steel, rust is always a potential enemy. When persistently damp they can corrode quite swiftly, and replacing them is a costly and time-consuming process, involving cutting out dozens of individual bricks from the outer leaf. Replacing corroded wall ties is more difficult where cavities are filled because the insulation first has to be removed around each

tie, and refilling the gaps left in the insulation can be difficult.

There's some debate about whether CWI actually hastens rusting in wall ties. In theory insulating can make corrosion more likely, because once the walls are stuffed full of insulation, warmth from the rooms will no longer be able to escape into the cavity, which will therefore remain colder than before, as will the outer leaf. The worry is that if any warm, moist air from inside the house manages to find its way through the inner wall and into gaps in the insulation it's more likely to condense on the colder wall ties.

Above: Patches visible prior to redecoration where corroded wall ties have been cut out and replaced

Right: Tell-tale horizontal cracking caused by expansion from rusted wall ties

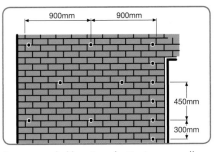

Recommended locations for ties in new walls

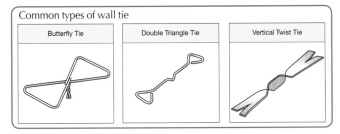

Common types of wall tie

| Butterfly Tie | Double Triangle Tie | Vertical Twist Tie |

On the other hand if they're totally sealed within insulation that shouldn't be a problem.

Probably more of a risk is where driving rain can get through the outer wall, making the insulation wet. As there's no longer any airflow within the cavity, dampness can't escape; and densely packed insulation that's harbouring moisture in close contact with metal wall ties is likely to accelerate corrosion.

Homes most at risk of wall tie corrosion are those built with wrought or cast iron 'fish-tail' ties prior to 1920, and those built with galvanised steel 'butterfly' ties between about 1964 and 1981. Salty sea air in exposed coastal areas also tends to hasten corrosion.

To pre-empt such problems homes are meant to be assessed by the contractor prior to installation, usually by peering into the cavity with a boroscope. However, the method recommended by experts at BRE is for two bricks to be removed on each elevation

(at high and low levels) and the ties tested for corrosion. This is a more effective method than using a boroscope, where you can't see the ends of the ties embedded in the mortar.

Types of insulation

The most common materials used to insulate cavity walls are mineral wool and bonded polystyrene beads. Polyurethane (PU) foams can also be very effective, with the additional benefit of providing a degree of structural reinforcement to walls.

	Thermal conductivity (Lambda value) W/m²K
Mineral wool and fibres	
Glass wool (some made from recycled glass bottles)	0.040
Rock wool / stone wool	0.039
Cellulose fibre (eg 'Warmcell')	0.40
Beads or granules	
Expanded polystyrene (EPS) beads	0.033–0.040
Expanded polystyrene (EPS) granules	0.030–0.038
Polyurethane (PUR) granules	0.022–0.028
Perlite beads	0.045
Foamed insulants	
Urea-formaldehyde foam (UF)	0.40
Polyurethane foam (PUR)	0.022–0.028

There are also some high-tech materials available such as silica-based 'Nanogel' with ultra-low thermal conductivity of 0.15, which is up to four times better than mainstream materials. This makes it suitable for use in some narrow cavities that would otherwise be 'unfillable'. It also has excellent acoustic resistance, but inevitably it's super-expensive and hence rarely used at present.

BLOWN MINERAL WOOL FIBRE

This is similar to the mineral quilt insulation used in lofts. Here it takes the form of small tufts that are blown down a hose into walls by a sort of reverse-thrust vacuum cleaner. Some types made from recycled glass have a similar texture to cotton wool. Although water-repellent it only has to become slightly damp to lose its insulation properties, potentially drawing heat out of the house.

Poorly installed blown mineral fibre can also suffer from cold gaps in the insulation, with resulting condensation patches developing on room walls. Concerns have also been raised about the long-term performance of mineral fibre in more exposed environments, but if pre-installation site checks are properly carried out this shouldn't be an issue. Fibre can also be prone to settling within the cavity over time, leaving cold voids at the top of the house. It's important that the contractors install the materials to the correct density, which for glass fibre mineral wool is around 28kg per m³, whereas natural cellulose fibre typically needs a much higher density of 60kg per m³.

BEADS AND GRANULES

Popular with mainstream housebuilders, polystyrene beads and granules provide good insulation qualities and are generally effective at achieving consistent gap-free coverage within cavities. Beads made from polyurethane can offer even better thermal performance. However, although beads and granules are waterproof there are reported cases where incomplete filling has left voids that allowed water to track across the cavity.

Photo: The Insta Group

Loosefill polystyrene beads

	Pros	Cons
Blown mineral wool fibre	• Relatively cheap. • Quick to install. • Water-repellent. • Vapour permeable. • BBA certified and can be CIGA guaranteed.	• Potential to retain water and wick across cavities. • Loses insulation properties if damp. • Can suffer from gaps in the insulation, if wrongly installed. • Prone to settling under its own weight. • Not recommended for some high-exposure locations.
Cellulose loose-fill	• Recycled paper content. • Safe to handle and non-irritant. • Fire-resistant. • Resistant to fungal attack.	• Can wick moisture across cavities. • Not tolerant of damp, so unsuited to high-exposure locations. • Can settle under its own weight. • Not CIGA guaranteed. • Limited BBA certification.
Bonded polystyrene beads	• Superior thermal performance to mineral wool fibre. • Inherently waterproof. • Non-irritant and safe to handle. • EPS is BBA certified and can be CIGA guaranteed. • Resistant to fungal attack.	• More expensive and takes longer to install than mineral wool. • Can suffer from gaps in the insulation if wrongly installed, due to 'static cling'. • Poor bonding can allow escape of granules. • Tops of cavities must be capped.
Foamed insulants	• PUR is one of the best insulating materials. • Foam seals all gaps, minimising air leakage, and can strengthen walls. • Inherently waterproof. • Resistant to fungal attack. • PUR is BBA certified.	• More expensive and takes longer to install than mineral wool. • UF foams cannot be used in high-exposure locations or high-rise. • Not all types are CIGA guaranteed. • UF foams unsuited in walls with galvanised steel 'butterfly' wall ties.

In most of the UK all three main cavity insulation materials can be used. However, some are better suited than others where conditions are more demanding.

EPS beads are spherical, with diameters varying from 2mm to 8mm. If you've ever punctured a beanbag you'll know from bitter experience that they're very free flowing! This means they require fewer injection holes through the outer leaf. Granules, being irregular in shape, are less free flowing. To limit the risk of escape through cracks and openings, specially bonded beads are coated with adhesive just prior to being injected into the wall. In some cases insufficient bonding has allowed loose beads to escape through airbricks or to pour out of the walls during later alterations. Others have suffered from careless installation, blowing out the top of the cavities into loft spaces and gutters.

FOAM INSULATION

The thermal insulation value of polyurethane (PUR) is amongst the best available. Applied in foam form in cavity walls it also has the ability to enhance structural strength as the foam seals gaps and moulds itself to wall contours as well as creating its own vapour control layer. The foam expands in the cavity and sets into a closed-celled rigid material, strongly adhering to both leaves and bonding them together. This can make it a useful material for stabilising walls where the metal ties have corroded.

Polyurethane foam consists of liquid ingredients mixed together and injected into the cavity via 12mm diameter holes through one leaf of the wall. But, as always, a successful outcome is dependent on good quality control on site.

Photo: Yorkshireinsulation.co.uk

PUR foam injected into wall

Urea-formaldehyde (UF) is a similar type of foam insulation that can be pumped into cavities, consisting of a resin and hardener solution. After injection the foam hardens and shrinks slightly as it dries, with a certain amount of thin spidery 'fissuring' developing. Although UF foam produces formaldehyde vapour as it hardens, good ventilation of any affected rooms should remove lingering traces. Concerns that it might accelerate corrosion in galvanised steel wall ties have not been borne out by research. However, some older installations have degraded over time, becoming cracked and powdery.

What does the job involve?

Although it's possible to hire the necessary equipment, when you factor in the cost and risks of attempting a DIY job it simply doesn't add up. Cavity wall insulation is a specialist job that should be carried out by an approved installer (registered by either BBA or BSI). Upon completion of the work they will arrange for the Cavity Insulation Guarantee Agency to issue a CIGA guarantee covering defects in materials and workmanship over a 25-year period. CIGA

Left: Make sure you get a cavity insulation guarantee

Above: 'Fibremaster' blowing machines can be hired

Photo: Firstinsulation.co.uk

are an independent agency, so should the contractor go bust in the meantime the warranty should still apply. If there are any post-installation problems the homeowner will need to contact the approved installer, who should inspect and remedy the problem free of charge.

Under the scheme, an approved installer is required to:

■ Carry out a pre-installation assessment of the property to determine its suitability.
■ Install the insulation in accordance with approved technical standards, and make good afterwards.
■ Provide the customer with a guarantee issued by CIGA on completion.

Key 'advance survey' checks

■ Is the wall of cavity masonry construction?
■ Is the wall taller than 12m?
■ Check the exposure rating of the wall.
■ Has it already been filled?
■ Are there any defects externally that need to be remedied, such as failed pointing?
■ Are there any defects evident inside, such as damp problems?
■ Note the position of any penetrations through the wall (eg flues and vents etc).
■ Are there any adjoining cavity walls (in terraced or semi-detached houses)?
■ Can the installer gain safe access externally?
■ Is there anything that would invalidate the provision of a CIGA guarantee?

Checking the suitability of walls

The contractor is responsible for checking the type and condition of the wall to determine whether it's suitable for filling. There are three key parts of the building that must be surveyed prior to installation work – the outer wall surface, the inner wall and the cavity itself:

■ External inspection

The outer wall surface should be free from defects such as significant cracking, eroded pointing or masonry and dampness. Wall heights must be checked in relation to their exposure to wind-driven rain and the correct type of fill selected. Any leaking gutters, pipes or worn sills etc that could cause damp penetration to the walls must be repaired. Houses with integral concrete 'Finlock' gutters (circa 1950s) are often damp at the tops of walls and may need to be lined.

■ Internal inspection

Walls should be free from damp, and any visible gaps to the inner leaf should be sealed so the insulation doesn't seep into the house. The tops of cavities in the loft should be checked and if necessary sealed to prevent the fill being blown into the loft. Any service pipes and cables, ventilation ducts and flues will need to be sleeved through both leaves of the wall.

■ Cavity inspection

Cavities must be at least 50mm wide to be eligible for a CIGA guarantee. This can be confirmed by drilling small holes in mortar

Old air brick replaced with new one sleeved through cavity

Photos: Knauf Supafil

joints near each corner and inserting a measuring stick. The total amount of fill to be used can then be calculated by multiplying the cavity width by the number of square metres of wall. Using a boroscope inserted through these test holes the condition of a sample of wall ties can be checked on each elevation, and cavities viewed to identify any blockages.

Airbricks at ground-floor level must be clear. Older ones (typically pre-1970s) often need to be sleeved through the cavity so the insulation doesn't block them (some 1950s houses with solid floors have air bricks simply for venting cavities).

Injecting the walls

Having confirmed that the property is suitable, the contractor may need to submit a Building Notice to Building Control, although most firms should be able to self-certify as 'competent persons'. This means that at least one person supervising on site needs to be 'carded' with BBA certification.

Although the installation usually takes only half a day or so to complete, the need for any extra repairs can significantly extend

Photos (pages 46 & 47): GreenPuzzle.co.uk

timescales. The work is done entirely from the outside so it causes little disturbance (other than noise from drilling injection holes and pumping the insulant).

The installation process

■ Before starting, a preliminary 'box test' is carried out. This involves pumping the fill into small test box to check that it's working at the correct density and that the pumping machine is calibrated correctly (see pics 1–3).

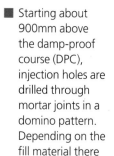

■ Starting about 900mm above the damp-proof course (DPC), injection holes are drilled through mortar joints in a domino pattern. Depending on the fill material there will be a recommended pattern of injection holes. For mineral fibre this is typically about 1.35m apart – ie approximately 5 bricks along and 17 courses up. Holes are drilled closer together around openings – typically 2 bricks away from the side of each window/door, and 3 courses above and below. Similarly where any pipes etc cross the cavity, extra holes are drilled above and below. A 22mm drill bit is used, specially designed to extract as much brick dust as possible, to minimise the amount entering the cavity. The final hole is drilled near top of the gable.

With rendered walls, the location of the mortar joints can be calculated once the first courses (usually of blockwork) have been located, or by measuring up from DPC level. A team of two can drill and fill – but not on the same vertical stretch of wall, in case brick dust gets into the insulation.

- To prevent the fill entering adjacent properties, cavity barriers need to be installed. To do this a hole is drilled at the top of the wall and a second hole directly beneath it at the base of the wall (about three bricks from the top and bottom). A long flexible length of plastic barrier (in brush form) is attached it to a length of thin chain. This 'pilot' chain is poked into the top hole, inserted vertically down the cavity and fished out via the lower hole, pulling the cavity barrier in its wake. Once the barrier is in place the fill can't get past.

- The cavity is filled from the bottom of the wall upwards. The fill material is pumped or blown in under pressure into each injection hole in turn, starting at one end of an elevation at the bottom of a wall. All the holes in the lowest row of the elevation should be filled before moving up to the next row, ensuring that no gaps are left in the insulation between injection points. At the very top it's not usually necessary to fully fill gable walls to the absolute peak, unless the loft space is used as living space, but it's best to continue about a metre above ceiling level to allow for future settlement.
- Periodic checks are needed during installation to ensure the wall is filling up evenly. It should be possible to see the insulant as it rises to the next layer of fill holes above. With some types of insulation such as foam, indicator sticks placed in the injection holes should twitch when that part of the cavity is full. The pump should automatically cut off when an area is full due to 'pressure blow-back', but vigilance is necessary to spot any fill squirting out into lofts etc. If the filling time is less than normal, the cavity may not be full; but if the filling time seems longer than normal, it may be leaking into adjoining walls next door! When the cavity is full, back pressure should stop the flow.
- On completion, the quantity of insulant used should be compared with the amount estimated at the outset. A remaining surplus of more than 10% may indicate missed areas. On the other hand, if a lot more has been used check the interior of the property to make sure that the fill hasn't entered the dwelling. Any fill that's entered air vents, service ducts, flues and weep holes should be cleared.

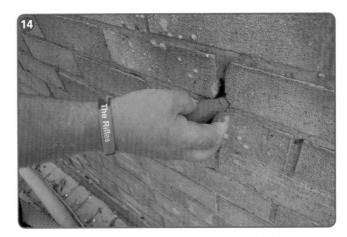

- The injection holes are made good with mortar or render after all checks and tests are complete. Mortar should be a fairly dryish mix and rolled into a sausage shape to apply into the fill holes. Dye can be added to the mix to obtain a colour match.

- Thermal imaging photography is a quick and reliable way of spotting any gaps in the insulation. Indeed, post completion spot checks carried out by some local authorities and CIGA increasingly utilise heat cameras for quality control checks.

EXTERNAL WALL INSULATION

Photo: British Gas

Photo: ECD Architects

Left: PUR boarding awaiting cladding with new outer leaf

Below: Transformation – before & after

Photo: British Gas

Above: Insulated render system comprising (R to L): inner parge coat air barrier; insulation batts (mechanically & adhesively fixed), base coat render with mesh + surface coat of silicone render

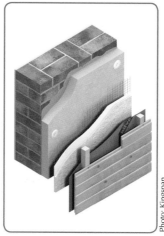
Photo: ECD Architects

Photos: Structherm

Photo: Kingspan

Right: Roof structures normally need to be extended where EWI thickness exceeds overhang

Before venturing outdoors in freezing weather we normally take care to wrap up warmly. Donning a thick woolly coat to maintain body temperature is a method that translates very effectively to preserving the comfort of our living spaces. In fact, wrapping lots of insulation around the outside of your house is one of the best ways to boost the thermal performance of solid walls, but there are, inevitably, pros and cons.

Benefits

Insulating the outside of your home offers major advantages. Unlike lining the walls internally, the insulation layer is more complete as it doesn't get interrupted by partition walls and floor junctions. This means there's less risk of thermal bridging and the associated problems of condensation and mould. And because the insulation's continuous, airtightness should be excellent. Unlike insulating internally, your rooms suffer no loss of floor space, plus there's relatively little disruption to occupants, (although temporary disconnections to services can cause a fair amount of inconvenience). The icing on the cake for homes that are a bit bland-looking, or even downright ugly, is that they get a free facelift, transforming their appearance. So as well as benefiting from lower future maintenance costs, this should enhance their 'kerb appeal', something that's likely to boost property values.

Once safely sheltered behind a thick protective coating, the walls no longer have to confront the worst that the British weather can throw at them. Instead, the thick new 'overcoat' should absorb the stresses formerly imposed on the structure of the building. Another benefit is that the walls inside remain untouched and retain some of the benefits of 'thermal mass', acting like a giant storage heater that keeps the building warm long after the heating has been turned off.

Downsides

For quite a lot of properties cladding the walls on the outside isn't likely to be a practical proposition. For a start you can rule out most period homes with charming historic features. Listed buildings and those in Conservation Areas would require planning consent for such a major alteration, with rejection the likely outcome. For terraced or semi-detached houses, as well as individual flats, it can look a bit odd if one owner 'goes it alone' with a newly bloated front elevation sticking out like a sore thumb. From a technical, as well as a visual, perspective it's better to upgrade such homes as a group.

On a practical level making your walls stouter will require some tricky modifications at window and door openings as well as at roof level. You may need to reposition rainwater downpipes and external lights, as well as reinstalling any pipework, cables and satellite dishes etc. But what really makes EWI a comparatively expensive solution is the need for scaffolding – unless, of course, you happen to be insulating a bungalow. That said, unit costs can be substantially reduced where a whole terrace or a complete block of flats is treated at the same time.

Who can do it?

Cladding systems need very careful design and installation – a badly done job can cause more problems than it solves. External wall insulation is most effective when carried out as part of a comprehensive refurbishment including replacement of windows and doors, and installation of new heating and ventilation systems. Approved installers registered with INCA (the Insulated Render and Cladding Association) should normally be used as they'll be familiar with the various specialist insulation systems. However, one-off jobs can sometimes be done by local builders if they have the necessary skill and experience.

External insulation is appropriate for:

- ■ Solid walls (ideally to detached houses that aren't Listed or located in Conservation Areas).
- ■ Cavity walls that are unsuitable for cavity fill, *eg* where cavities are thinner than 50mm, or buildings of non-traditional construction.
- ■ Homes where insulating internally would make room sizes too small or cause too much disruption.
- ■ Shabby-looking exteriors that could do with a radical facelift.
- ■ Walls with old render in need of major repairs (adding new insulation saves the cost of hacking it off and replacing it).
- ■ Walls that aren't sufficiently weathertight, suffering damp, draughts and heat loss.
- ■ As part of a larger refurbishment scheme for high-rise or mass system-built housing.

Critical detailing

Cladding the outside face of a wall means carefully designing the detailing at a number of key areas:

Eaves and verges

At the tops of walls, the roof slopes normally overhang at the eaves to afford protection from the weather, as well as to look 'right'. So if you suddenly make the walls 100mm or so thicker it can cause problems, especially where the overhang is quite small. To maintain the original proportions of the house it may be necessary to extend the roof slopes by an equivalent amount – significantly bumping up the cost. So if any roof work is due to be carried out in the near future it makes sense to extend the roof at eaves and gable ends in preparation for installing the wall insulation.

A simpler alternative can be

EWI often requires a deeper fascia - *hermowood* cladding used here adds a touch of style

to leave the roof as it is and cover the top of the insulation with special guttering.

Gable end walls can be easier to deal with. These large triangles of masonry usually form the end to an uninhabited loft, so they may not need insulating much above ceiling joist level. The insulation can therefore be capped horizontally along its top forming a small ledge, with a shallow outward slope to disperse rainwater. However, the resulting protruding shelf-like ledge may look a bit weird. Where this isn't visually acceptable, the gable can be lined to its full height.

Special super-wide gutter to eaves and verge extension provides a neat solution avoiding the need to extend the roof

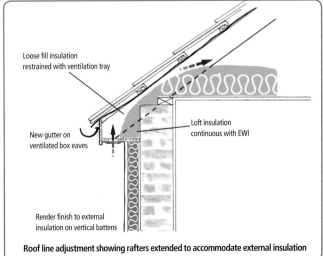

However the verges at the edge of the roof slopes typically only project about 50mm – less than the width of insulation you want to install. These may therefore need to be extended by constructing a timber 'ladder' framework that's then tiled, with a new bargeboard fixed under the verges secured through the insulation.

Loose fill insulation restrained with ventilation tray

New gutter on ventilated box eaves

Loft insulation continuous with EWI

Render finish to external insulation on vertical battens

Roof line adjustment showing rafters extended to accommodate external insulation

Thermal bridging and air leakage

The insulation should be fitted evenly over the existing walls. A simple modern 'box' house will be much easier to treat than those with complex features. It can be difficult to maintain an even thickness and coverage of insulation whilst accommodating balconies and bay windows etc. Detailing at junctions is key to avoid thermal bridging and preventing air leakage. Sealing of joints should prevent both water getting in and heat leaking out.

Photo: ALUMASC Swisslab insulated render

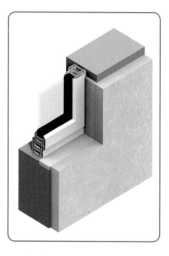

Above: Special wide window frames awaiting EWI to be overlapped

Left: Snugly insulated reveals – but thickness is normally limited by the width of the window frame

Photo: ECD Architects

Photos: ECD Architects

Insulation installed below DPC level to avoid heat loss from solid floors to the ground (eg extruded polystyrene boards). This may require repositioning of some underground drainage, gulleys and waste pipes

Junctions with windows

As with internal wall lining, you need to continue insulation around the corners at reveals to windows and door openings to reduce thermal bridging. But the usual problem applies – space here can be very limited. The best option technically is for the insulation to butt up to and overlap the window frame. But if you can't see the window frames because they're now engulfed within the thicker wall it can make the house look rather odd. One solution is to use a thinner high-performance material such as aerogel to line the reveals.

Below: New window taped to masonry ready for parge coat to be applied and lapped

Below: New windows in position with DPCs awaiting lapping to EWI

Photo: ECD Architects

Photos: SEArch Architects / Greening The Box

It's also important for window sills to project clear of external wall surfaces so that rainwater is dispersed well away from the building. The sills will therefore need to be extended in order to accommodate the thicker walls. The easiest way to do this is for window replacement to be carried out at the same time. New custom-made windows can be specified with deeper sills and wider frames to accommodate thicker insulation.

The base of the wall

Traditionally, render is designed to stop short of the ground just above DPC level, terminating with a 'bellmouth drip' to disperse rainwater. However, if you leave the bottom few courses naked there can be a risk of thermal bridging. To prevent this, insulation can be installed to the lower wall below DPC level, taking care not to bridge the DPC. Below ground, thick strips of extruded polystyrene can be installed to help insulate floor junctions.

Services

When you think about it, the list of items protruding through the main walls of an average property is surprisingly long. As well as rainwater downpipes there may be waste pipes serving kitchens and bathrooms, a large vertical soil and vent pipe, plus assorted extractor vents, air grilles, flues, satellite dishes, telecom boxes and cable runs. These will all need to be temporarily removed and relocated on the face of the new insulation. Where

Downpipes need to be re-fixed to accommodate thicker walls

the cladding isn't up to providing the necessary support a timber pattress can be inserted to carry the load through to the main wall.

Fixings and movement

Clearly the walls being clad must be sufficiently strong to support the weight of the new insulation and its fixings (allowing for extra stresses from wind pressure and suction). Fixings should be corrosion-proof and the system needs to allow for a certain amount of movement to the building. Where a building has movement joints in the existing structure, the external insulation will usually need joints at the same locations.

High-rise dwellings

As a rule, tower blocks aren't known for their beauty. Some architects have a soft spot for them, but many were shoddily built from cheap concrete panels with very poor insulation qualities. So as well as the usual benefits of improved comfort and thermal efficiency, cladding the outside walls can also transform the appearance of acres of stained, streaky concrete. It will

also protect vulnerable joints, giving these unloved buildings a new lease of life and a fresh persona.

External insulation is ideally suited to high-rise structures, especially those with exposed concrete frames and consequent thermal bridging problems. The fact that this method causes minimal disruption to residents is also a major benefit.

However, multi-storey buildings present special challenges, not least because even a minor failure at high-level could have fatal consequences. One key factor is the inclusion of firebreaks in claddings to prevent the potential spread of flames.

Historic buildings

When it comes to historically sensitive buildings, radically altering their appearance isn't usually acceptable. However, there are some situations where external insulation may be appropriate. The best advice is to start by consulting your local authority Conservation Officer.

The values of period houses can plummet if their kerb appeal is trashed. So obliterating charming original architectural features such as string courses and moulded window surrounds behind layers of insulation is tantamount to self-harming. Original brick or stonework is a major part of the charm of even the humblest houses, and appearances can be drastically altered by deepened window and door reveals and unsympathetic alterations to sills, downpipes and eaves. Even where walls are already rendered, making them fatter can give the house a squat, dumpy feel.

From a technical perspective, old buildings made of soft materials like earth or straw rely for their structural strength on the walls being kept neither too wet nor too dry, so they may not be suitable for wall cladding of any type. However, EWI can sometimes be appropriate where traditional tile-hung or timber-weatherboarded facades can be insulated behind the original cladding, which is later reinstated. If such works are carried out with care this can reap major thermal benefits with little visual impact (see 'Period timber frame' below).

Materials

It's important that the choice of insulation is compatible with an old solid wall's need to breathe, so that any moisture is free to evaporate harmlessly away. Modern plastic-based materials are unsuitable as they're impermeable and hence trap moisture, causing damp problems. To retain the necessary 'breathability', natural materials with a low vapour resistance are preferable such as woodfibre panels and hemp-lime composites. Each layer added to the exterior should be more breathable than the last, as this draws moisture outwards.

Wood-fibre 'Diffutherm' insulation with mesh and render coat being applied

To protect the new insulation from the weather and physical damage, a compatible moisture-permeable finish will need to be applied, such as a traditional lime render with a breathable natural paint.

Period timber frame

External insulation is technically the most effective means of insulating walls, bridging cracks and protecting the frame and panels from the weather. But obscuring traditionally exposed timber frame walls behind new cladding will radically change an old building's character, and normally won't be acceptable. Where there are no such restrictions, natural breathable insulation materials, such as sheep's wool and wood fibre, can be fitted to the external face of the timber frame behind a vapour permeable breather membrane to help protect it from driven rain.

However, many historic properties in more exposed locations were originally built with an external cladding of tiles or timber weatherboarding to protect them against the wind and rain. This can make the task of insulating much easier where it's possible to temporarily strip the timber boarding or tile cladding and install insulation within the thickness of the timber frame. In some cases it may be feasible to go one better and install an additional external layer of insulation over the newly infilled timber frame, such as tongued and grooved wood-fibre board; but inevitably this would make the wall a bit thicker, with the consequent need for complicated revisions to window reveals and downpipes etc. Before reinstating the original cladding a breather membrane layer should be laid, as this significantly improves the performance of the insulation by reducing air infiltration. It should also intercept any rain that penetrates the cladding, so it can run freely away down the face of the membrane. Allow a certain amount of slack when fitting the membrane to accommodate future movement.

What is external wall insulation?

External insulation systems consist of three key components – a layer of insulation, some method of securing it in place, and a protective finish such as render or cladding.

INSULATION

Photo: Knauf

A number of types of rigid or semi-rigid insulation can be used:

- Mineral fibre – glass fibre quilt or wool batts.
- Foamed plastic rigid boards, eg PIR, PUR or PF.
- Polystyrene rigid boards, eg EPS, XPS or enhanced EPS (also used below damp-proof course).
- Natural materials, eg wood fibre boards, hempcrete blocks.

Photo: DOW Styrofoam – GreeningThe Box

FIXINGS

- Adhesives, eg chemical anchors.
- Mechanical – supporting tracks and frameworks or anchors (made from polypropylene, nylon, aluminium or stainless steel).
- A combination of 'glue and screws'.

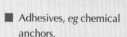

Below: Base track fixed to lower wall

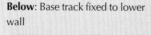

Below: PUR Insulation boards resting on base track are secured to wall with plastic anchors (and bedding adhesive if required)

Photo: ALUMASC Swisslab insulated render

EWI systems & finishes

There are two main types of external wall insulation – those with wet render finishes, and dry 'rainscreen' cladding systems. There's also a third type: bespoke designs. The most common systems use wet render. But for all systems there are key points to consider, such as the initial cost, whether it's covered by an insurance-backed guarantee, and the frequency of future maintenance and decoration. It's also important that cladding is sufficiently durable to withstand the weather, resist cracking, and look good over many years (coping with dirt and algae etc).

Wet render systems

The idea of applying thick coats of render to boost a building's defences against foul weather has been around for donkeys' years. The main difference today is that the walls are first lined with a layer of insulation.

The first job is to fit the insulation boards (*eg* mineral fibre batts or rigid foamed plastic) to the wall. Normally a horizontal base track is screwed to the wall just above DPC level to support the insulation boards. To prevent thermal bypass it's important that there are no continuous gaps behind the boards, so any surface irregularities on the wall should first be smoothed out by applying a 'parging coat', which also helps ensure airtightness. Adhesive is combed on to the back of the boards to create a continuous surface (but flexible enough to allow initial adjustment). Once boards are glued in position they can be further secured by inserting special anchor fixings that have plastic sleeves to prevent cold bridging.

Next, the fitted insulation boards are coated with a special high-performance 'polymer-modified' render base coat. Wet systems are typically built up in two or three coats over a reinforcing mesh (glass fibre, plastic or metal) that's applied over the insulation to provide a key. Synthetic 'polymer modified' systems have exceptional strength despite being only 10–15mm thick – much thinner than traditional cement-sand mixes (which are no longer used). The addition of polymer makes the render more workable on site and improves weather protection and flexibility. Thin polymer modified coatings have a high degree of crack resistance and their reduced weight can be especially advantageous for use in high-rise buildings. These coatings don't need movement joints (unless the wall itself has them).

Once dry, a primer and final decorative coat can be applied. This could take the form of a through-coloured finish such as acrylic or silicone, or a brick-effect render system where the top coat is scored to give the appearance of brick. Alternatively special thin brick slips (approximately 20mm thick) can be glued to a plastic carrier board fixed directly to the insulation, a relatively quick process. Once these imitation bricks are pointed up with mortar they can look surprisingly realistic and are easily mistaken for the real thing.

Plastic corner bead bedded and fixed in place

Photo: ALUMASC Swisslab insulated render

EWI refurbishment

Photos courtesy: Structherm

1 Before refurbishment
2 Installation of insulation boards
3 Base coat rendering
4 Applying reinforcing mesh to base coat render
5 Embedding mesh with second layer base coat render
6 Door reveal rendering
7 Optional application of coloured top coat finish
8 After refurbishment

New brickwork outer leaf will enclose insulation within cavity, like newbuild construction

The thickness of insulation needed to meet the Building Regs target of 0.30W/m²K will obviously depend on the materials used, but it's possible to significantly beat this figure and achieve a U-value of only 0.15W/m²K by using a 120mm thickness of phenolic foam (PF) – one of the best performing materials – applied to a typical 230mm solid wall.

Dry cladding systems

Cladding walls with tiles or timber boarding to protect houses from foul weather is a tradition that dates back centuries. Based on the same principle, modern 'dry cladding' systems are used to give large structures like tower blocks a new lease of life. But instead of simply hanging tiles from battens, these comprise thick layers of high-performance insulation encased within a protective outer cladding of panels or boards. However, dry cladding is relatively expensive, and hence generally uneconomic for use on individual houses.

The insulation material applied to the walls typically comprises rigid boards or compressed mineral wool batts, similar to those used with conventional wet render finishes. These can be fixed directly to the wall, although it's more common for dry cladding systems to employ supporting aluminium

Photo: Kingspan

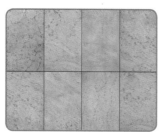

Simulated brick and stone cladding panels

Photo: Thorvertonstone.co.uk

frameworks that also secure the outer cladding. Because frameworks can span large areas of wall they're ideal for uneven wall surfaces, or for buildings with restrictions on where fixings can be anchored, such as some high-rise dwellings. Provision of a ventilated cavity also allows walls to breathe when used in conjunction with a natural insulation such as wood fibre boards, but reduces thermal performance.

Clearly the appearance of the cladding is a key factor and a wide range of colours and textures are available, including:

Photo: Whetherby

Brick slips fixed with adhesive - once pointed up can look very authentic

- Resin-impregnated laminates (eg epoxy resin laminate board).
- Fibre cement board.
- Fibre-reinforced calcium silicate aluminium panels.
- Terracotta rainscreen cladding or tiling.

To achieve a neat decorative finish, edging trims and profiles can be added to corners, window reveals, roof verges and copings, as well as at DPC level.

Bespoke systems

Designed by architects for individual projects, custom-made systems tend to have simple detailing that enables non-specialist building contractors to construct them. A typical design might consist of a rainscreen (eg traditional oak weatherboarding) fastened to a masonry wall via a simple timber framework forming a traditional ventilated cavity. But a wide variety of possible finishes can be used, including stone, glass, terracotta and tile hanging. Being tailor-made to suit the building makes it easy to specify sustainable materials, but the downsides are its relative expense plus the fact that there's no manufacturer's guarantee.

The design will need to consider detailing in the same key areas as mainstream methods – eg prevention of water ingress, supporting loadings, fire protection, durability and future maintenance. If solid timber studwork is used, it can be bracketed proud of the wall to prevent thermal bridging. Alternatively, lightweight composite I-beams of low thermal conductivity can be used.

Installing external wall insulation

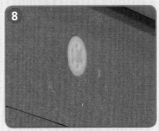

1. Aluminium starter track / rail screwed to base of wall above DPC …
2. …extended around corner
3. EPS insulation boards (graphite impregnated 'Thermoshell') are bonded to wall…
4. …and secured in horizontal and vertical tracks
5. Hole drilled through insulation into wall …
6. …plastic anchor inserted
7&8 … and hammered into wall
9&10 Hot knife used to slice off surplus
11. Hand rasp used to smooth cut ends
12. Render base coat applied
13&14 Reinforcing mesh adhered to base coat
15. Mesh cut to shape around openings
16. Render coat applied over mesh
17. Final render coat applied
18. Decorative finish

Photos courtesy: Knauf Insulation

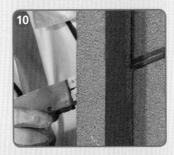

Photos: ECD Architects

Left: Foil-backed polyurethane insulation pinned and foamed to an internal wall. Battens form a service zone ready to receive plasterboard finish
Above: Timber stud lining with infill mineral wool or wood-fibre insulation

IWI is best:

- ■ As part of a refurbishment you were going to do anyway.
- ■ For individual terraced and semi-detached houses.
- ■ For period properties with attractive facades and those in Conservation Areas.
- ■ For individual flats – you can't externally insulate just one flat.
- ■ For multi-storey buildings where external access is difficult and expensive.

IWI is less suitable:

- ■ For rooms with detailed period features (although ornate plasterwork can be concealed or reproduced, and wood panelling removed and reinstated).
- ■ Where walls are damp (until remedied).
- ■ Where room sizes are very small (although the typical loss of only 125mm or so floor space on one or two walls in a room is usually imperceptible).
- ■ Where disruption to fittings such as pipework and electrics would be excessive.

Millions of older homes have walls of traditional solid masonry construction. But it's not just quaint period properties where the option of squirting insulation into a handy cavity doesn't apply. In the post-war period large numbers of Council houses and flats were erected using innovative methods of construction in concrete or steel; and although some of these walls have cavities, they're unsuitable for filling.

Whatever the provenance of your home, when it comes to boosting thermal efficiency to solid walls there are two options – insulating on the inside or the outside. The external option may technically be the better choice, but as we've seen, it's often highly impractical, with complex detailing issues and major planning implications, plus there's a pretty god chance it will seriously cheese-off the neighbours.

IWI is the next best thing. The good news is that it costs a lot less and is easier to install (no need for scaffolding), plus the materials are readily available. Inevitably there are some drawbacks: it involves more disturbance (but can be installed in one room at a time to minimise disruption); making the walls thicker on the inside inevitably means sacrificing a small amount of floor space; and unless the job's done competently there's a danger of condensation causing localised damp problems.

Left: Cut away showing support batten behind insulation
Right: Mould due to water vapour condensing on cold walls

PUR insulation boards can be fixed to a timber batten framework to accommodate unevenness in old walls

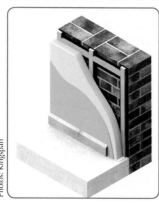

Photos: Kingspan

Danger – water vapour!

Probably the greatest concern with internal wall insulation is the control of moisture. As we saw earlier, once your walls are lined with lots of thick insulation the original surface of the wall, now concealed behind it, will be colder than before since it's now separated from the warm atmosphere of the room. So any moist indoor air that's able to leak through the insulation layer will quickly cool and condense into water as soon as it comes into contact with colder surfaces. This may not sound too alarming, but if a lot of clammy dampness accumulates over time behind your new insulation it can lead to mould growth, rusted fixings or decay to nearby timbers (such as floors or studwork frames supporting the insulation).

There are two ways that water vapour can penetrate through walls and cause such 'interstitial condensation': by diffusion, where moist air seeps through the insulation material itself; and

Solving thermal bridging

Thermal bridges are more likely to occur at certain 'critical details', where full depth and coverage of insulation can be difficult to achieve, eg:

Window and door reveals

The 'classic' place for thermal bridging is around window and door openings. Reveals can be lined by returning the insulation round the corner up to the frame (taking care not to block trickle vents). But these areas can often be difficult to line effectively due to a lack of space, because the amount of visible window or door frame isn't thick enough to accommodate much insulation. The simplest solution is to use thinner strips of insulation board such as special lining boards of expanded PVC, or super-high performance aerogel or vacuum panels (but these are expensive). If space is very limited, plaster may need to be stripped away to create more room. Where windows are being replaced the new jambs can be designed to accept a decent thickness of insulated lining.

Window ledges and the walls under them can be vulnerable to damp from condensation running off the windows and dribbling down. So these can similarly be treated with thin strips of high-performance insulation placed under the ledges on the walls beneath them. It may also be necessary to insulate the heads above doors and windows where the lintels are of metal or concrete (typically post-1930s), as opposed to 'warmer' traditional timber.

Super-thin, high performance vacuum panels can be used in areas where space is restricted

Internal partition walls

Thermal bridges can also occur where internal walls (eg partition and party walls) meet the main external walls. These structures act as a 'heat sink', channelling warmth from indoors to the external walls and out of the building. Ideally you'd want to thermally separate them by inserting a slice of insulation at the point where the walls meet, to block heat from being conducted out.

This is never going to be easy, but it may be possible to insert strips of insulation where partition walls are of timber studwork construction (which is a lot of extra work, given the fact that stud walls are less 'cold' than those of solid masonry).

In practice the best way to resolve this problem it is to lap the insulation so it continues along the internal walls. So instead of stopping dead where the main wall finishes you keep going round the corner so that the insulation is 'returned' 300–600mm along the internal wall. The thermal bridge may never be entirely eradicated, but the problem will be substantially reduced.

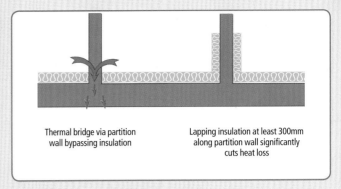

Thermal bridge via partition wall bypassing insulation

Lapping insulation at least 300mm along partition wall significantly cuts heat loss

Wall junctions to ceilings and floors

Where floors meet the main walls they have the same potential for heat loss as partition walls. There are two types of ceiling-to-wall junctions:

Ceilings to the floor of rooms above

The challenge here is to isolate the cold strip of outside wall that's sandwiched between the ceiling and the floor above. Where the joists run parallel to the wall (ie the floorboard ends abut the wall), there's normally a gap between the wall and the nearest joist. This can be filled with a strip of PIR board that effectively links the insulation in the rooms above and below. The face of the insulation is then lined with a vapour barrier.

Where the joists ends are embedded within the wall, complete sealing of the timber joists in their sockets isn't recommended. Any moisture that builds up must be free to evaporate. So to reduce thermal bridging, mineral wool, or a similar breathable material, can be stuffed between the joists for the first half-metre or so.

Upper-floor ceilings to cold loft above, ground floors to cold basement below

These areas can be treated by ensuring that the wall insulation overlaps with the loft (or floor) insulation laid between the joists above. This is the same approach to overlapping partition walls, with the wall insulation returned along ceilings for at least 300mm. Any gaps can be sealed with expanding foam or silicone.

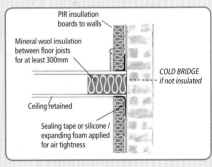

PIR insulation boards to walls

Mineral wool insulation between floor joists for at least 300mm

COLD BRIDGE – if not insulated

Ceiling retained

Sealing tape or silicone / expanding foam applied for air tightness

Wall corners

Where you have one wall with internal insulation and the other with external insulation, thermal bridging is avoided by overlapping the internal insulation approximately 400mm from the corner.

Fixings

Gluing boards to walls with suitable adhesives should minimise the risk of thermal bridging. But where 'cold' metal screws are used to anchor the plasterboard, penetrating through the insulation, there's a risk they can transmit cold and attract condensation. To reduce this problem, fixings should have plastic spacers or caps to help isolate them. Stainless steel screws should be bedded in 'warm' nylon wallplugs (stainless steel has lower thermal conductivity than ordinary steel and is resistant to corrosion).

BGas IWI

Insulation returned along party walls to minimise heat loss via thermal bridging

Multifoil laid to a thickness of 30mm is claimed to achieve a U-value equivalent to over 200mm of mineral wool – approx 0.20 W/m²K. Joints must be overlapped at least 50mm and taped to give an airtight finish. Multifoil can be fixed in place with battens to provide the necessary air gap (minimum 25mm) before plasterboarding.

(far more significantly) by 'air movement', where it can seek out any cracks or gaps in the surface and between insulation boards.

Fortunately it's fairly easy to control the passage of warm, moist air into the wall by fitting a vapour barrier (aka vapour control layer) on the warm indoor side of the insulation. This commonly takes the form of large polyethylene sheets laid over the insulation before it's covered with plasterboard. Alternatively, some types of plasterboard and insulation boards are manufactured with a foil backing which acts as a ready-made vapour barrier. Either way, care must be taken to ensure that the vapour barrier is continuous. But to completely banish moist air from entering the structure, any cracks and gaps must be fully sealed. This relies on accurate cutting and installation, taking special care to seal potential weak points at joints between the boards and where pipes or cables penetrate the lining.

Materials

As we saw in Chapter 2, there's a large variety of insulation materials on the market, everything from hemp and denim through to foils, foams and space-age gels. For lining walls internally, popular materials include:

- Rigid boards, eg PUR, PIR or PF.
- Batts of mineral wool or sheep's wool for studwork.
- Interlocking boards of woodfibre.

In terms of thermal performance, the best results can normally be achieved using large rigid boards of polyurethane (PUR or similar). To save the hassle of having to separately fit the insulation followed by separate sheets of plasterboard, you can buy them both combined as 'insulated plasterboard'. Specifying the foil-backed variety can save even more hassle because the foil acts as a built-in vapour barrier (although it can be difficult to ensure the vapour barrier is continuous at joints).

To meet the U-value target of 0.30W/m²K is likely to require an insulation thickness of 80–120mm, depending on the material used. In fact 100mm of phenolic foam-backed plasterboard should be able to beat this handsomely and achieve a U-value of 0.23 or better.

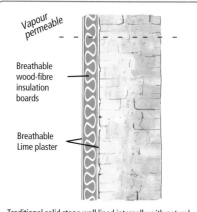

Traditional solid stone wall lined internally with natural vapour permeable insulation. No vapour control barrier so any moisture in the wall can evaporate out.

Vapour permeable

Breathable wood-fibre insulation boards

Breathable Lime plaster

Super-thin high performance aerogel strips used to line 'cold' battens behind insulated plasterboard

Lining a wall with woodfibre boards

Victorian house with breathable wood-fibre boards applied using insulated fixings and lime-based adhesive. Base coat and mesh applied over boards prior to lime plaster finish. Original cornicing retained with neat 'shelf' formed to top of insulation (but a potential risk of thermal bridging)   Photos: NBT

For areas where space is restricted, such as window reveals, there are special mould-resistant lining boards, slim 12mm PIR rigid strips or, best of all, those made from super-thin, high-performance aerogel or vacuum panels.

Installation

Whatever type of insulation takes your fancy, they all have to be fixed in place using one of the following methods:

Fixed directly to the wall

■ Glue

Where an existing plastered wall is dry and its surface is reasonably even, rigid insulation boards can simply be glued directly to the wall with adhesive. This minimises the amount of space lost within the room, so you may only lose about 65mm in total (depending on the thickness of insulation used). But you can't just use any old Pritt stick – special drywall adhesive or plasterboard sealant is normally best (but check what the manufacturers recommend). The adhesive is applied in thick bands about 200mm wide, to the centre of the board and around the edges (set in about 50mm). To prevent any risk of boards collapsing off the wall in the event of a house fire, it's recommended that additional support is provided with screws extending at least 35mm into the wall.

■ Plaster dabs

If a wall is uneven (eg where the plaster's been stripped) rigid boards can be bonded in place using dollops of plaster, provided the wall is dry. The edges of the finished boarded wall must be filled, including those around windows. It's important these are

Insulated dry-lining on dabs

Photos courtesy Kingspan insulation

1 Prepare the surface, ensuring that it's dry and free from loose or flaking material
2 Apply adhesive dabs
3 Place board against adhesive
4 Any mechanical fixings (eg hammer anchor plugs) should be positioned at the tapered edge
5 Apply dabs at higher levels
6 Ensure insulated plasterboard is cut accurately
7 Place boards against adhesive ensuring a tight fit around the edges
8 Use expanding foam sealant to fill any gaps

Insulating between battens

This system uses glass mineral wool ('Earthwool Eco-batts) fitted between insulated studs. 'Ecostuds' are a composite of extruded polystyrene (XPS) and Oriented Strand Board (OSB) with superior insulation qualities to timber. A thickness of 80mm should improve the thermal performance of a typical uninsulated solid wall by around 80% (from 2.10W/m²K to at least 0.35W/m²K).

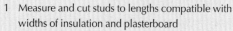

1 Measure and cut studs to lengths compatible with widths of insulation and plasterboard
2 Pre-drill pilot screw holes in studs
3 Hold studs to wall and drill into wall using a long bit
4 Insert anchor plug into hole for long length hammer screws
5 Hammer the screw anchor through studwork part way into wall
6 Fix screws fully into wall using cordless screwdriver
7 Cut notches in studs and insert around pipework. Extend any electric cables (protected in conduit as necessary)
8 Skirting removed to fit base studs at floor level
9 Any unevenness to the wall can be packed using plywood strips
10 Apply insulation between studs taking care not to leave gaps
11 & 12 Align plasterboard over insulated studwork and vapour barrier if required (or 'moistureshield' type plasterboard)
13 Place shims under base of boards to adjust position of plasterboard
14 & 15 Drive home drywall screws to secure plasterboard
16. Seal gaps at edges with silicone mastic and tape board joints prior to skim plaster coat and decoration
17 Insert backing boxes for any sockets and switches and pull through electric cable, connect up and fit covers.

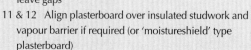

Photos courtesy: Knauf Insulation

fully sealed with a continuous band of plaster to stop cold air creeping into the room and reducing its effectiveness. As with the adhesive method, additional screw fixings should be provided as backup.

Screws

Special screws can be inserted into wall plugs embedded in masonry walls, but because metal conducts cold there's the potential risk of 'cold bridging', so this is the least preferred option. However, for houses of modern timber frame construction, where the main walls comprise a timber panelled inner leaf the insulation boards can be screwed through the plasterboard directly into existing timber studwork. A new vapour barrier should first be provided over the existing wall as a precaution against moisture penetrating the timber inner leaf.

Fitted to battens

Where walls are lumpy and uneven, a timber framework of preservative-treated battens can be screwed to the wall. They need to be at least 50mm x 100mm to accommodate the required thickness of insulation, and the dimensions should be compatible with sheets of plasterboard. Insulation can be fixed between the studs or over them, or for best results you could do both.

Insulation between timber battens

The insulation is fitted between the studs by being squashed into individual panels between the framework. This suits a wide range of 'squishable' materials such as wool quilts or batts of wood fibre or cellulose. Alternatively, thick rigid boards can be cut to fit, but because it can be difficult to accurately cut and tightly fit them a good alternative is to cut them 'slack' and fill the gaps with expanding foam.

A vapour control plastic sheet is then stapled across the whole surface (ensuring the sheet edges are overlapped and sealed) before being plasterboarded over. Joints are taped and a skim plaster finish applied (where breathability is an issue in some older buildings a breather membrane can be used instead of a vapour barrier). The loss of floor area in the room would be about 115mm, including the plasterboard and skim finish.

In terms of performance, the addition of 100mm thickness of mineral wool fitted between studs fixed directly to a typical 230mm solid brick wall should reduce the U-value from 2.10 to around 0.35W/m^{2}K – which almost meets the current target of 0.30W/m^{2}K.

Insulating over timber battens

Rigid insulation boards can be screwed over the timber framework. The studwork needs to be built to dimensions that

Slim aerogel pre-bonded boards applied direct to wall for minimal loss of floor space

Photo: Proctorgroup.com

Slim aerogel pre-bonded boards applied to timber battens

Photo: Proctorgroup.com

Insulation over battens

1. Treated timber battens are screwed vertically to the wall over protective strips of DPC.
2. Place sheets of insulated plasterboard against the timber studwork
3. Fix the boards in place with drywall screws
4. Horizontal timber studs and noggins provide support to board edges
5. Each board should be firmly screwed to studwork behind
6. Drill through boards to create holes for wiring
7. Pull cables wires through insulated plasterboard
8. Seal around penetrations with vapour resistant mastic sealant
9. Fill any remaining gaps with expanding foam sealant
10. Ensure all the edges are airtight

support all four sides of the boards. However, this increases the overall thickness to around 160mm. The Energy Saving Trust describe this method as suitable for 'walls that have previously been damp *eg* after curing rain penetration or reducing condensation'. However, a ventilated 'floating wall' is probably a better solution in such cases (see below).

Alternatively you can use sheets of heat-reflective multifoil, lapped and taped at the joints. This is sometimes combined with mineral wool insulation stuffed between the panels of the studwork frame behind the layer of multifoil. The insulation is held in place with a series of horizontal battens on top, on to which plasterboard sheets are fixed. These battens provide the necessary air gap of at least 25mm which this type of insulation requires for optimum performance.

An independent 'floating wall'

For properties where the walls have been exposed to damp, or where there's potential for moisture (*eg* from rain penetration in severe weather) the best method is to build an independent 'floating wall' with an air gap to act as a break in any moisture transmission path. The space behind this 'inner lining' must be

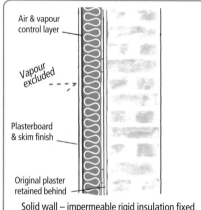

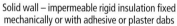

Air & vapour control layer

Vapour excluded

Plasterboard & skim finish

Original plaster retained behind

Solid wall – impermeable rigid insulation fixed mechanically or with adhesive or plaster dabs

Left: Celulose insulation can be applied by spray

Below: Scrubbing wall surface flush

Photos: Warmcel

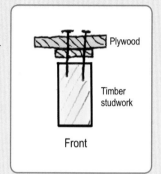
ventilated to the outside so any humid air can escape.

A timber stud wall is constructed (using studs of at least 50mm x 100mm), but set away from the main wall leaving a clear gap of at least 30mm, so you're likely to lose nearly 150mm of floor space. The studwork spans between the floor and the ceiling, like a partition, and isn't physically connected to the main wall. Panels of rigid insulation are then cut and pressed between the studs; alternatively you could use mineral wool batts. It's best to fit a small backing 'lip' on the cavity side of the studs to prevent any risk of insulation later slipping into the void and bridging the cavity. A lining of plasterboard (or insulated plasterboard) can then be applied over a vapour control sheet across the face of the studwork. Alternative materials include sheets of multifoil as described above. Finally, the plasterboard joints should be taped before skim plastering.

Design considerations

Before you start installing IWI, there are a number of issues to mull over:

Is the wall damp?

Any damp issues must be resolved before insulating, otherwise lining the walls could make matters worse. Damp in walls is frequently due to high ground levels, leaking pipes, overflowing gutters, eroded window sills and defective roof flashings. Condensation is another common source of damp, and is characterised by black staining or mould to unventilated, cold, poorly insulated surfaces. Improved ventilation is key to resolving such problems, such as fitting extractor fans to bathrooms and kitchens – see Chapter 3.

Once the source of the damp has been cured the walls must be allowed to dry out, which can take about a month per inch thickness of wall (most solid brick walls are 9in thick). In exposed locations subject to severe driving rain it may be worth considering cladding them externally with a ventilated protective covering, *eg* traditional tiling.

Loss of room space

Lining your walls is obviously going to make them a bit thicker, which will eat into your floor space. In most cases it won't make much difference, except in some very small cloakrooms, bathrooms, and kitchens, and may limit your choice of insulation. Rigid boards bonded directly to the wall with adhesive generally take up least space, typically at least 65mm (50mm insulation + 12.5mm plasterboard plus about 2mm plaster skim). Alternatively, constructing stud walls to support the insulation can reduce room space by 150mm or more.

Bumps and gaps

Any gaps or cracks in the walls can cause draughts and heat loss, undermining the performance of the insulation, so it's important they're filled prior to insulating. Once skirting boards and architraves have been temporarily removed check the exposed surfaces for gaps.

In most houses the walls aren't perfectly smooth. Adhesive can be used to seal and smooth out surfaces before sticking boards directly to walls, but where bumpiness is an issue an independent stud wall can be a better solution. This can also provide a convenient space for service runs, such as cables or pipe conduits – see 'Services' below.

Airtightness

An airtight vapour control membrane is key to the performance of the insulation (the exception is where you're dealing with historic buildings where the walls need to breathe – if in doubt check with your local authority Conservation Officer). Unless fully sealed, air leakage can take place in both directions, with cold draughts from outside seeping in, and warm air leaking out, condensing en route to form damp patches inside the insulation. So vapour control membranes are placed on the warm side of the insulation (ie facing the room) prior to plasterboarding. The easiest way to do this is by using foil-faced PIR board and sealing the joints with aluminium foil; alternatively lay large sheets of polythene vapour barrier over the insulation before plasterboarding.

Where boards are fixed to the wall with plaster dabs, or an insulated inner studwork wall is built, there will be air spaces left behind the insulation. So it's important there are no leakage paths where cold air from lofts or underfloor voids could penetrate into these spaces, making the surface colder.

If any cold air from outside does get into the space behind the insulation, the vapour barrier provides a secondary line of defence to stop it leaking through any gaps into the room. Hence the importance of making sure the vapour control layer's airtight. Any exposed edges around the perimeter of the insulation boards must be sealed with adhesives or battens so that moisture can't bypass the vapour barrier. Also be sure to seal junctions where the insulation meets adjoining walls, floors and ceilings.

Services

A major chink in your home's thermal armour can occur anywhere that pipes and cables penetrate insulated walls. So, for example, there's a risk that gaps can allow air leakage at switches and sockets. To make matters worse, metal pipes such as those serving radiators can act as a 'cold bridge' through the insulated layer. One solution is to use modern plastic pipes, which are less

cold than copper. Where possible pipes and cables should be run along the surface of the wall rather than being embedded inside it. Pipe runs can be discreetly boxed-in within skirting panels or neatly concealed running up the corners of the room. Where possible services should be relocated to adjoining internal partition walls. Where you can't avoid the occasional pipe or cable penetrating the vapour barrier they must be fully airtight. Holes can be sealed using special vapour-resistant tape or acrylic sealant.

Light switches, power outlets and wall lights will all need refitting. This should be fairly straightforward as there's usually a bit of excess cable that can be pulled through. Also, any waste pipes, wall-mounted boilers and flues, air vents and phone cables etc will have to be relocated on the face of the new plasterboard lining.

Where you've got a lot of pipes or cables a good solution can be to build an independent studwork inner wall leaving sufficient space to run them. Alternatively, where insulation boards are bonded directly to the wall, a shallow channel can be cut, in either the wall or the insulation. If you're using polystyrene insulation, avoid direct contact with electrical cables as it can react with the PVC cable sheathing, making it brittle. To prevent any risk of overheating and short-circuiting, cables covered by insulation should be protected inside conduit with a cover strip. Most at risk are cables carrying higher loads, such as to cookers and shower units. But as long as the system is reasonably modern, the lighting and ring main circuits are unlikely to exceed their current-carrying capacity when covered with insulation.

Sound transmission

As well as making your home warmer, the new layers of thermal insulation should help reduce noise transmission, which can be of particular benefit to flat-dwellers. However, the acoustic performance of some materials is better than others. Where sound insulation is important, a mineral wool wallboard can be used to achieve good results. This can be fixed to a new independent timber studwork partition fixed clear of the wall, and the frame filled with a minimum of 50mm thick mineral wool quilt or batts. For best results the frame should be covered with two layers of 12.5mm wallboard with staggered joints. For more information on acoustic insulation see website **www.homeinsulating.co.uk**.

Timber batten inserted within insulated wall to support fixings

Supporting fittings

To gain access to the interior wall surfaces in some rooms, fittings such as kitchen units, cupboards, boilers, basins and WCs will have to be temporarily taken down. So it makes sense to schedule insulation work when these fittings are due to be replaced anyway.

All these fittings are fairly

heavy, so remounting them needs to be carefully planned in advance in order to ensure there's sufficient support. Before the insulation is installed their fixing positions should be noted. In stud walls, thick timber battens can be strategically positioned to align with fixing points. In masonry walls, screwing through to the underlying brick, stone or blockwork should provide strong support, but can risk thermal bridging (unless you use insulated plastic anchors).

Standard plasterboard isn't strong enough to support much weight. However, there are some specially developed fibrous insulation boards designed to accommodate fixings, or you could line the insulation with a layer of timber boarding (eg plywood or OSB) under the plasterboard to provide support for fixings. Any radiators will also need to be temporarily removed, and either refitted later to a different wall, or the pipework extended slightly to accommodate the new insulation depth.

IWI in historic buildings

For older buildings, the alternative to using vapour control membranes is a modern 'breather' membrane compatible with natural breathable insulation such as hemp, sheep's wool, cellulose or wood-fibre boards.

Don't damage heritage features

Works that damage the appearance and character of old buildings can slash values, and in some cases may be illegal. Traditional features, such as plaster cornices and picture rails, skirting boards and door architraves, are all likely to be affected by internal wall insulation. Where possible these should be carefully removed and reinstated on the new wall surface. Where this can't be done without damage, one option is to conceal them safely behind new independent insulated studwork walls and suspended ceilings, preserved for posterity. Alternatively, there are specialists who can copy the precise design of period cornicing and skirting boards etc and recreate the original elegance of the room – at a price.

A skilled plasterer can re-creating period cornicing

Photo: SURE Insulation

Timber frame

Lining the inside face of historic timber-framed walls is not normally an option because it would mean sacrificing the aesthetic appeal of exposed posts and beams.

However, in some properties where the frame is already covered by lath and plaster, lining the walls can be a realistic proposition. Only natural, vapour-permeable insulation should be used, together with a lime plaster finish internally so that any moisture can easily evaporate out.

Where the main timber posts and beams are thicker than the old panels in between, there may be scope to beef up the panels by adding insulation internally, leaving the frame exposed. Historic infill

panels should normally be retained, but sometimes the panels have to be removed anyway, eg to facilitate structural repair to the frame, or because they've failed or have been damaged with cement render. This can provide the opportunity to replace them with new insulated panels made from natural materials such as of hemp lime, wood fibre or sheep's wool, finished in traditional lime render.

Leaving a gap

In period properties of solid masonry or timber frame construction, conservationists often recommend building an insulated inner leaf with a gap left to the original wall, as described earlier. The difficulty is ensuring this void is adequately ventilated to the outside so that any moisture that finds its way into the cavity can be dispersed. Without ventilation there would be insufficient air movement, and damp air could collect, causing rot in concealed areas. The challenge is to discreetly locate vents in the external wall so they're acceptable visually (eg inserted in horizontal mortar joints). In properties with a ventilated underfloor void additional vents can be set into the floor. However, there's no point ventilating to the rooms inside as the air movement would simply bypass the insulation, rendering it ineffective.

Woodwool boards (magnesite bound) are breathable and can be lime rendered – here shown hammering oakum caulking into gaps at panel edges to timber frame

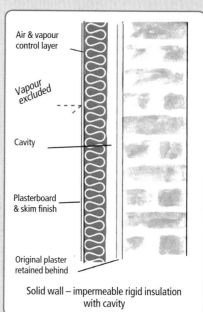

Air & vapour control layer

Vapour excluded

Cavity

Plasterboard & skim finish

Original plaster retained behind

Solid wall – impermeable rigid insulation with cavity

Natural wall insulation for historic buildings

INSULATING WALLS WITH REED BOARD

Natural reed board is ideal for insulating walls in historic buildings, especially those of timber frame, earth or rubble stone construction. It is screwed in place using stainless steel screws with plastic washers to prevent thermal bridging and provides an excellent base for plastering.

Wall being prepared for insulation.

The board is marked and cut to size (the reeds are bound with zinc-coated wire).

Reed board can be cut with a saw (hand or powered). Wire cutters or secateurs are used to cut the wire.

Boards can be held in place with dabs of plaster, then carefully trimmed and the wire adjusted. A minimum of 20mm must be left at the edges of cut boards to avoid the wire slipping.

Drilling for special fixings.

Bedding the reed in lime mortar helps to prevent voids.

Reed partially fixed to wall.

INSULATING WITH WOOD-FIBRE BOARD

Wood-fibre boards provide thicker breathable insulation, ideal for bathroom and kitchen walls.

Reed insulation fitted around oak window and slate sill, ready for lime plastering.

Wood-fibre insulation board fixed in place on the inner face of an external wall.

The board is secured in place with easy-to-use insulated fixings.

Lime plastered wall ready to decorate.

Fully redecorated in vapour permeable paints. The ceiling is left as original as possible to retain its history.

(All images courtesy Mike Wye & Associates Ltd)

INTERNAL WALL INSULATION

(Courtesy SURE insulation)

Insulating walls internally is quite a complex job and must be done to a good standard to be fully effective. In this example we're using rigid insulation boards of PIR (polyisocyanurate) – one of the most thermally efficient materials for lining walls.

PREPARATION AND STRIPPING OUT

Tools and materials
- In addition to normal construction tools an oscillating multi-cutter power tool is useful
- Protective dust sheet to cover floors
- Expanding foam
- Plastic mesh

Health and safety
- Dust mask
- Heavy-duty gloves
- Latex gloves for expanding foam/adhesive
- Goggles

 SAFETY FIRST!

It's essential to turn off the power before attempting any electrical work.

PREPARATION

Preparation work should be done with the room as empty as possible, in preparation for all the dust and mess. Allow a couple of hours to clear the room of furniture etc and lift the carpet. Alternatively, the furniture can be moved well away from the work area and protected with dust sheets. If the house is occupied, the spread of dust can be minimised by sealing gaps around doors with tape and hanging protective sheets across open hallways.

1 Set up spaces for waste and to park any materials that can be reused.

2 Fit a self-adhesive carpet protector.

3 Materials can be bulky and heavy.

4 Note order of stacked materials: flooring chipboard on top, then PIR board, then plasterboard.

5 Set up a workspace with plenty of room.

6 Keeping the workplace tidy improves safety.

STRIPPING OUT

Next the wall to be insulated must be cleared by disconnecting any electrical and plumbing fittings. After draining down the central heating system, disconnect and remove radiators. Turn off the power at the consumer unit to the electrical circuits being worked on. Then unscrew the faceplates to electrical wall sockets and switches etc, disconnect the wires, and set aside the faceplates. Temporarily protect exposed bare wires with strips of electrical tape.

The timber joinery to the wall can now be stripped. As well as skirting boards, this may include architraves and linings to windows and doors and sometimes dado and picture rails. These can normally be removed using standard hand-tools, but care is needed because it's easy to splinter the wood, as the fixing nails can be very firmly embedded. Once removed, set these aside for possible later refixing.

It's normally difficult to remove any coving or cornicing near ceiling level without destroying it, unless it's modern stick-on type (which is easy to replace). Coving can be removed with a hammer and masonry chisel, having first run a sharp knife along the top and bottom edges of the coving to loosen it from the existing wall and ceiling.

Because the wall will be thicker once it's insulated, any skirting on adjoining partition walls (which aren't being

1 Remove the skirting board.

insulated) will need to be cut to accommodate this. So a piece of adjoining skirting must be cut away where the end of the new insulation will butt up against it. This will typically be about 125mm deep – comprising the depth of the PIR board (say 100mm) plus 12.5mm for the plasterboard with an allowance for the adhesive. A multi-cutter tool is ideal for this job.

Similarly a small length of coving may need to be cut away on adjoining walls to accommodate the depth of insulation. However, a better solution that helps minimise thermal bridging is to extend the insulation along partition walls for at least 300mm, so it laps around the corner.

2 Remove architrave and other woodwork.

3 Cut out a section of coving to make space for the insulation and plasterboard.

4 Large hole found behind a skirting board.

5 Large gap into the external wall found behind window reveal.

6 Large gap above window head into the external wall.

1 Holes in the external wall found under a window ledge.

2 Repairing a wall section near a window.

3 Deep crack between a party wall and an outside wall.

4 Filling the crack with acoustic sealant.

FILLING HOLES

Any gaps and holes in the wall surface should be filled to prevent ingress of cold air that could otherwise swirl around behind the insulation. Some repointing to the external brickwork may be necessary if it's deteriorated. Air leakage paths around pipes and at the edge of floorboards will also need to be sealed.

Any gaps behind window reveals and window heads etc can be sealed with expanding foam. For larger gaps, first fit lengths of plastic mesh folded into a 'U' shape to hold the foam in place as it cures. For deep cracks at wall junctions an acoustic sealant can be used.

5 Hole found near external vent.

6 Demonstration of amount of air blowing out of a wall cavity.

INSULATING

Tools
- Plasterboard cutting tools
- Sanding tool for shaping the edges
- Work table
- 'Celotex' saw
- Long straight edge
- Spirit level
- Long-bladed knife for trimming cured foam

Materials
- Plasterboard
- PIR rigid insulation board
- Aluminium tape (at least 75mm wide)
- PU foam adhesive and silicone sealant
- Wallplug fixings
- Expanding foam
- Plastic mesh
- Thermal-break foam sheet
- Structural board (eg 'FermaCell') and hammer plug fixings
- Construction-grade adhesive
- Dry-wall screws
- Plasterboard gap filler and metal edging

Health and safety
- Dust mask (when cutting PIR board)
- Latex gloves (when using expanding foam or adhesive)

WALLS NEAR WINDOWS AND EXTERNAL DOORS

When insulating around door or window reveals, space is often limited. However, it's important for part of the door or window frame to be left visible, otherwise it'll look a bit odd and imbalanced. The lack of space means it may be necessary to use a thinner depth of insulation board for these areas. Alternatively, special thin, high-performance foam sheets can be inserted behind the plasterboard to act as a thermal break. To make more space the existing window linings and any defective plasterwork can be hacked off, but exposed brickwork surfaces will need to be stabilised before insulating by applying a coat of diluted PVA. Before plasterboarding it's important to ensure that the vapour barrier is continuous between the window reveals and the internal surface of the wall.

INSULATING WALLS WITH PIR BOARD

Start with the largest areas. Measure the wall area to be lined and place a piece of PIR board on the work table with the front facing upwards. Cut the board to shape – a specialist 'Celotex' saw creates less dust than a wood saw. Ensure you keep the saw cuts square, especially when cutting board thicker than about 50mm. An airtight seal must be formed where the PIR board meets adjoining walls, floors and ceilings.

1 Stripping the linings can reveal holes and gaps.

2 Wire mesh fitted above window head ready for foam. Gap at side into external wall already filled.

3 Injecting foam into the window head. Note the use of an extended nozzle on the can of foam.

1 Attach a strip of aluminium tape to board edges that will touch adjoining surfaces to walls, floor and ceiling. The tape should be folded so it laps over the front of the board as well as the edges.

4 The cured foam before being trimmed.

5 Using PVA to seal the brickwork before gluing.

6 PIR board on the reveal and extra foam near the window ledge. Aluminium tape will be used to create vapour barrier across the cut edge of the board.

2 Turn the PIR board over and apply a bead of foam adhesive to the rear foil face around the complete edge of the board. Apply additional lines of adhesive across the centre of the board. Allow to cure for 5–10 minutes (the cooler the room the longer the cure time).

3 Apply a generous bead of silicone sealant to the wall and floor where the PIR board will touch them. This will form the airtight seal. Also apply a line of adhesive to gaps at the floor edge between the floor and wall.

4 When the adhesive has started to cure, offer the PIR board up to the wall, ensuring it's vertical. Apply pressure for a few minutes and hold or wedge the board in place until the bond is firm.

5 Ensure the joints are tight to avoid air gaps and thermal bridging. Then apply a bead of foam adhesive to the edge of the previous board to ensure a good seal to the next one.

6 Use a spirit level and a long straight edge to create a flat surface across multiple boards.

The insulation boards can be glued to the wall with construction-grade adhesives (*eg* dry-lining adhesives such as 'Pinkgrip' or PU foam adhesive), but it's good practice to additionally secure them with 4–6 wallplug anchors per board. These must be long enough to extend through plasterwork into solid masonry – *ie* about 60–75mm longer than the depth of insulation. Holes can be drilled for the wallplugs once the foam adhesive has fully set (30–45 minutes after the board has been fixed on the wall). For a 150mm thick PIR board this will typically require a 300mm drill. Drill the required holes about 100mm in from the edge of the PIR board. Tap in the body of the fixing, ensuring that the head is flush with the surface of the board. Then hammer the anchor pin into the fixing.

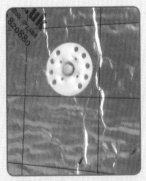

7 Continue around the room until the entire surface is covered. Fix smaller pieces at the top of the wall.

8 At window and door reveals pieces of PIR board can be cut so they overlap the insulation on the main wall. Where the wall is very uneven, apply extra adhesive to the board or wall for support and grip.

9 Fit wallplug insulation anchors to each board. Then put aluminium tape over the heads.

10 Deep fill any remaining gaps between PIR boards, or between boards and the wall/floor/ceiling, with low expansion foam or foam adhesive.

11 When the foam has cured it can be trimmed flat. All joints between boards, and any tears in the foil surface and heads of fixings, must be sealed with strips of adhesive aluminium tape. This is crucial to create the airtight vapour barrier.

12 Ensure the entire surface is airtight.

PLASTERBOARDING THE WALL

Foil-faced PIR insulation boards have a built-in vapour control layer (the foil), so the joints between boards need to be sealed with aluminium tape. Alternatively, a polythene vapour barrier needs to be placed across the entire insulated wall, overlapped and taped at joints. Plasterboard sheets can then be installed as a surface layer. Where heavy fittings such as kitchen units and radiators need to be attached to the wall, a timber structural board can be fitted instead of plasterboard. This is attached using 'hammer plugs' through the insulation into the wall. In rooms with a lot of fixings, such as kitchens and bathrooms, the structural board can be fitted in place of plasterboard across the entire wall surface.

Where skirting boards need to be mechanically refixed in place (as opposed to being glued), a 150mm tall strip of structural board can be fitted at the base of the wall. Similarly installing a strip above each window will make it easy to attach curtain rails (approximately 150mm tall extended beyond the sides of the window reveals by about 200mm). And where radiators need to be refitted, vertical strips of structural board can be attached to correlate with the radiator brackets.

The surface of the structural board may require treating with a bonding agent prior to the plaster skim. The remainder of the wall surface can be covered with plasterboard stuck on with adhesive. Gaps between sheets of plasterboard larger than a couple of millimetres should be filled with a flexible filler. All joints are then covered with a scrim tape. The edges and top of boards adjacent to walls and ceilings should also be scrim taped. External corners should have metal or plastic stop-edging attached. It's useful to apply a continuous bead of adhesive behind this edging for extra support. The wall is then ready for the plaster skim final coat.

1 Typical locations of structural board inserts.

2 Structural board fixed behind radiator brackets.

3 Applying adhesive to the back of the plasterboard.

4 Scrim tape across all joints and tops of boards.

5 Applying the plaster skim. Note the metal edging on the external corner.

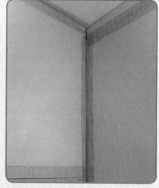

6 The finished, skimmed wall.

PARTY WALLS AND STAIRWAYS

Party walls and stairways can be tricky to insulate, due to limited space. Party walls tend to be relatively cool for about the first metre closest to the external wall, so this is the key part to insulate. They also commonly have chimney breasts occupying part of their length. This means it may only be practical to insulate the stretch between the chimney breast and the external wall, which in most cases should provide adequate cover to the cooler parts.

Another potentially cold stretch is found in houses with unheated cellars, which are outside the property's 'red line' insulated defences. Here the partition wall between the living space and the stairs down to the cellar may be very thin and thermally leaky. In many Victorian terraced houses this wall is made of pine matchboarding vertically fixed to timber studwork. These walls can be insulated with PIR board, similarly to the main walls. The main difference is the restricted space that may limit the depth of board that can be applied.

Space is often particularly tight where stairs run alongside an external or party wall. Where the stairs are fixed to the wall, the timber side of the staircase – the 'string' – can be insulated. Above each step the visible triangular part of the string can be lined with a piece of insulation board, which can then be covered with a thin decorative strip of timber boarding. To reduce cold bridging, the underside of the stairs can then be filled with mineral wool and boarded over with structural board or plasterboard.

1 Typical cellar stairway with wooden side wall.

2 Cellar stairway with first PIR board in place.

3 Beneath an internal stairway.

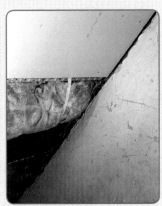

4 Mineral wool held in place with tape until board fitted.

5 PIR board fitted on top edge of stair string.

6 Surface layer fitted to surface of stair string.

DEALING WITH ELECTRICAL FITTINGS

Tools
- Bradawl
- Spirit level
- Long-bladed knife
- An oscillating multi-cutter power tool can be useful
- Set of templates to make cut-outs in the insulation and plasterboard

Materials
- Electric cable
- Dry-lined wall backing box/pattresses (typically about 30mm deep)
- Socket and switch fronts
- Screwless crimp connectors
- Earth wire sleeving
- Silicone sealant
- Insulation tape
- Adhesive aluminium tape
- Conduit

Typical cable sizes and power ratings
- Lighting: 1.5mm^2 twin and earth cable (maximum 14A).
- Ring mains for socket outlets: 2.5mm^2 twin and earth cable (maximum 24A).
- Cookers and showers etc: 6mm (maximum 40A) or 10mm cable (maximum 53A).

⚠ HEALTH AND SAFETY

It's essential to turn off the power before attempting any electrical work. Part P of the Building Regulations allows refitting or replacing of switches and sockets and limited extending of circuits. All other electrical work must be done by an officially registered 'competent person' (eg NICEIC registered electricians) or Building Control must be notified in adavance.

Most walls will have electrical sockets or light switches and some have wall lights. Fused switches are sometimes also found, serving higher amperage devices such as heaters, showers and kitchen appliances. New backing boxes will need to be placed within the insulation, and the existing cable pulled through or extended as necessary. The existing socket faceplate or switch can be reconnected to the new backing boxes, or new ones installed. This can also be a good opportunity to change the position of electrical sockets or install additional ones. The use of conduit to contain long cable runs is required to avoid cables being embedded in thick insulation, risking overheating.

PREPARING THE EXISTING SOCKET

Gently pull the wires out a little – there's often sufficient slack available without any need for additional cable. Otherwise individual wires will need to be extended.

Any new cable used to extend the existing must be of the correct size and power rating (see panel). Using a higher capacity cable is advisable where it runs through insulation, as lower resistance means less heat is generated. The cable must also be of sufficient length to make it easy to pass through the insulation (about 500mm long). Crimped connectors can be used to connect the new extension cable to each of the existing live, neutral and earth wires. Measure the distance from the centre of the socket to the floor and to the nearest wall.

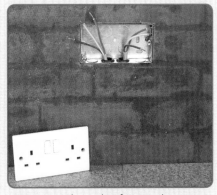

1 Remove the socket front and prepare the cables for the extensions.

2 Fit crimp connectors to the existing wires.

3 Remake the ring by attaching a loop of new extension cable. Note the heat shrink sleeving over the live and neutral crimps.

4 Measure the distance of the centre of the old backing box to the floor and to an adjacent wall.

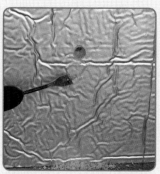

5 Drill a hole in the PIR board to be fitted for the wires to pass through.

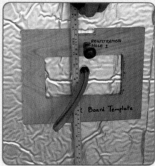

6 Use the first template to mark the position of the recess cut-out in the PIR board. Measure the position of the registration hole for later.

7 Cut out the recess to a depth of about 30mm – sufficient to accommodate the plasterboard backing box.

Templates

The specialist socket templates for use in this project can be downloaded and printed from **www.SUREinsulation.co.uk/template**.

FITTING CABLES THROUGH INSULATION

Before fitting the PIR board to the wall, measure where the electrical cable is to appear and mark the position on the board. Make a hole through the insulation for the cable, just large enough to pass the conduit through. It's best to use a power drill with a long 25mm wood bit.

Place the PIR board face up on the work table. Using the large template (see panel), mark the recess for the backing box.

Remove a depth of 30mm of insulation from the front face. Insert a length of conduit the same depth as the remaining PIR board into the cable hole. Use a knife or multi-cutter tool to cut the recess in the main PIR board to a depth of 30mm along the line drawn using the first template.

The PIR board can now be attached to the wall. Lengths of aluminium foil tape vapour barrier can be stuck around the sides and back, overlapping on to the original surface. The hole around the cables should be deep filled with silicone sealant. Note the position of the socket from the nearest wall and its height from the floor.

FITTING CABLES THROUGH PLASTERBOARD

A similar process is now carried out with the plasterboard. Mark the point where the cable is to appear through the plasterboard. Then make a small hole and pass the cable through it before fixing the plasterboard to the wall. The wall can now be skim plastered. Once dry, use the templates and the location measurements noted earlier to mark the position of the backing box and cut it out.

This should line up with the recess made earlier in the PIR board. Fit the pattress and connect the socket front. When the new fittings are safe, reconnect the power to the main circuit. Test the electrical circuit.

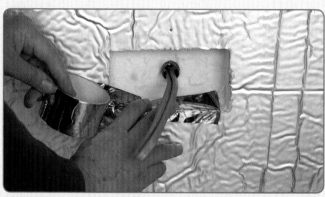

1 Use aluminium tape to reform the vapour barrier at the back of the recess.

2 Deep fill the space around the cable with silicone sealant.

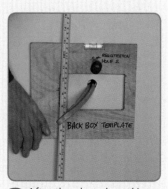

3 After the plasterboard is fitted mark the registration hole and use the smaller template to mark the position of the new backing box.

4 Fit the backing box.

5 Connect the socket cover plate.

6 Insulated draughtproofed door to electrical fuse/meter cupboard

REINSTATING THE WOODWORK AND COVING

Tools and materials

- A multi-cutter power tool may be useful
- A router may be needed
- Skirting board and coving to match that in the room
- MDF or other material to make window ledges
- Construction-grade adhesive

1 Complex pine skirting board installation.

The final stage before decorating involves reinstating the original skirting boards, or fitting new ones cut to size. (NB: Original joinery is often damaged during removal and may need to be repaired, *eg* glued and clamped, and also trimmed to fit the reduced wall dimensions after insulating.)

Joinery can be attached to the wall with adhesive. Where skirting boards are particularly tall or made of wood rather than MDF it's advisable for additional screw fixings to be made into the structural board facing described above. Similarly architraves around windows and doors can be glued and screwed in place.

Because the depth of the window reveals will now be larger, it may be necessary to make new window ledges to accommodate the increased depth. These can be made from 18mm MDF, and a router can be useful to form a curved front edge.

If new coving or cornicing is to be fitted it'll need to match any existing adjoining cornicing. A template can be made to recreate the shape of old cornices, although for more complex designs a specialist in decorative plasterwork should be able to replicate the originals. Alternatively it may be possible to leave the finished surface without coving.

2 MDF skirting board along a flat wall.

3 Creating a bull-nose on a new MDF window ledge.

4 An extra-wide window ledge fitted in place.

5 Two insulated walls with new coving fitted, extended window ledge and curtain rail in place.

5 ROOFS

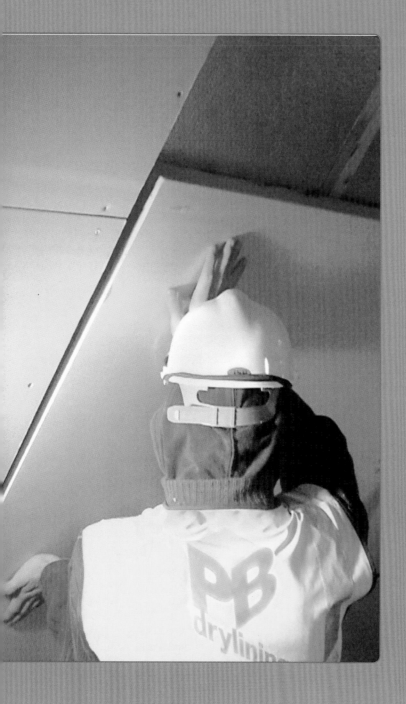

In the war against narcotics, sophisticated thermal imaging cameras operated from police helicopters are increasingly employed to identify covert 'drugs factories'. Where a roof is shown to be glowing suspiciously 'white hot', it can indicate the presence of heat-emitting infra-red lighting in the loft. And unless the occupants happen to be sun-bed fanatics, the only other plausible explanation is a secret cannabis farm. Unfortunately, in a number of embarrassing high-profile slip-ups, officers have found that the glowing was simply due to the central heating being turned up full blast, with large amounts of heat pulsating through poorly insulated roofs.

Roofs are particularly prone to heat loss. Externally they're highly exposed to the elements, whilst inside the house the warm air rises, concentrating at the top of the building. This explains why the Building Regs stipulate a tougher U-value target for roofs than for anywhere else.

In the summer months the same factors combined with 'solar gain' can make rooms at the top of the house prone to overheating, so insulating the roof will also combat this problem.

Applying loft insulation may be a relatively straightforward measure but, as we shall see, it isn't without its challenges. Roofs can also be insulated higher up at rafter level, creating a warm roof space that could potentially be converted for habitable use. However, some of the worst offenders in terms of heat loss are flat roofs, which are often devoid of any form of insulation.

As always, the first task is to ensure the fabric of the building is sound and leak-free – there's no point installing lots of insulation if its going to get soggy and actually make the house feel colder. So before insulating, any slipped or missing tiles must be fixed and defective flashings and valleys repaired.

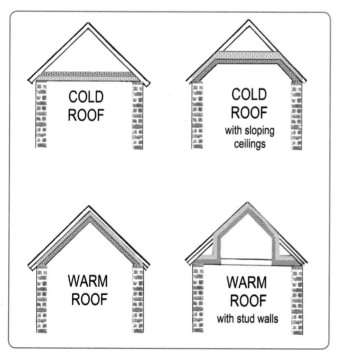

Roof insulation

Easy options

Loft insulation is an improvement that can be made at almost any time. It's relatively cheap and cost-effective to top up loft insulation to at least the recommended minimum depth of 270mm – or ideally as much 450mm.

Golden opportunities

If re-roofing work is due to be carried out, it makes sense to insulate the roof from above whilst you've got access. Indeed, the Building Regulations require you to upgrade insulation when making improvements to any thermal element. And if you're planning on doing a loft conversion it'll need to incorporate high levels of insulation to comply with Building Regulations.

Period properties

The roofs of historic buildings are often relatively complex, sometimes incorporating several more modern additions. This can make access internally quite difficult. The need to preserve historic features can also impose restrictions, such as retaining old lath and plaster ceilings in attics, unless they're genuinely beyond repair. Be aware also that the plaster 'nibs' that protrude between the laths to old ceilings can easily suffer damage when laying loft insulation. Most importantly, be aware that some old ceilings may not be able to bear much extra weight, so care must be taken when clambering around in lofts – use crawler boards to walk on and spread the load.

Above and below: *Natural materials are compatible with period buildings – but take care with fragile lath & plaster ceilings*

Materials

The most appropriate materials for buildings of traditional construction are the natural fibre-based type, such as sheep's wool, wood fibre, hemp lime and cellulose. Being 'breathable' these materials are compatible with traditional lime renders and plasters. This is particularly important where old timbers are vulnerable to rot or beetle attack. Natural materials are generally good at retaining their insulation qualities even when damp.

Lead-lined valley gutters can be insulated from below like flat roofs

Lead valley and parapet gutters

Many traditional buildings with pitched roofs have valley or parapet gutters, normally lined in lead. If the roof is to be properly insulated it's important these areas are also treated, and can be regarded technically as small flat roofs.

Photo: Andrew Osmond Thatching

Thatch

Thatch is the traditional way of keeping houses warm. Like giant tea cosies made from reed or straw, they're much better insulators than conventional roof coverings, with the added advantage of being highly soundproof.

Buildings of this age and type will almost certainly be Listed, so most insulation work, including internal improvements, are likely to need the approval of the Planners. Where historic ceiling and wall plasterwork survives it'll need to be retained.

Thermal efficiency

A typical thatched roof can come close to meeting modern standards for thermal insulation, and many will require no upgrading at all. They can be extremely energy efficient provided they're well maintained. U-values depend on the thickness and density but a mere 300mm depth can achieve between 0.23 and 0.29W/m²K, compared to the target of 0.18W/m²K in the Building Regs for roofs retro-insulated at rafter level. The tradition of 'overcoating' – building up layers of thatch over time rather than stripping – means many roofs are extremely well-padded roofs, and the addition of further insulation will often have little benefit.

However, thatch can sometimes be quite draughty at junctions with adjoining walls, stacks and tiled roofs, so a few simple repairs may be all that's needed to boost thermal performance and reduce heat loss. Heat leakage is often worst from non-thatched parts of the roof, such as dormers or tiled roofs, and lead-lined valley gutters.

In properties with conventional loft spaces these can be insulated as normal with quilt. Alternatively, an insulated false ceiling could be constructed beneath the existing ceiling (conserving historic lime plasterwork). However, many cottages don't have lofts as such, because the bedrooms occupy the space under the roof. It may be possible to apply insulation beneath sloping ceilings, with rigid boards (eg wood-fibre) fixed through the existing lath and plaster into the rafters.

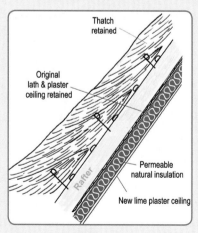

Thatch retained

Original lath & plaster ceiling retained

Rafter

Permeable natural insulation

New lime plaster ceiling

Insulating your loft is one of the cheapest and most effective ways of improving energy efficiency. It is by far the most common thermal improvement to British homes, generating major savings in heating bills for a relatively small outlay, often paying for itself within a couple of years. Yet despite these well known benefits it's estimated that nearly half of UK homes have still only got 125mm or less of the stuff, and would gain enormously from 'topping up'.

Laying rolls of loft quilt is a job that a reasonably competent DIYer should be able to manage. But that doesn't necessarily mean it's going to be an easy and enjoyable afternoon's exercise.

For a start, you're going to have to shift all those dusty old boxes, suitcases, plastic Christmas trees and bits of old tat that you (or your partner) simply couldn't bear to part with.

Once the loft space is nice and clear, you may notice that some areas aren't so easy to reach with conventional human limbs; and when you factor in various hazards and obstacles – bulky water tanks, intricate pipework, timber struts, shallow roofs devoid of headroom and quite possibly the odd wasps' nest or piles of bat poo – it'll become evident that this is a job for those of a robust constitution. The good news is that the old itchy skin-irritating mineral wool has today been largely superseded by softer, easier to use materials.

Doing it right

There are a number of key points to bear in mind when venturing up to your loft:

Don't fall through

Violently jamming your leg(s) through the ceiling wouldn't be the best of starts, so if hopping across ceiling joists isn't your cup of tea it's a good idea to place temporary crawler boards across the joists and set up some decent lighting so you can see what you're doing. It's also advisable to wear a mask, as dust and fibres in the air can be irritating. Avoid doing the job in hot weather or the sauna-like conditions will turn you into a sweaty dust-magnet.

Avoid thermal bypass

'Thermal bypass' can occur anywhere large gaps are left within the quilt (or between layers). It's surprisingly common, even in new houses, to find voids where the builders couldn't be bothered to finish the job. Loft insulation is rather like a giant duvet placed above your bedroom ceiling, so it stands to reason that any thin patches devoid of feathers won't be so snug. To avoid cold patches it's important to ensure the insulation quilt is well packed into all the awkward areas.

A useful way of testing loft insulation is by pointing a heat-sensitive 'thermograph' camera at the ceilings in the rooms below. This should reveal any pockets of cold air where the quilt is lifted by pipes or protruding bits of the roof structure. At the eaves it'll highlight thermal bypass caused by cold air circulating under the edges of the insulation. It'll also identify any bits you've missed, where a sheet of plasterboard might be the only thing between the inside of the house and the cold loft space.

Above: Many lofts have gaps in the insulation
Below: Replacement OSB ceiling lining provides airtight barrier when taped & sealed

Keep it ventilated

Over the years a lot of well-intentioned folk have meticulously sealed up every nook and cranny in their roof spaces in a determined effort to draughtproof the whole house. But the fact is, lofts are meant to be draughty and unheated above the insulation level – hence the name 'cold roof'. In contrast a 'warm roof ' is where the insulation is fitted higher up at rafter level, or on top, allowing the loft space to be heated and utilised.

Loft vent trays

Slate vent

Thermal bridging

One of the key objectives with laying loft insulation is to cover the whole ceiling area to a consistent depth. In reality, however, all the various obstacles mean that this can be hard to achieve. But as long as you don't leave any areas completely un-insulated, or with significantly differing depths of insulation, the risk of cold spots attracting condensation (and mould on ceilings below) should be tolerable. As far as possible this should join up with insulation to the walls below (which is more feasible where the walls are insulated internally rather than externally).

Above: A cold ceiling is a potentially moist and mouldy ceiling
Below: Lofts in period properties sometimes have mini walls which also need insulating

Thermal bridging can also occur in lofts at junctions with chimney breasts, party walls and main walls (eg at gable ends). To minimise this problem the quilt should be turned up against the wall to a height of at least 200mm. Where adjoining masonry walls are damp, placing insulation against it can reduce its performance if it becomes wet. So physically separating it with a vapour-permeable 'breather membrane' should help to keep the insulation dry.

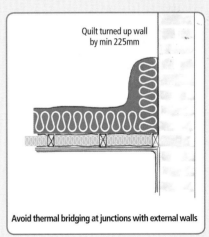

Quilt turned up wall by min 225mm

Avoid thermal bridging at junctions with external walls

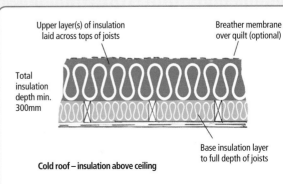

Upper layer(s) of insulation laid across tops of joists

Breather membrane over quilt (optional)

Total insulation depth min. 300mm

Base insulation layer to full depth of joists

Cold roof – insulation above ceiling

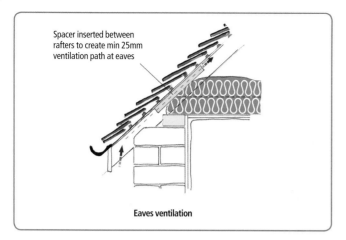

Spacer inserted between rafters to create min 25mm ventilation path at eaves

Eaves ventilation

Once your loft is fully insulated at ceiling level, the room warmth should stay where it belongs – in the rooms below. This means the loft will now be colder, so any moist air that gets in can condense on cold surfaces, such as the underside of the roof covering. In most houses there'll be a layer of old, black bituminised 'sarking felt' under the tiles, which over time can become moist and mouldy. So it's important to maintain a good flow of ventilation in order to waft away any moist air before it has a chance to morph into condensation making the roof timbers damp.

In most properties, air for ventilation enters via small vents at the eaves, and it's a common mistake to shove insulation quilt right up to the edges (ie where the rafters meet the ceiling joists), blocking these air paths. Alternatively, some properties have air vents in gable walls or at ridges, or there may be special tile vents fitted to the roof slopes. Older houses built without any sarking felt underlay often rely on small gaps between individual slates or tiles for a decent breeze.

So when laying insulation care must be taken to maintain ventilation across the roof space and not to obstruct any vents (see page 81). Of course, a big part of the solution is to minimise the risk of moisture entering the roof-space in the first place…

Reducing air leakage from the rooms below

If warm humid air from the rooms below – especially steamy bathrooms – can seep into the cold loft it'll condense, causing damp. Cracks or holes in the ceiling can also allow draughts to whistle down into the rooms below. But unlike insulating walls, it's not realistic to fit vapour barriers retrospectively in lofts. For one thing there are too many obstacles to form a continuous airtight layer. So careful attention must be paid to any gaps in your loft's defences, such as pipes or cables penetrating through the ceiling, notably in airing cupboards. Gaps around pipes and extractor fan ducting etc should be sealed with a flexible filler and sealed with tape from the ceiling below. Hairline cracks along plasterboard joints are very common and normally only need to be scrim taped and filled, and perhaps finished with a thin skim coat of plaster. But where ceilings are riddled with lots of gaps they may need to be replaced or boarded over with a new layer of plasterboard (ideally incorporating a vapour barrier sheet).

Alternatively, if headroom permits, constructing an independent suspended ceiling approximately 200mm below the existing is an excellent way of boosting both thermal performance and sound resistance. See 'Tricky areas' below.

How much do I need?

The Building Regulations set a U-value target of $0.16W/m^2K$ for insulation at ceiling level. This should be easily achievable with the stipulated total depth of 270mm mineral fibre wool. But the recommended depth is likely to increase in future, and mineral wool is relatively cheap, so while you're at it you may as well get the maximum bang for your buck and super-insulate your loft to 400mm total thickness.

Rolls of mineral wool quilt are sold in a range of thicknesses, eg 100mm, 150mm, 170mm, 200mm and 220mm. Allow about six rolls of 150mm deep quilt to cover $50m^2$ of loft with a single layer, and another six rolls on top. If you prefer natural materials, a slightly deeper thickness of sheep's wool, hemp or cellulose fibre (about 300mm) should do the trick in meeting the minimum target.

Most houses have got a smattering of ancient, sad-looking, mineral wool quilt nestling between the ceiling joists, often little more than 60mm

First fill any gaps in the existing insulation

deep and distinctly patchy. This should be left in place and covered by new quilt. But there are usually a number of areas with bits missing or bare expanses of ceiling visible. So the first job is to fill any glaring gaps with tufts of new quilt so that it's reasonably even.

Rolling it out

The new insulation is best laid in two layers. The first is applied between the ceiling joists (in line with them) over any existing insulation. A telescopic decorators' pole can be used to push insulation into hard-to-reach corners. This is then crisscrossed by rolling the second layer across the top, at right angles, over the joists.

Ceiling joists are typically about 100m deep, but even if they're taller than this they should be filled to the brim or above, before laying the top roll, so there's no air gap between the two layers of insulation. Wool insulation can be stretched to fill small gaps. Larger gaps can be filled with a small quantity of loose-fill insulation, eg cellulose fibre.

Quilt is sold in widths suitable for joists spaced at 600mm centres (in most houses built since 1970) and also for joists spaced about 400mm apart (older traditional roofs). But in some period buildings the ceiling timbers are 'roughly hewn' and may be spaced at irregular intervals.

It's also important to consider how access can be safely gained in future to tanks, wiring, aerials etc.

Not everyone is superbly nimble, and

Unrolling wool quilt

Photo: Thermafleece

now that the loft comprises a woolly sea lacking any clues to the whereabouts of the joists there are dangers afresh. So to reduce the risk of people stepping between the joists, injuring themselves and damaging ceilings, boarding for walkways can be provided. The icing on the cake is that you can now buy insulated timber loft boards for even greater thermal efficiency.

The final job is to return all the stuff that you painstakingly cleared away at the outset. But as we've seen, putting even fairly lightweight goods on top of insulation is likely to compress it, causing significant loss of effectiveness. If you don't want to go to the trouble of finding a new home for all the old clobber you could erect storage platforms. However, this isn't as simple as just whacking down a bit of old chipboard. Because the top layer of insulation projects well above the joists the new boards will need to be fitted in a way that doesn't unduly compress it. One way to create a storage area is to fix additional timbers or I-beams at right angles to the existing ceiling joists, insulate between them, and attach flooring-grade chipboard panels on top.

Don't forget the hatch

For some reason, even in the best-insulated lofts, access hatches are sometimes left devoid of the barest modicum of insulation. A poorly sealed, un-insulated hatch can single-handedly undermine all the improvements carried out elsewhere. They're a surprisingly common cause of cold bridging and a source of draughts, with gales howling around ill-fitting rims.

Professional installers are wise to such elementary oversights and consequently ensure hatches are lined internally. This might take the form of a 100mm rigid insulation board cut to size and glued to the inner face with adhesive, or could simply comprise some spare loft quilt encased in a plastic sheet and stapled to the hatch. Where there's a fixed loft-ladder, it may be necessary to extend the mounting brackets to create space to fit the insulation.

The opening will also need to be carefully draughtproofed. This can be done using special rubber strips nailed around the perimeter. These have a soft 'lip' that forms a tight seal under pressure when the hatch is closed. Some installers also fit small hooks to clamp the hatch down and resist wind uplift, but these can be a bit annoying when access is needed, and most hatches are heavy enough to stay in place without assistance. New purpose-made hatch and frame combos can be purchased pre-insulated and ready to install between ceiling joists.

Photos courtesy: Greenpuzzle Insulation

Installation checklist

It's not a bad idea to sketch out a plan of the loft before you start and mark down any difficult areas. The following are useful questions to ask:

Wasps nests are surprisingly common in lofts (but are often unoccupied)

- ■ Are there any hard-to-reach areas, such as sloping ceilings?
- ■ How is the roof ventilated? Is it sufficient? Will special eaves vents be needed so the insulation doesn't block air paths?
- ■ Is the loft boarded, and if so is it fixed in place or loose?
- ■ Are there any water tanks and pipes?
- ■ Note the routes of electric cables and positions of any recessed lighting.
- ■ Do you have any wildlife in residence, such as bats or nesting birds, which are protected by law?
- ■ Is there any old asbestos pipe lagging?

Avoid crushing the insulation

The effectiveness of loft insulation is greatly reduced if heavy items are placed on top, crushing the air pockets between its fibres. So once the job's done try to avoid chucking all the stuff you cleared earlier back on top of it. Crushing can be avoided by constructing a decked platform above the top of the insulation.

Left: Decking can be laid for safe access, but…
Above: …avoid squashing insulation as it reduces performance
Below: Insulated loft storage boards

Materials

Mineral fibre quilt (glass wool or rock/stone wool) is the most common material used for loft insulation. Loose-fill insulation such as cellulose is also used fairly widely. This is supplied in bags for hand filling or can be blown into position with specialist equipment by a registered installer (who should be able to provide a guarantee). Loose-fill has the advantage of forming a continuous insulation layer, and is especially useful for filling hard-to-reach areas.

Spraying loosefill cellulose should cover all the awkward spots - approximate coverage 5 sq m to 150mm depth

SHEEP'S WOOL

Sheep's wool is a popular natural alternative to mineral wool, but how does it compare?

Mineral wool quilt

Sheep's wool

Photo: Matthew Clements

What's good
- * Relatively cheap.
- * Available in DIY stores.
- * Good thermal performance.

- * Fully breathable.
- * Retains thermal performance even when damp.
- * No health risk.
- * Production uses minimal energy.

What's not so good
- * Some older types are irritants – not very user-friendly.
- * Poor performance when damp and can retain moisture.
- * Produced using larger amounts of energy.

- * More expensive.
- * Greater thickness needed to achieve equivalent U-value.

Tricky areas

No loft is completely devoid of annoying obstructions. Some may boast the whole repertoire of awkward obstacles discussed below. Where there's a profusion of lights, cables and pipes at low level one option can be to board over the tops of the all joists, *eg* in plywood decking, and then lay the insulation on top of this (ensuring that cold air from eaves vents can't penetrate under the boards).

Eaves and edges

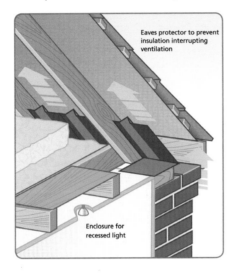

It's important for detailing at the eaves to be done correctly. If ventilation paths become blocked it could promote condensation and damp. On the other hand, you don't want blasts of cold air disappearing straight underneath the insulation, nullifying its effect. Fortunately special 'eaves vents' are available to help get this right. These are basically plastic ducts that you slide down between the rafters to maintain an air path. Once they're in place you can push insulation quilt into the eaves to your heart's content. Alternatively, you could make your own protected air channel using strips of timber board designed to direct air up between the rafter feet, over the insulation and into the loft. Or you could wedge strips of rigid insulation board between the rafters above the wall plate, maintaining a clear air passage of 50mm directly under the tiles (or underlay). Compressible board systems are available for this purpose.

Fitting rafter vents prevents blocking air paths at eaves

Polystyrene vent wedges inserted into overlaps in underfelt can improve ventilation

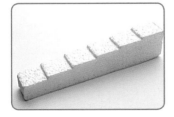
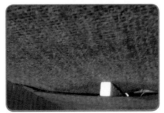

Higher up the roof slopes, some installers insert special polystyrene wedges into overlaps between sheets of underfelt to widen the gaps, thereby assisting ventilation emanating from small gaps between the tiles. Alternatively, to improve cross-ventilation, new vents can be fitted into gable walls, or special terminals inserted in roof slopes.

Recessed downlighters

Where you've got downlighters in the ceiling, covering them with thick layers of insulation can cause overheating, so the usual advice is to leave a clear space around them. The problem is this blows a gaping hole in your carefully planned insulation strategy, allowing torrents of humid air to flood straight up into the cold loft. The heat from the light fittings actually promotes upward air leakage, making matters worse.

The simplest solution (apart from not having recessed lighting) is to replace the existing inefficient bulbs with high-performance LEDs (which don't generate any significant heat) and then insulate the space above as normal. Better still, you could swap the old recessed light fittings for new shower-proof fittings capable of using high-brightness LED bulbs. Unlike ordinary recessed lighting these are safety-sealed so no draughts enter, and insulation can be laid above them.

Another option is to box-in the individual lights and continue the insulation seamlessly above the new enclosure. This can be done by fixing strips of timber boarding or plasterboard over the ceiling joists on either side of the light fitting and closing off each end (leaving an air space of about 100mm either side of the light). Quilt can then be laid around and above the boxed-in lights. Note however that transformers for low-voltage lighting are very sensitive to overheating and should be placed above the insulation. Check with a qualified electrician before making alterations.

If funds and headroom permit it's a good idea to construct a new 'false ceiling' beneath the existing one to house recessed lights and provide a handy route for assorted cables, ducts and pipework.

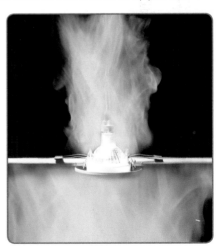

Right: Warm, steamy air from bathrooms can seep into cold lofts around downlights

Below left: Replacement MR16 dimmable LED reflector bulb

Below Right: Fit sealed showerproof fittings

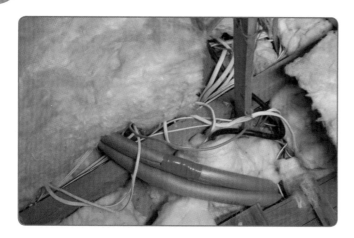

Electric cables

Electric cables give off heat when current flows through them. Where they're covered by insulation some can be at risk of overheating and short-circuiting. This risk is increased if combustible loose-fill or polystyrene-based insulation is used rather than quilt.

However, this is more likely to be a problem where you have cables supplying large loads, such as those serving cookers and storage heaters (rarely run in lofts) and electric showers. Cables serving lights are less likely to be prone to overheating, and these are the ones usually found running above top floor ceilings. But older cables, especially those pre-dating modern plastic sheathing (*eg* encased in rubber or flax) are a serious risk, and in any case will be long overdue for replacement.

Electric cables should either be clipped out of the way (*eg* above the insulation on its 'cold side') or sheathed within conduit with an air space left around the cable. Groups of cables can be run in large diameter (100mm) conduit. Junction boxes should ideally be relocated above the level of the insulation. So before installing insulation some localised rewiring in the roof space may be needed, where possible using thicker, higher capacity cable as this will generate less heat.

Water tanks and pipes

Traditionally, the roof space at the top of the house was where cold water tanks resided, the height advantage boosting gravity-powered water pressure to the taps. But over the last 20 years there's been a major move towards mains-supplied systems, such as combination boilers and unvented pressurised cylinders. These have no requirement for a supporting network of water tanks and associated pipework. So if your boiler and hot water system is likely to need replacing any time soon it's worth having this done before insulating the loft, so all the redundant paraphernalia can be removed, freeing up the loft space.

However, in most lofts the presence of a large cold water tank together with a smaller feed and expansion tank (serving the heating system) can pose one of the classic insulation dilemmas. The standard advice is that ceilings directly below water tanks should be kept free of insulation in the belief that warm air from rooms below will percolate up through the ceiling and prevent the tank from freezing. But for this to stand any chance of working the insulation needs to be draped over the tank like a tent engulfing the void underneath, lapped seamlessly at the bottom into the loft insulation. In reality there will often be large gaps in

the 'tent' or it'll be entirely absent, so any exposed cold surfaces to tanks and pipes can be prone to condensation, which can drip down, causing damp patches to ceilings below. And if timber decks supporting tanks become soggy, they can be prone to sagging or collapse.

The best advice is to lay insulation across the whole ceiling including the area directly under the water tanks. The tanks should then be fully insulated, including the base. This can be achieved by emptying the tank and slipping a thick rigid board of flooring-grade polyurethane underneath between the tank and its deck; alternatively mineral wool can be stapled to the underside of the deck (where accessible). Ready-made lagging jackets can be bought at DIY stores, and proper tight-fitting lids should be installed to water tanks to seal off this potential source of water vapour. For details of how to lag pipes and tanks, see Chapter 8.

Tanks should be supported on a stout insulated plywood deck (not chipboard, which softens when damp). The deck should in turn be supported on three or more thick timber bearers secured from the roof structure, or from a load-bearing masonry wall below. However, the ideal arrangement is to install a modern hot water system so that the tanks and pipes can be removed – and with them a potential source of moisture and condensation. The structure of the house will most likely also breathe a sigh of relief as heavy water tanks weighing 230kg or more no longer need to be supported.

Right: Taping quilt to underside of tank deck

Below: Bald patch where insulation moved to fit new water pipes to shower (note also electric cable into wall)

Lofts you love to hate

Not all lofts have easy access; some are positively claustrophobic. Especially tricky customers include:

- Shallow pitched roofs, where anyone over eight years old will struggle for headroom in the loft. Common in 1970s houses.
- Small rear addition lofts leading off the main roof, common in Victorian houses. Some Victorian terraces may also be missing 'firebreak' party walls, meaning your neighbour's humid air can invade your cold roof space; so new firebreak walls need to be constructed adding considerable cost.
- Houses where the lofts have been converted but there's a tiny, residual loft space beneath the ridge (plus small eaves cupboard lofts at the sides).
- Some older houses may have no loft hatch, or one that's so narrow you have to cut down on curries to stand any chance of squeezing through – or a new opening will need to be cut.
- Small lean-to roofs and porches with no means of access, short of physically ripping out the ceiling.

Obstructions

Unrolling blankets of quilt may not be the most challenging job in the world, but the average loft will present an array of obstacles that need to be navigated with care. Modern trussed rafter roofs have W-shaped timber webbing sprouting from ceiling joists, and horizontal bracing timbers that can restrict bodily access around the loft. Where there are a lot of obstacles loose-fill insulation can be blown into tricky corners and used to fill inaccessible pockets that are difficult to reach with quilt. For other obstructions, such as clumps of pipes, sections of mineral wool can be cut to size and stuffed around them.

Sloping ceilings

Ceilings to top-floor rooms are sometimes sloped near the eaves, which can make the job of insulating considerably more difficult.

The chances are no one bothered to insulate these areas when the house was first built, so a thermal imaging photo would probably show massive heat leakage around the edges of the roof. Such localised weak-spots are highlighted when the rest of the ceiling in the loft has been super-insulated. As with insulating eaves, a major challenge with sloping ceilings is maintaining ventilation, because simply stuffing quilt down them will block crucial air paths. But there are a number of possible solutions discussed below.

Whichever method you choose, the amount of insulation you can fit between a pair of rafters will obviously depend on how deep they are. Although typically 100mm thick, rafter depths can vary considerably from a slender 70mm in modern trussed roofs to more than 200mm. You normally need to leave a 50mm air space between the rafters on the outer side (*ie* under the tiles/above the insulation).

There are four options when installing insulation to sloping ceiling areas with restricted access:

PUSHING DOWN FROM ABOVE

For short slopes it may be possible to slide rigid insulation boards or batts down into place, working from within the loft. The insulation should sit directly above the plasterboard of the ceiling, leaving a 50mm ventilation gap above. Rigid boards are the easiest type of insulation to install, squashed tightly between the rafters.

This method has the advantage of minimal disturbance and cost, but it can be difficult to get the insulation fully in place or tight fitting. It also risks forcing debris into the eaves at the bottom and blocking the ventilation path. Care must be taken with old lath and plaster ceilings that you don't snap off the plaster nibs when pushing in rigid boards.

INSULATING BENEATH EXISTING CEILINGS

The simplest solution is often to line the underside of the existing sloping ceiling. New sheets of insulated plasterboard can be fixed in place using dry-wall screws secured into the rafters through the existing ceiling. This is a relatively inexpensive option with good access for working, and also has the advantage of preserving existing air gaps and ventilation. However, the thickness of insulation will reduce the internal room space and if there are any roof windows the detailing is more complex.

REPLACE THE CEILING

The existing sloping ceilings can be removed and replaced with new insulated ceilings. This allows insulation to be positioned between the rafters without the need to remove the roof tiles, retaining the necessary ventilation air gap above it. This should achieve good U-values at a reasonable cost but can be very messy.

INSTALLATION FROM ABOVE

The 'nuclear option' is to temporarily remove the roof coverings, battens and underfelt above the sloping ceiling area. The insulation is then installed between the rafters, maintaining an air gap under the roof coverings. This has the advantage of leaving historic ceilings intact, and provides an opportunity to fit a modern high-performance breather membrane to the roof. With good access the job can be done to a high standard. But it's a major project that's expensive, largely because of the need for scaffolding. In terms of performance, the most effective option is to create a true 'warm roof', with insulation boards fitted above the rafters. But this may not be viable for small areas of sloping ceiling, as adding a layer of insulation will raise the height of the roof, which can alter a building's character and normally requires planning consent.

INSULATING LOFTS

Tools
- Hammer
- Screwdrivers
- Scissors
- Telescopic decorators' pole

Materials
- Mineral wool quilt insulation
- PIR insulation board pieces
- Cable conduit and cable clips
- Pipe insulation
- 'PinkGrip'-type adhesive
- Draught stripping

Health and safety
- Lighting
- Dust masks
- Knee pads
- Head torch
- Crawler boards

Preparation

Preparation is the really time-consuming part of the job – clearing the loft space of stored items. The actual laying of the insulation is relatively straightforward, although dealing with all the fiddly pipes, cables and light fittings can add a couple of hours. Prepare the area by setting up lighting and crawler boards, if required, to make moving around easier.

You need to dress for the occasion, donning protective clothing including a dust mask. Other useful equipment includes gloves, knee-pads, a head torch and crawler boards. Wearing a mask is essential as old mineral wool materials emit itchy fibres when disturbed, which are irritating to eyes, skin, throat and lungs. Also, it's not unknown for rodent droppings to be present, so be sure to wash your hands afterwards.

Fortunately, it's extremely rare to find old asbestos-based insulation (usually in the form of lagging to pipes), but if spotted this must be professionally removed, as it's potentially hazardous (see page 131). Old loose-fill vermiculite insulation isn't common, but if present be sure to wear a dust mask and avoid disturbing it (see page 21).

1 Ensure the loft is well lit

2 A head torch can be very useful in confined spaces.

3 Typical disarray of wires and poorly insulated loft area.

4 Downlighters fitted into ceiling of room below.

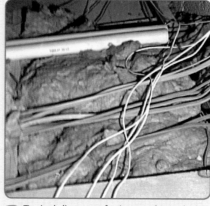

5 Replace downlighters with sealed shower lights with LEDS, so insulation can be laid on top.

6 Sections of large conduit ready for fitting.

7 Pipes with poor insulation should be lagged and joints taped. Gaps around pipes and cables should be sealed for airtightness with silicone sealant.

8 Unwrap insulation and rolls up into the loft.

9 First layer of quilt laid between joists.

10 Second layer laid across first layer.

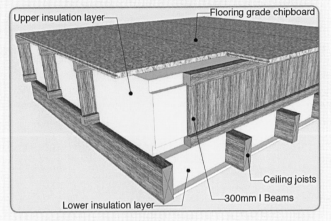

Upper insulation layer

Flooring grade chipboard

Ceiling joists

300mm I Beams

Lower insulation layer

11 Storage platform raised on timbers to create more space for insulation underneath.

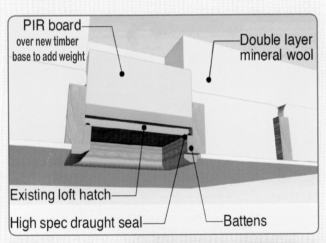

PIR board over new timber base to add weight

Double layer mineral wool

Existing loft hatch

High spec draught seal

Battens

12 Draughtproofed loft hatch with PIR board glued to top surface.

13 Loft ladder with insulation fixed to hatch.

RAFTER INSULATION

Not every property has a conventional loft space. Some older houses were built with sloping ceilings that follow the line of the roof, often embracing chilly attic rooms traditionally used as servants' quarters. A lot of other properties have had their lofts converted, although many such conversions will be significantly under-insulated by current standards. Even where your house has a loft, you might prefer the idea of insulating it higher up to make the most of the available space. The challenge, then, is to upgrade the thermal performance to the roof slopes. This can be done by insulating above, between or below the rafters, or more likely a combination of these methods.

Insulation on top

Insulating externally is the most thermally efficient method. This is known as 'warm roof' construction, because the roof structure and living space are located within an 'insulated capsule' and hence remain warm. This method is very effective at minimising heat loss, as it's easier to achieve an excellent standard of airtightness. Maintaining 'thermal continuity' is also easier, with the insulation overlapping any wall insulation below.

Because lining the outside of the roof structure will involve working at height, and hence the need for scaffolding, it's best to combine this with any scheduled work to overhaul or replace defective roof coverings. This would provide an excellent opportunity to insulate over the tops of the rafters at minimal additional cost. Crucially, however, this will result in the height of the roof being raised slightly, so a planning application will normally need to be made. Also, unless the house is detached it can look a bit odd if one house sticks up higher than its neighbours; plus getting the detailing right at party walls can be complex.

Photos: Kingspan

Photo: Knauf Earthwool

PUR insulation boards laid over rafters and sealed for airtightness

Even where matters such as these conspire against you, it's still worth considering this method for upgrading smaller, less prominent lean-to roofs (which may have no access for insulating internally).

The first job is to expose the basic skeleton of the rafters, by stripping the tiles or slates, and removing the battens and

Materials

A number of materials are commonly used for insulating roofs at rafter level:

Over rafters
- Rigid PIR, PUR or PF insulation boards, with aluminium foil facing
- Rigid EPS insulation boards
- Wood-fibre boards

Between rafters
- Rigid PIR, PUR or PF insulation boards, with aluminium foil facing
- Rigid EPS insulation boards
- Mineral wool quilt or batts
- Sheep's wool quilt or batts
- Wood-fibre batts

Under rafters
- Rigid PIR, PUR or PF insulation boards with aluminium foil facing
- Rigid EPS insulation boards
- Wood-fibre boards
- Multifoils

Between the rafters

In many properties, stripping the roof to insulate it from above simply won't be feasible, given the expense and likely planning issues. But an inside job is obviously going to be more disruptive for occupants. This is essentially the same challenge that you faced when converting a loft. To achieve a U-value of 0.18W/m²K you may need to insulate between the rafters (eg 75mm PUR board) as well as underneath them (eg 50mm PUR board).

Modern roofs with breather membrane underlays require little or no air space directly underneath. This solution combines natural wood-fibre batts between the rafters with multifoil beneath.

1 Wood fibre insulation batts beneath breather membrane
2 Combined multifoil insulation and vapour control layer with airspace either side
3 Rafters are extended internally with battens to create airspace around multifoil and support plasterboard

underlay. A layer of insulation can then be applied over the top of the rafters, normally in the form of high-performance rigid boards such as PIR or PUR. For airtightness, a vapour control sheet can first be applied over the rafters, although this is less critical with warm roofs, because any humid air that finds its way through the ceiling from the rooms below should only encounter relatively warm surfaces, thanks to the thick layer of insulation perched on top. Hence condensation is less of a risk.

On the outer side of the insulation boards, timber battens (minimum 28mm x 38mm) are fixed down the line of each rafter to secure the insulation board in place. These 'counterbattens' are screwed or nailed through the insulation into the rafters beneath. New horizontal battens are then fixed across a breather membrane laid over the counterbattens, forming a ventilated air space above the insulation. Finally, the tiles or slates are hung conventionally from the battens.

Rigid insulation materials are best suited for use on warm roofs. Natural materials in board form, such as wood fibre, are vapour-permeable, which in combination with breather membranes can make them better suited to older houses.

To achieve super-high performance, a new roof can be constructed above the original rafters, which are first overclad with 9mm OSB timber boarding over a polythene vapour barrier. An incredibly low U-value of 0.09 can be achieved by installing new rafters made from engineered timber I-beams (400mm deep) over the existing roof structure. These can then be packed with semi-rigid batts of mineral fibre before being finished with insulated boarding, breather membrane and roof tiles.

Quilt can be stuffed between rafters but must maintain the necessary air space behind

This loft conversion is only 15 years old, but polystyrene boards between rafters are very thin and have come loose – rendering it useless

Right: Breather membrane laid from inside between and under the rafters, ready to receive insulation between and under them, with vapour check and plasterboarding

Photo: ECD Architects

In most roofs built from about 1950 to 2000, a thick layer of black hessian 'sarking felt' underlay can be seen sagging ponderously between the rafters. Although most have seen better days, it's normally best to leave it in place, unless you're prepared to get up on the roof and strip off all the tiles and battens in order to replace it. Any large torn strips dangling down should be taped and secured, but otherwise the condition isn't particularly critical (as long as the roof is watertight). Older roofs (pre-WW2) were generally built without underlay and relied on small gaps between tiles to ventilate away any moisture that entered the loft. Most houses built since the turn of the 21st century have modern breather membranes which cleverly act as a barrier to rainwater getting in, yet allow any moisture in the roof structure to escape.

Before embarking on fitting the insulation, bear in mind that you normally need to leave a 50mm deep ventilation path on the upper side. The exception is where you have a roof with a modern breather membrane, because unlike old impermeable underfelts these already permit a certain amount of ventilation; but it's still advisable to leave a ventilation path of about 20mm.

Obviously the amount of insulation you can fit between the rafters will depend on their depth (less the necessary ventilated path). As we've seen, the depth of rafters can vary from as little as 70mm up to as much as 200mm, but typically they're around 100mm. This won't accommodate an enormous amount of insulation. One solution is to install deeper rafters screwed alongside, ie 'doubling up' the existing rafters with new ones, say 150mm deep.

Even allowing for the ventilation path you should now be able to fit a more substantial 100mm depth of insulation. The boards are then cut to shape (or slightly larger to friction-fit). But before pressing them home, thin lengths of timber batten should be fixed up the rafters to form a guide rail or lip for the boards to sit

on (allowing a clear 50mm air space on the outer side). This helps secure them so they can't slip and block the air void.

Once the boards are firmly wedged in place any gaps should be sealed with expanding foam to prevent blasts of cold air leaking into the house.

In old roofs without any form of underlay beneath the tiles, it's a good idea to install sheets of breather membrane before fitting the insulation boards between the rafters. Of course, working from inside severely limits how this can be done; but even draping it between and under the rafters, stapled in place, can provide a useful secondary line of defence in case rain gets through, thus helping keep the insulation dry.

PURLIN WALLS

To save having to insulate the lower roof slopes, short purlin walls can be constructed in 100mm thick timber studwork. These create a useful eaves cupboard area to the sides, and effectively block off the lower one-third of the rafters. Eaves cupboards are basically 'mini lofts' ventilated to the outside and can therefore be very cold. So their floors need to be insulated to keep the rooms down below

warm and to achieve continuity of insulation with the main walls. Use a telescopic decorators' pole to position mineral wool in hard-to-reach corners, but avoid blocking ventilation paths at the eaves.

The stud walls also forms a boundary between the cold mini loft area and the heated living space so it's important that they're fully insulated and airtight. Insulation can be applied both between the studwork and lined across the inner face to the room. To achieve a U-value of 0.30W/m²K you could for example fit 80mm rigid PUR board between the studs with at least 25mm PUR lining internally.

Where access is possible, however, insulation can be fitted from inside the eaves cupboard, eg with PIR board attached to the studwork using dry-wall screws. Alternatively, mineral wool can be hung in a curtain across the entire surface, held in place using long nails hammered into the frame of the stud wall (eg 220mm nails for fixing 200mm mineral wool). Before attaching the

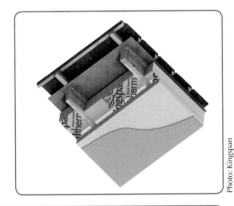

PUR board fitted between rafters on batten rails to leave air space behind, plus rafters lined with insulated plasterboard internally – should comfortably exceed target U-value

Photo: Kingspan

Hinged access door showing PIR board

Photo: SURE Insulation

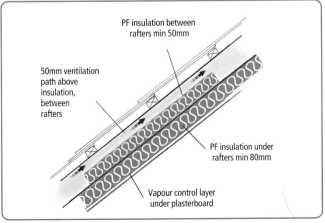

PF insulation between rafters min 50mm

50mm ventilation path above insulation, between rafters

PF insulation under rafters min 80mm

Vapour control layer under plasterboard

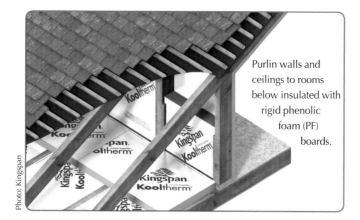

Photo: Kingspan

Purlin walls and ceilings to rooms below insulated with rigid phenolic foam (PF) boards.

Lining rafters with multifoil

■ Starting at the top, staple horizontal layers of multifoil across the rafters (using min 14mm galvanised staples). The upper edge of each layer should lap the one above by at least 50mm to the loft side. At the bottom of the rafters, staple the lower layer to the timber wall plate.

■ Where insulation has already been fitted between the rafters, leave a clear space (min 25mm) between it and the multifoil.

■ Tape each joint with 100mm wide purpose-made tape to achieve an airtight finish

■ To permanently hold it in place, fix timber battens (min 25 x 35mm) horizontally across the rafters (or vertically along the rafters). Foil-backed plasterboard can be screwed to the battens, leaving an air gap (min 25mm) between the insulation and the plasterboard.

mineral wool any gaps and holes in the stud wall should be sealed with silicone sealant or wood strips and adhesive.

Lining for the room-side face can similarly be attached using dry-wall screws.

Small gaps can be sealed with expanding foam. Cables and backing boxes for electric socket outlets and switches will need to be accommodated.

Access doors must be insulated and draughtproofed. An offcut of 100mm PIR board can be glued to the void-side face of the door and draught strip fixed to a lip running round the sides of the door frame. The door can be made to close tightly by fitting a positive-closure catch.

Below the rafters

Lining the underside of the rafters with insulation boards (typically 50–100mm thick) is usually carried out once insulation has first been fitted between them. With foil-backed insulation the foil provides a vapour barrier, but it can be difficult to make this airtight. Alternatively, to ensure airtightness a polythene sheet vapour-check membrane should be draped across the 'warm' inner face of the insulation prior to plasterboarding, with all joints in the sheeting lapped and taped.

In houses with attic rooms, or where the loft has been converted, the rafters will be inaccessible, concealed behind the plasterwork of sloping ceilings. Builders are very good at advising that old ceilings are torn down, but not so good at predicting the stupendous amount of mess as centuries of accumulated dust and ancient plaster engulf your formerly pristine home.

Many period properties have their original lath and plaster ceilings which are much thicker and lumpier than modern plasterboard, with better sound and thermal insulation qualities, so it makes sense to preserve them.

A useful compromise can be to apply a fresh insulated lining over the old plasterwork (subject to headroom). However, extra-long dry-wall screws will be needed to firmly secure it. To achieve sufficient grip these

will need to extend through the new insulation and plasterwork into the timber rafters behind. So this is likely to limit you to about 50mm depth of insulation (+12.5mm plasterboard), which alone is probably insufficient to achieve the target.

To overcome these limitations, special 'extension rafters' can be fitted to support thicker levels of insulation. These are C- or Z-shaped in section and are screwed to the joists so they project underneath, cradling the insulation boards. For example, a Z-beam can accommodate three 50mm thick layers of PU insulation. Alternatively, it might be worth considering fitting a multifoil lining secured with battens.

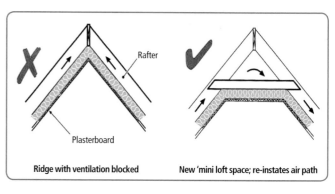

Rafter

Plasterboard

Ridge with ventilation blocked   **New 'mini loft space; re-instates air path**

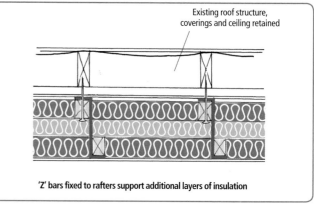

Existing roof structure, coverings and ceiling retained

'Z' bars fixed to rafters support additional layers of insulation

FITTING INSULATION TO RAFTERS

Tools and materials
- Fine tooth saw
- Hand padsaw
- Surf rasp (plane)
- Craft knife
- Cordless screwdriver
- Insulation boards as specified
- Foil-backed 12.5mm plasterboard or insulated plasterboard
- Dry wall screws 75mm & 100mm
- A can of polyurethane expanding foam

The products used here are phenolic foam (PF) insulation boards by Kingspan.

Health and safety
- Mask, goggles and gloves

Insulating a roof at rafter level can make sense if you want to use the loft space, *eg* as an occasional den or insulated storage area. See *Haynes Loft Conversion Manual* for use as habitable space.

Insulating at rafter level is more likely to suit traditional 'cut timber' roof structures rather than modern trussed rafters, which have a lot of W-shaped webbing obstructing the loft. (NB: Roof timbers must never be cut or removed without consulting a structural engineer.)

The best approach to this project is to consider the loft as an insulated box, so any adjoining external surfaces such as gable walls and subsidiary roofs will also need to be lined.

The main roof slopes are insulated in two stages. First an outer layer of insulation is wedged between the rafters, then an inner layer of insulation is fixed across the underside of the rafters prior to plasterboarding. Here insulated plasterboard is used to combine the last two stages. This should easily exceed the target U-value of 0.18W/m²K.

1 Before insulating, it's essential to leave a 50mm ventilated air space under the existing roofing felt (or in older unfelted roofs, directly under the battens). This means the insulation can't just be stuffed all the way in otherwise it would block the airflow between the rafters. To prevent the risk that the insulation boards could later slip and block this ventilation path, the first job is to fit timber battens along the rafter sides. These act as 'guide rails' for the slabs to rest on, and are nailed in place 50mm in from the outer face of the rafters (using sawn treated 25 x 38mm battens).

2 If necessary, the existing rafters can be made deeper in order to accommodate a thicker depth of insulation. Here the traditional 100mm deep ('4in by 2in') rafters are being extended by nailing 20mm thick battens along their inner faces, to achieve a total depth of 120mm.

3 Before installing the first layer of insulation between the rafters, an extra row or two of horizontal battens (say 25 x 38mm) may need to be fixed between them, flush with their inner face. This will later provide extra support for the inner layer of insulation in stage 8.

4 Next, insulation boards are measured and cut into suitably sized chunks to fit between the rafters using a fine tooth handsaw. To achieve a tight 'friction fit' the board can be cut slightly oversized on one side, or cut at a slight angle. Alternatively, boards can be cut 'slack' and gaps filled with expanding foam (the boards held temporarily in place with battens as it cures). The insulation shown is 70mm thick.

5 Push the chunks of board between and flush with the face of the rafters. A small amount of adjustment and trimming can be done in situ using a handsaw. If required, screws can be used to hold boards in place. Any gaps should be sealed with expanding foam.

6 The second stage involves applying a layer of insulation across the inner face of the rafters. Mark the boards and cut to size with a handsaw. To achieve a snug fit the sides of the boards can be planed with a small rasp.

7 All edges of boards must be supported on rafters or battens. In this example, 62.5mm thick insulated plasterboard sheets are used (50mm insulation combined with 12.5mm plasterboard).

8 Secure boards in place with dry-lining wall screws.

9 To maintain ventilation across the roof structure, a mini-ceiling is constructed with horizontal battens. The insulation to the rafters need not continue any higher than the new ceiling.

10 Where the insulation boards meet the new ceiling they need to be cut at an angle to neatly butt against its surface. If you're using 'all-in-one' insulated plasterboard, a neat joint here is especially important as this is the final surface. If you're fitting standard insulation boards then a separate finish layer of plasterboard will later be needed, ideally with a separate vapour barrier sheet first installed (or using foil-

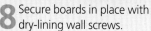

backed board). The plasterboard is secured with dry-wall screws through the insulation into the rafters, which also helps hold the insulation in place.

11 Where you've constructed a stud wall 'eaves cupboard', the lower rafters behind the wall can be left un-insulated. Otherwise the insulation will need to continue down to the wall plate, taking care not to block the eaves' air vents.

Window reveals

Where your loft has roof windows, these can be insulated as follows:

1 To achieve a neat, well-insulated joint around roof windows, the best approach is to board right across the room, as described above, including the windows (temporarily). Before this is done, the dimensions of each window opening are first marked in pencil on the board.

2 Using a pad saw, a rough hole is cut allowing some light in, leaving at least 25mm extra board protruding inward around the window opening.

3 The reveals around the window are filled with pieces of insulation cut to fit, typically about 50m thick.

4 The opening is then neatly cut and trimmed using a padsaw so that it's flush with the surface of the insulated reveals.

5 Strips of plasterboard are then inserted over the insulated reveals and pushed firmly into a purpose-made slot in the window frame. The inner edges are trimmed to achieve a neat finish prior to taping or skimming.

FLAT ROOFS

Flat roofs give surveyors the collywobbles. From bitter experience they know that most have cheap, short-life coverings that are guaranteed to start leaking – usually sooner rather then later. At best insulation levels are poor, and frequently non-existent. So this is an area with serious potential for boosting energy efficiency. The good news is that where coverings are likely to need replacing in the not too distant future the cost of upgrading the insulation can partially be absorbed by being piggy-backed on the scheduled work.

A lot of properties have fairly large expanses of flat roof on extensions, and upgrading these can often be a relatively straightforward job. It's the smaller roofs to porches, bays and dormers that tend to be relatively tricky in terms of detailing and access.

The preferred method of upgrading is simply to place thick rigid boards over the existing structure and apply a new waterproof layer on top, to create a 'warm roof'. Where this isn't possible, improvements can either be made within the structure or to the ceiling below.

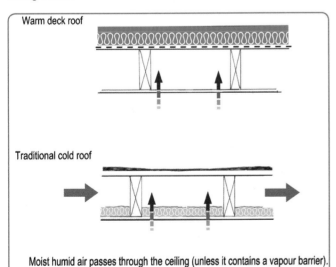

Warm deck roof

Traditional cold roof

Moist humid air passes through the ceiling (unless it contains a vapour barrier). In a cold roof it condenses, depending on decent ventilation to disperse damp. In a warm roof (top) the air stays warm and shouldn't condense

Construction

Before getting too engrossed in boosting the thermal performance of flat roofs, it's worth taking a quick look at how they're constructed. In essence, most domestic roofs are simply built in the same way as timber floors, with a series of joists covered on top with boards or some other kind of decking. The main difference is the addition of a waterproof covering to keep it dry. Of course, flat roofs aren't actually flat, since a sufficient slope or 'fall' is necessary for rainwater to disperse. Any roof less than about 12° officially counts as flat, with the slope normally created by the insertion of wedge-shaped 'firrings' on top of the joists.

Traditionally decking was made using softwood boards, later superseded by plywood or OSB. The analogy with floor construction doesn't extend to the use of chipboard, however, which although widely used for decks has one killer drawback – dampness causes it to lose its strength and turn to mush.

Solid reinforced concrete flat roofs are comparatively rare on residential buildings other than some apartment blocks and small additions and bays on some 1930s to 1950s houses. But one thing that flat roofs of all shapes and sizes have in common is the need to cope with expansion and contraction of the coverings. All roof materials expand in strong sunlight, none more so than metals.

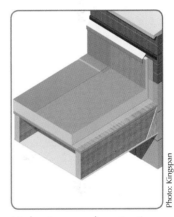

Photo: Kingspan

Modern 'warm roof' construction with rigid high performance insulation boards laid on top of deck

Sheet metal

Being the most durable form of protection, cladding roofs in metal makes them virtually bulletproof, but is relatively expensive. Metal sheet is laid in sections with movement joints in between. Typically joints that cross the slope of the roof are formed as a step or 'drip' in the deck, whilst joints parallel with the direction of fall are formed as rolls or welts.

Although many roofs of this type will still be functioning after 100 years or more, most will contain zero insulation, and few will have sufficient ventilation or any method of vapour control necessary to cope with modern lifestyles.

Despite their remarkable longevity, special care is needed when insulating metal sheet roofs because they're vulnerable to corrosion on their undersides. Hence the importance of good detailing to prevent moist air getting into the structure from the rooms below, and effective ventilation to disperse any moisture that does percolate through.

Lead

Often lasting well over a century, lead is a high quality material, having gained a certain notoriety in recent years for its popularity amongst the ecclesiastical roof stripping fraternity. Being weighty it requires a strong roof structure. Also it's very prone to expansion and contraction, so detailing of joints is critical.

Zinc

A cheaper material than lead, zinc was widely used for small flat roofs to bays and dormers in the Victorian era.

Copper

The Rolls-Royce of roofing materials, copper is highly resistant to corrosion but is very expensive and hence not that common on domestic buildings.

Continuous coverings

If you think about it, human skin is the ultimate 'continuous covering', being both flexible and water-resistant. The same principle can be successfully applied to flat roofs. Instead of relying on joints at regular intervals to accommodate thermal expansion and contraction, the materials themselves are flexible enough to absorb this natural movement. The downside is that over time they tend to lose their flexibility and become brittle. Several types of continuous covering material are used on flat roofs:

Mineral felt

The most widely used material for flat roofs, being relatively cheap. It's made from bitumen-coated fabric, usually applied in layers bedded in hot bitumen. It's a relatively short-life material, lasting only 10–15 years, although longevity is improved by protecting the surface with solar reflective coatings such as stone chippings.

EPDM synthetic rubber etc

A variety of artificial rubber/thermoplastic or fibreglass compounds are available with superior performance to cheaper roofing felts. Perhaps the best known is EPDM (ethylene propylene diene monomer), a highly durable synthetic rubber. As always, workmanship and detailing are key to longevity.

Bituminous coatings

Asphalts from natural rock were used to coat flat roof surfaces in Victorian times, later superseded by synthetic bitumen made as a by-product of oil refining. However, surfaces must be well protected with solar reflective paint or light stone chippings. In recent years the durability of bituminous coatings has improved, with claimed lifespans of up to 50 years.

Insulation materials

You don't normally think of flat roofs as having lofts, but the void between the ceiling and the deck on top traditionally functioned in the same way as conventional lofts, with a meagre layer of insulation under a ventilated air space – the classic 'cold roof'. There are three main types of insulation suitable for flat roofs:

SOFT FIBRE QUILT OR LOOSE-FILL MATERIALS
Mineral wool quilts, sheep's wool and loose-fill cellulose are popular materials for laying above ceilings. However, being 'floppy' they can't support their own weight, and are therefore suited to being laid loose with nothing over them. If they get heavily compressed the air is squeezed out, dramatically reducing performance. On the plus side they're easy to install around awkward shapes, minimising gaps and cold bridging. Loose-fill materials are ideal for filling awkward voids above old irregular ceilings.

SEMI-RIGID INSULATION BATTS
Batts of mineral wool, sheep's wool or wood fibre etc are rigid enough to support their own weight without slumping. This makes them well suited for wedging between joists. Although squishing them can result in a small performance penalty, their compressibility makes them ideal for fitting between irregular timbers found in older buildings. They're also easy to cut for fitting around awkward shapes.

Thermal bridging

Placing insulation on the outside is always technically the better option. A warm roof with the insulation boards placed on top solves the problem of thermal bridging. Here the roof structure itself is encased by the insulation and can't transmit cold from outside (but the relatively exposed joists at the ends may need insulating).

Thermal bridging is more of an issue on older 'cold' roofs where the joists form a direct link or bridge between the cold deck above and ceilings to the rooms below.

Condensation within the structure ('interstitial condensation') can cause corrosion to metal roof coverings, as well as posing a risk to roof timbers; and once most types of wool or loose-fill insulation become even slightly soggy their performance plummets. There are four main ways to prevent this:

- Insulate carefully – get the detailing right and don't leave gaps. The roof insulation should be overlapped with insulation to the walls below to maintain continuity.
- Install a vapour check membrane to prevent moist air getting in from the room below.
- Provide ventilation above the insulation, so any moisture that gets in can evaporate swiftly away.
- Reduce the amount of moist air in the house with extractor fans and lifestyle changes.

RIGID BOARDS

Large rigid insulation boards (*eg* polyurethane or polystyrene) are highly resilient and durable, making them suitable for use on top of the deck. For additional strength boards are sometimes bedded and jointed with hot bitumen. Some are designed with sufficient rigidity to perform the combined role of deck and insulation and can be laid directly over the joists. These boards can span several metres and are resistant to compressive loads and are also widely used in 'inverted roof' systems – see below. Alternatively, insulation boards can be cut to size and wedged between joists above ceiling level, or can be fitted underneath the joists as insulated ceilings.

Equivalent natural materials available in rigid board form include wood-fibre and compressed hemp-fibre. Some are available with tongued and grooved edges to improve airtightness and structural rigidity.

New warm roof – insulation boards anchored to existing deck with EPDM type covering laid on top

Rubber roofs

Photos courtesy: Rubber4Roofs

1 The existing roof covering can be kept in place if the roof deck is in good condition. Remove any loose gravel or debris from the roof and strip the lower 2 or 3 courses of tiles from adjoining roof slopes. But where the existing roof deck is rotten it will need to be replaced with new plywood or OSB3 board with a minimum thickness of 18mm.

2 Standard foil-backed rigid PUR type insulation boards are laid directly over the old roof covering (which acts as a vapour barrier). At the edges, the fascia will need to be extended to accommodate the new insulation depth. A length of timber may need to be fitted behind the fascia to provide a solid surface to fix into.

3 Board over the insulation in 12mm plywood (or 9mm OSB3). Although roofing felt is often laid directly over the insulation, with EDPM you get a much better finish with a separate base. Alternatively, composite insulation boards can be used which are bonded to a 6mm timber deck on top.

4 The boarding and insulation can now be secured in place. Screws need to be long enough to pass through the boarding, insulation, and the old roof covering so that they're fixed securely into the deck or joists. But check for any hidden electric cables and water pipes passing through the roof void.

5 Unpack the rubber membrane and lay out on the new roof deck to 'relax' it for at least 30 mins. This should remove any creases prior to bonding.

6 Special water-based adhesive is applied in even strips using a paint roller. Starting at one edge, roll the rubber membrane tightly towards the centre of the roof. While the adhesive is still wet, roll the membrane outwards towards the other edge of the roof. The adhesive shouldn't be applied to the whole deck all in one go or it could dry out before the rubber roof can be rolled into place. The adhesive shouldn't be applied right to the edge of the roof – leave a 150mm strip bare ready for the contact adhesive…

7 Using a mini roller or paint brush apply contact adhesive thinly to the strip of un-glued boarding under the membrane and the back of the rubber. It should also be applied to any up-stands and where the membrane is folded down over the edges. The adhesive should be touch-dry prior to rolling the membrane into position (depending on the temperature etc this can take between 2 to 15 mins). If the membrane is positioned too early bubbles will appear from the gas given off by the drying adhesive.

8 Where the membrane abuts the main tiled roof slope, the roof tiles can be nailed back in place. Fascias and edge trims can now be fitted around the edges.

Installing insulation

To achieve the target U-value of 0.18W/m²K or better, a 100mm depth of PIR boarding or similar laid on top of the deck should be sufficient. But check with the insulation manufacturer for recommended depths for different products. Just as important to performance is where you put the insulation. There are several options – on top, below or in between – or if you really want to impress the neighbours, there's nothing to stop you combining all three!

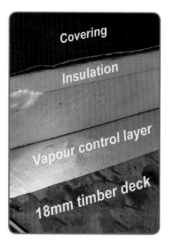

Covering

Insulation

Vapour control layer

18mm timber deck

1 On top – a new warm roof

No matter how cold and draughty your old roof, laying thick high-performance insulation boards on top of the deck should transform it into a snug 'warm roof'. In most cases this is the best option, the main constraint being whether raising the height of the roof by up to 150mm presents any problems. For example, if there's a very low window on an adjacent wall it could make the detailing tricky (eg where the covering is tucked into mortar joints at upstands). The guttering and fascias are also likely to need modification. And where you're planning to fit external wall insulation, the eaves and fascia will need to be extended to accommodate it.

Once the old roof covering has been stripped, the condition of the deck can be checked. If this shows signs of rot or damage a new deck of plywood or OSB should be installed, and the

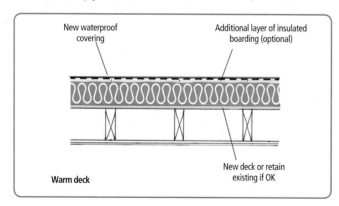

New waterproof covering

Additional layer of insulated boarding (optional)

New deck or retain existing if OK

Warm deck

Natural wood-fibre insulating boards with high compression resistance can be used for balcony roofs and floors

insulation boards can be laid on top. Alternatively, special rigid insulation boards can be used to replace the deck. Where the fall of the roof is insufficient the addition of wedge-shaped timber firrings can support a new slightly raised deck above, or in place of, the existing one.

The attraction of upgrading roofs from above is that it's generally easier and less messy than taking down and replacing old ceilings. Plus warm roofs have inherent immunity to condensation. However, where scaffolding is needed it will significantly add to the cost.

2 On top – an inverted warm roof

An 'inverted roof' is a modified version of a warm roof potentially allowing it to be used as a balcony. Instead of stripping away the old covering it's left it in place with the insulation simply placed on top. As long as it's in sound condition, retaining the original waterproof covering below the new insulation can provide a ready-made vapour barrier. Unfortunately, this is rarely an option because the vast majority of flat roofs are covered in short-life felt, and it's not worth hanging on to grotty, worn out old coverings.

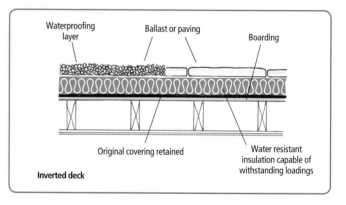

Waterproofing layer

Ballast or paving

Boarding

Original covering retained

Water resistant insulation capable of withstanding loadings

Inverted deck

With inverted roofs, sheets of loose-fitting waterproof insulation (such as rigid EPS or PUR) are positioned on top of the existing covering. To prevent them disappearing with the first gust of wind, or floating off on a tide of rainwater, they need to be securely held down. Ballast is often applied for this purpose, or, if you want to create a walkway, paving slabs can be used. Obviously, it's essential that the roof structure is strong enough to support the increased weight.

Some designs allow rainwater to percolate down through the joints between insulation boards and drain away along the top of the existing waterproof layer below. But because this can introduce 'cold spots', it makes sense to first place a sub-layer of insulation on top of the old covering to form a warm base. The new layers of insulation will protect the existing covering from the sun whilst keeping the roof structure below warm. The main disadvantage of inverted roofs is the increase in loadings which may necessitate some strengthening to the structure.

3 Beneath the ceiling

Sometimes raising the height of the roof isn't feasible for planning or technical reasons. So unless the roof needs recovering anyway, it may be simpler to tackle the job from below, keeping the existing 'cold deck' arrangement in place up above. Without the need for scaffolding, this should also be a cheaper option.

This doesn't necessarily mean consigning the old ceiling to

oblivion. Of course, there may be cases where replacing the existing ceiling with a new insulated one makes perfect sense. But if you can avoid the unbelievable amount of dust and mess that taking down ceilings creates, so much the better. There are two main ways you can insulate from below:

- Fix a new layer of insulated plasterboard directly on to the existing ceiling. First apply a vapour control sheet so it's sandwiched above the new layer to keep moisture at bay. Then, using long dry-wall screws, secure the new insulation board through the existing ceiling into the joists. Finally, apply a skim plaster finish.
- Where your rooms are blessed with reasonably generous ceiling heights, the prospect of losing up to 200mm of headroom should hold few terrors. So a new false ceiling incorporating

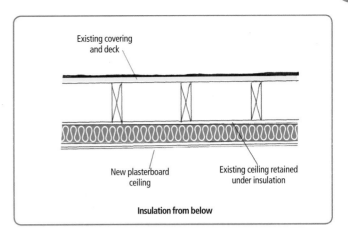

Existing covering and deck

New plasterboard ceiling

Existing ceiling retained under insulation

Insulation from below

Insulating between the joists

1 & 2. Old leaky roofing felt temporarily covered with tarpaulin

3 Removal of felt reveals disintegrating chipboard deck

4 Damaged deck is stripped away to expose joists with wedge-shaped firings

5 Top of ceiling visible once old (damp) insulation quilt is cleared away

6 New insulation boards fitting above ceiling abutting tightly to joists with no gaps; ventilated air space left above

7 New plywood deck laid to falls over existing joists

8 Completed new deck abutting pitched main roof

9 New felt covering bedded on bitumen lapped under adjoining tiles with lead flashing to stack

Photos courtesy: Matt Coleman

A suspended ceiling can be packed with insulation and is a useful place to run pipes and cables

a vapour barrier can be constructed beneath the old one, using fairly shallow joists (eg 100mm x 50mm depending on the span). Where space allows, a gap of at least 50mm can be left so the new structure 'floats' independently of the old ceiling. The void can then be packed with mineral wool quilt, which has the added advantage of providing excellent soundproofing.

4 Within the structure – a cold deck

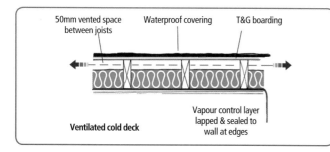

50mm vented space between joists   Waterproof covering   T&G boarding

Vapour control layer lapped & sealed to wall at edges

Ventilated cold deck

Where head-height in the rooms below is limited, it's possible to do things the old-fashioned way by 'filling the void' between the existing joists, leaving a 50mm ventilation path on top. So with typical 200mm deep joists you should be able to squeeze 150mm of insulation above the ceiling.

Where access is possible, adding insulation is often easier from above, as it saves taking down the ceilings. But clearly this will require the temporary removal of the roof covering and deck – something that's best done when coverings need replacing anyway.

Alternatively, you could tackle the job from below, taking down the ceiling and stuffing semi-rigid insulation batts between the joists before fitting a new plasterboard ceiling (but then you may as well go the whole hog and fit a new insulated plasterboard ceiling).

If any small gaps are left in the insulation it can allow humid air to penetrate, making the insulation soggy and useless. So a vapour control layer should be installed across the underside of the joists prior to plasterboarding, especially to ceilings above steamy bathrooms and kitchens. It's obviously not a good idea to make holes in the new ceiling, which rules out recessed lighting (except sealed shower lights).

One problem with this method is where the joists aren't very deep (eg on some small roofs). This can seriously restrict the depth of insulation that can be squeezed in, allowing for a ventilation path above, unless you raise the height of the deck (but then fitting a higher-performance warm roof would be a better option). If you crammed in the maximum insulation between joists to their full depth without ventilation, the control of condensation build-up in the structure would rely entirely on the vapour-check membrane below the insulation. To improve ventilation, small holes can be drilled into fascia boards. But avoid cutting joists to improve ventilation, as it will weaken them. Vents should be protected with mesh to keep wasps and flies out.

Insulating above & between the joists

A new roof structure is erected above the old flat roof, and set to with a very shallow fall (which still counts as 'flat'). Natural wood-fibre insulation is applied between and above the joists.

1. New wall plate, timber deck (OSB) and joists erected above existing flat roof
2 & 3. Breather membrane stapled over joists supporting thick flexible wood-fibre batts
4. Insulation fully fitted between joists
5. Rigid wood-fibre insulation boarding applied over new joists
6. Timber battens fixed above new deck
7. Roof clad with corrugated PVC awaiting new guttering.

DORMERS

Dormer windows lead a lonely existence. Projecting at high level they are often sadly neglected. Even if the rest of your house is generously cosseted and warm as toast, this uncared for part of the building may be distinctly cold and leaky, potentially compromising the energy efficiency of the whole roof.

Over the years dormer windows have been built in a wide variety of shapes, sizes and materials – everything from tiny 'cottage' windows to massive 'full-width dormers'. But in essence they all comprise a box-like framework with a pair of side walls, some

Right: Modern 'large box' dormer
Below: New small dormer showing typical timber studwork construction
Below right: Modern version of a traditional dormer – but many have little or no insulation

form of roof perched on top plus a window at the front. Something else they have in common is that they can be tricky to insulate, with lots of awkward junctions. To make the job even harder, it

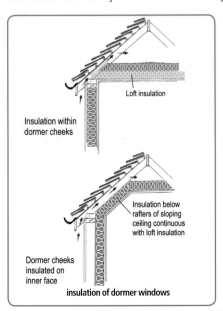

Loft insulation

Insulation within dormer cheeks

Insulation below rafters of sloping ceiling continuous with loft insulation

Dormer cheeks insulated on inner face

insulation of dormer windows

can be difficult to achieve U-value targets without changing their outer appearance, which may not be acceptable on older buildings.

The same rules apply to dormers as for insulating the rest of the house, so it's important to seal any draughty gaps and upgrade the whole structure, not just the easy bits. However, the available space in

TARGETS
The relevant thermal efficiency targets in the Building Regulations are:

	W/m^2K
Dormer sides/walls	0.30
Refurbished flat roofs	0.18
Refurbished pitched roofs	0.18

which insulation can be fitted is usually quite restricted, hence the thickness you can apply may be less than to the main roof. So to reduce the risk of condensation it's important to line the warm inner side of the insulation with a suitable airtight vapour barrier (or in older buildings a breather membrane).

Rigid boards such as PIR/PUR or wood fibre can be used to insulate the inner or outer faces of the dormer frames. Where insulation is placed between rafters or studs, flexible batts or quilt can also be suitable.

In an ideal world work to dormers would be carried out at the same time as the rest of the roof. However, this isn't always possible, so here we look at how to treat each element in turn.

Roofs
Many small dormer and bay window roofs are simply mini versions of the main roof, and can generally be insulated in the same way. This might take the form of a pitched roof with a central ridge and a small triangular gable above the front window, or might be hipped with a slope to the front. Flat roofs are also common.

Pitched dormer roofs can be insulated externally, internally or between the rafters. The best option is to strip the tiles and battens to insulate on top, although this will raise the height of the roof. Alternatively, where there's access to the small loft void above the ceiling (*eg* from the main loft) quilt can simply be laid over the ceiling joists. Where there's no access, a section of the ceiling may need to be removed.

However, a lot of ceilings are sloped, following the underside of the rafters, so there may be no loft space. Where access is difficult, the ceiling can be lined underneath, taking care not to obstruct the window or sacrifice too much headroom – see next page.

Mono-pitched 'cat slide' roof

Most large dormers have flat roofs. These are best insulated on top of the deck, raising the roofline slightly, but can also be upgraded internally or between the joists – see 'Flat roofs'. Where ventilation needs to be improved, vents can be added to fascias, eaves, gables or roof tiles.

Walls

Dormer side walls (known as 'cheeks') are generally made from lightweight timber studwork, clad with tiles, lead sheet, timber boarding or rendered lath. The front walls incorporating the windows are likely to be of the same design, although traditionally these were sometimes built up in masonry above the main walls. Internally the studwork will be lined with plasterboard or, in older houses, lath and plaster. These walls are often quite narrow, with studwork sometimes no more than about 80mm thick.

As with roofs, the best option technically is to insulate externally, ideally combined with insulation placed within the frame. But making the walls thicker may require the roof overhang to be extended to accommodate it. On older buildings the visual change may only be acceptable where dormers aren't so visible, such as those facing a hidden valley. Some types of external cladding, such as tiles, can be removed to install insulation and reinstated afterwards, but lead and rendered cheeks aren't so amenable.

Cheeks insulted with rigid PIR board within framework, plus insulated plasterboard applied to inner face

Where space permits, lining the walls internally can be the next best option, but often there'll be limited room for manoeuvre without blocking the window. So the only space available may be within the frame itself – but to gain access you either have to disturb the external finish or rip out the interior lining. Even then, this may only accommodate an insulation thickness of 80mm or less, which may be insufficient alone to meet Building Regulation targets. To work effectively the insulation should be firmly packed into all corners. But because the frame can act as a cold bridge (despite the fact that timber has a moderate insulation value) it's a good idea to line the inside or outside surface with a thin strip of high performance insulator such as aerogel. Alternatively, the use of polyurethane foam strips or multifoils could be considered – even 20mm can significantly reduce cold bridges and boost the overall insulation value.

Windows

Perhaps the most obvious way to improve the performance of dormers is to upgrade the window itself. But that doesn't necessarily mean replacing it. The simplest solution is to eliminate most of the draughts by ensuring the window fits well and is in good repair. Adding draughtproofing and secondary glazing can achieve substantial thermal and sound improvements without affecting the appearance or character of the window. See Chapter 7.

INSULATING DORMERS

(Courtesy SURE Insulation)

Tools
- Work table
- 'Celotex' saw
- Long straight edge
- Spirit level
- Auger wood bit
- Long-bladed knife for trimming cured foam

Materials
- PIR board
- Aluminium tape (at least 75mm wide)
- PU foam adhesive
- Foam adhesive applicator
- Silicone sealant
- Plasterboard
- Wallplug-type fixings (shorter than those to masonry walls)

Health and safety
- Dust mask (debris in voids)

SLOPING CEILINGS

Insulating sloping ceilings can be a time-consuming operation because of the complexity of the angles. Working in confined spaces such as attic eaves and dormers can extend the time needed to complete a task by two or three times.

The insulation can be applied directly over the existing ceiling. The rafter positions can be located using a bradawl or by test drilling with a small-diameter bit. Only a few screws will be needed since further fixings are used when the plasterboard is attached.

For rooms with limited headroom it may be possible to remove the ceiling to expose the rafters. The space between the rafters can then be filled with PIR board, ensuring an air gap of at least 50mm is left on the roof side of the insulation. The insulation boards must be fitted with no gaps at their edges. One way to do this is to cut the board slightly narrower than needed and then use expanding foam adhesive to seal the sides. Fill any remaining gaps with foam and then seal all of the joints with aluminium tape. Boards can be temporarily held in place with battens as the foam cures, then any excess foam trimmed with a sharp knife. A second layer of insulation boards can be applied across the underside of the rafters, secured with dry-wall screws (and adhesive if required) and a vapour control sheet installed before plasterboarding. After sealing the plasterboard joints as normal with scrim tape and fitting metal edging to the external corners, a finish coat of plaster skim can be applied.

1 Drilling the fixing holes in the sloping ceiling with an auger wood bit.

2 A shaped piece of PIR board.

3 Attaching PIR board to the sloping ceiling.

4 Remaining gaps filled with foam and the joints taped.

5 Plasterboard and scrim tape in place.

WALLS

Even fairly small dormers can take several hours to insulate because of their complexity and restricted access. If new windows are to be installed this should be done first, allowing extra depth at the sides of the frame to accommodate a sufficient depth of wall insulation.

To gain access to the wall studwork the existing plasterwork will need to be stripped out using a craft knife and ideally an oscillating multi-cutter power tool. Strips of PIR board can then be fitted between the wall studs and adhesive foam used to seal the edges around the boards. Alternatively (or in addition) the inner face of the wall can be lined by securing insulation boards through the existing plasterwork to studs with dry-lining screws. With a vapour barrier sheet fitted, the walls can be lined with plasterboard and plastered.

2 Space for insulation within the frame of the dormer.

4 PIR board fitted to dormer cheek, sloping attic ceiling and purlin.

1 Stripping out the dormer sides.

3 PIR board fitted tight between the roof timbers.

5 Plasterboard in place ready for skim.

6 FLOORS

Photo: John McKay

Floorboards being re-fixed over a vapour
control layer laid over floor insulation

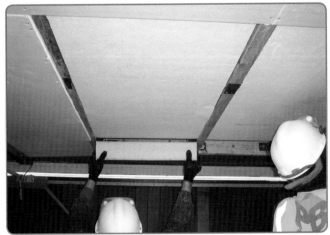

Rigid phenolic foam (PF) insulation wedged between joists from below

There's only one part of the home that our bodies maintain consistent physical contact with. Yet despite comprising a sizeable chunk of the building's thermal envelope, floors are commonly overlooked when it comes to insulating. In a typical home as much as 15% of the total heat loss is through the ground floors, and to stem this effectively will require something more than the time-honoured remedies of woolly rugs and furry slippers.

Before assessing the various options it's worth bearing in mind that some insulation works involve significant disruption, particularly if the height of the floor needs to be raised or fitted units have to be moved in kitchens and cloakrooms etc.

Construction

As a general rule, most houses built from the Victorian era up to the 1950s will have ground floors made predominantly of suspended timber. These were superseded by solid concrete slabs, which remained fairly standard until the advent of modern 'beam and block' suspended concrete floors in the late 1990s. However, many properties have a combination of solid and suspended ground floors. Upper floors made from timber are found in homes of all ages, although traditional softwood floorboards started to be substituted by cheaper chipboard panels from the 1970s.

Floor insulation

Easy options
Eliminating draughts is an inexpensive and reasonably straightforward measure. And where access is possible, insulating suspended timber floors can be relatively cheap, with minimal disruption when accessed from below.

Golden opportunities
Where repair work is needed anyway, such as replacing a decayed joist or the odd beetle-ridden board, it's a good opportunity to insulate and draughtproof the floor. Provision of underfloor heating to concrete floors requires the addition of insulation.

Thermal bridging
Anything that directly links the warm inside of a building to the cold outdoors can potentially form a 'thermal bridge'. Although wood has better insulation properties than concrete, thin timber floorboards can transmit cold up from the void beneath.

Even with solid floors, which are physically connected to the ground, this isn't normally a serious concern. More of a worry are modern suspended beam and block floors with concrete joists, although these *should* have been fully insulated when constructed. Condensation is also less of a risk with timber floors because wood has better insulation properties than concrete, and ventilation through under-floor voids should disperse any moisture that could otherwise accumulate.

More serious concerns are found in blocks of flats with cantilevered concrete upper floors that extend out of the wall to form balconies, the perfect arrangement for transmitting warmth from indoors to cold outdoors and vice versa. A similar problem can occur in buildings (circa 1950s and '60s) where the concrete floor slab was built through the walls and exposed externally. Such properties can benefit greatly from external wall insulation.

SUSPENDED TIMBER FLOORS

Traditional timber floorboards can add real charm to a home, and estate agents never fail to highlight the lure of stripped pine. If however you put your thermal-imaging specs on, their appeal would be somewhat diminished as you watched all the warmth from the room gushing through them. The fact is, timber ground floors can be a source of considerable heat loss, particularly where there are draughty gaps between the boards and around the edges of the room.

When it comes to upstairs floors, because they're already located snugly within the building's thermal envelope they rarely need upgrading. Only where there's an unheated space below, perhaps to a garage or passageway, would insulating be essential. However, introducing insulation into upper floors may be useful for sound-deadening or fireproofing.

How timber floors work

Suspended ground floors were originally introduced as a defence against damp. Physically separating the floor structure from the ground below with a deep void of air was a major improvement on traditional 'ground' floors (aptly named since some originally comprised little more than compacted earth). In order for floor joists to span the full length of a room they're supported every 2–3m on thick timber floor plates, which in turn rest on brick piers or short 'sleeper walls'. But the problem with timber is that it can become attractive to wood beetle and prone to fungal decay where moisture levels are consistently high (above about 15% and 20% respectively). So to prevent the build-up of damp air under the floor structure, ventilation is provided through the void via airbricks or metal grilles set in the lower walls. This flow of air keeps humidity levels low and the timber structure in sound condition, but can be a significant source of heat loss.

Before you start

Insulating a suspended floor should significantly reduce heat loss, as well as eliminating draughts from the ventilated void below. Once under the floor, it's often possible to access the whole of the timber ground floor from underneath, so you may as well do it all in one go.

But before deciding which approach to adopt, there are a number of key issues to consider.

The condition of the floor

If a floor is unsound, the worst thing you can do is cover it up and hide the problem. So the first task is to check that it's structurally OK. Any significant defects should have been flagged up if you had a survey done when you bought the house. Otherwise a little judicial stamping and jumping should reveal any localised softening or excessive springiness. Normally, as long as the walls aren't damp and there's a decent flow of ventilation under the floor, the risk of defects should be low. To keep damp at bay the external ground levels should be at least 200mm below floor level, preferably sloping away from the building. However, it's only once the floorboards are lifted that the true picture will emerge.

One of the most common defects to floors on all levels is where joists have been weakened by inappropriate cutting for central heating pipes and cables. Notches should be cut no deeper than one-eighth the depth of the joist, and not within the first quarter of the span from the joist ends. Where this is excessive some localised strengthening may be required to the joists.

Although it was standard practice traditionally for joist ends to be built into masonry walls, the quality of the timber in many older buildings combined with good ventilation has helped to keep damp at bay and resist decay. But any new timber in contact with potentially damp masonry should be protected with a strip of plastic DPC.

Floorboards

Before lifting any floorboards you need to figure out how they're secured, which isn't always obvious. Floorboards were traditionally fixed in place with special flat-sided nails called 'brads', hammered into the boards in pairs about 25mm from each end. In some more expensive properties interlocking tongued and grooved boards were laid, in a bid to eliminate draughts. These allowed 'secret nailing', with the nail heads hidden. Lifting floorboards of this type will require the use of specialist joinery tools to avoid damage.

As a rule, the wider the boards the older and more historically significant they're likely to be. The floorboards are an important part of the character of many older buildings, and where they've remained undisturbed for a century or more lifting them requires great care. It can sometimes be difficult to lever them up in one piece without splitting, so this may require the services of a joiner. To ensure they're replaced in the correct order it's a good idea to mark each board and take photos before and during the works. With luck there may be alternative access to the void below, perhaps via a cellar or a hatch in the floor. Otherwise it should be possible to cut a neat access hatch in the floors of all but the most historic of Listed buildings.

Insulated hatch to underfloor void showing PIR board and draught strip

Underfloor ventilation

As noted above, the health of timber floor structures depends on maintaining a decent flow of air through the void below to magic

away excess moisture. It's therefore important to ensure a clear intake of air, so be sure to check that the air bricks aren't obstructed.

One unintended consequence of sealing gaps between boards to draughtproof rooms is that the air formerly blowing up through the floor may have helped create a good through-flow of air across the underside of the floor. So sealing off these gaps could have the undesirable effect of making the air below damp and stagnant. To compensate, new vents may need to be inserted in the lower main walls where they're lacking or where ventilation paths have been blocked by extensions etc.

Services

Most floors conceal a variety of pipes and cables secreted away where the sun don't shine. The problem is, anything out of sight tends to get forgotten about. But unlagged hot water pipes run under ventilated floors mean you're effectively paying to heat up the cold outdoor air. Lagging pipework is covered in Chapter 8. Worthwhile improvements include:

- Lag any hot water supply pipes and central heating pipes within the floor structure to prevent wastage of heat.
- Lag any cold water supply pipes as they're vulnerable to freezing and bursting when attacked by frost.
- Attention to airtightness is important where pipes or cables pass through the floor surface. Gaps must be carefully sealed, eg with a flexible mastic.
- Electricity cables running through floor voids are generally those supplying ring main sockets (white or grey cable). There's normally a fair amount of slack, so they tend to dangle down within the void (where they're cooled by wafts of air). It should be possible to retain this arrangement once the floor itself is insulated. If it's not possible to avoid running electric cable within thick insulation (especially those supplying higher currents, eg to cookers, heaters and showers) to prevent any risk of overheating they can be run in conduit or substituted with higher capacity cables which

will generate less heat. Some localised re-routing of cables may therefore be required. Also, make sure you have a modern consumer unit with safety cut-out switches (MCBs and RCDs).

Materials

Quilt insulation materials such as mineral wool batts are a popular choice, being relatively cheap and fairly easy to handle and install. Loose-fill or floppy materials need to sit in some form of 'tray' between the joists, such as sheets of breather membrane.

For older buildings conservationists recommend the use of natural breathable materials such as sheep's wool, hemp fibre, cellulose and wood-fibre board. When placed next to timbers these allow moisture to escape. However, mineral wool quilt also has the benefit of being air permeable and shouldn't therefore trap moisture. This is a useful quality in households with young children because, as parents will know, spillage of drinks is a surprisingly common source of damp!

Above: Wood-fibre batts between joists over membrane, battens and plasterboard ceiling to room below – for improved sound and thermal insulation
Below: Sheepswool can accommodate irregular joists in older buildings

Foamed plastic materials like PIR and PUR are excellent insulators and in many cases it should still be acceptable to use rigid PIR-type boards in older properties, because a typical 200mm-deep floor joist only needs to be 'filled' with insulation to the upper 100mm depth, with the lower half remaining well ventilated. But the floor timbers must be dry and not exposed to moisture. The downside with this material is that accurate cutting and fitting of rigid boards in historic buildings with irregular shaped joists can be difficult.

How much insulation?

The Building Regulations set a U-value target of 0.25W for upgrading existing floors. Obviously the greater the depth of the joists the more space there is to fill with insulation. So as little as 150mm depth of mineral fibre quilt or sheep's wool between the joists should meet the required standard, assuming air infiltration is well controlled (eg with breather membranes). But, while you're at it, it makes sense to 'go for gold' and fit 200mm or more. As always, high-performance materials such as PIR/PUR boards will require less thickness to achieve the same result.

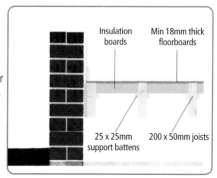

Insulation boards
Min 18mm thick floorboards
25 x 25mm support battens
200 x 50mm joists

Draughtproofing

Suspended timber floors are notoriously draughty, so a spot of diligent sealing can achieve impressive results with virtually zero upheaval – it's estimated this can save a typical household as much as £40 per room per year on energy bills. Draughtproofing may be the best option where the floorboards cannot be lifted (*eg* where they're historically valuable) and there's no other means of access. Although sealing cracks and gaps won't do much to reduce heat loss from conduction, it should significantly boost comfort levels by reducing the amount of cold air blowing in. Draughts are particularly wasteful of energy because as well as allowing expensively heated air to escape they make the occupants feel cold; and the natural reaction when you start shivering is to turn up the thermostat to compensate.

Floorboard Draught Filler

Floorboard filler strips can seal gaps of varying sizes and once fitted appear almost invisible. Being flexible they can be applied to a wide range of gaps which will be completely sealed. No adhesive is required. Filler strips can also be used to seal gaps under skirting boards. Strips are available in three sizes – small, medium and large (respectively for gaps of 3mm or less, 2–7mm and 6–11mm).

Photos courtesy: Draughtex.co.uk

Key areas that need to be targeted include:

- Gaps in floorboards are more evident in plain square-edged boards than the interlocking tongued and grooved variety. Larger gaps can be sealed with purpose-made slivers of timber. This a good option where the floor surface is visually important. However, such tapered strips of wood aren't likely to fit with 100% accuracy so they need to be bedded in place with sealant. Papier mâché is another traditional part of the floor-repair kit. But perhaps a better modern solution is to fit compressible foam rods or beads, which come in a range of diameters and are simply pressed into place. These rods remain flexible to accommodate any subsequent movement in the floorboards. Silicone frame sealant can also be used, either clear or 'colour-matched' (brown).

- Around the edges of the room to the skirting boards there's often a gap of centimetre or more. Strips of artificial rubber draught seal can be compressed and inserted, or expanding foam carefully applied. For smaller gaps silicone sealant can be useful.

- Where pipes or cables penetrate the floor from below any gaps and holes can be sealed with tightly packed mineral wool, or by squirting expanding foam or silicone sealant into the holes.

- Where there are extensive gaps, draughts can be reduced by screwing hardboard sheets over the boards and sealing the edges. The hardboard should be taped at the joints and sealed at the edges prior to laying carpeting or a wood/laminate finish.

- Fitted carpet laid over rubber underlay can be very effective at reducing draughts.

- Any access hatches to floors will also need to be draughtproofed and insulated (as per loft hatches).

Insulating from above

In most properties insulation can be fitted between the joists, having first lifted the floorboards to gain access. In all cases care should be taken to insulate tricky areas, such as the gap between the wall and the nearest joist running parallel, preferably with a breathable insulation material so any moisture is free to evaporate. Different materials require different techniques to install:

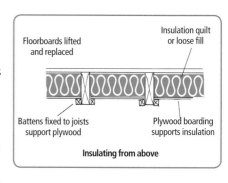

Floorboards lifted and replaced

Insulation quilt or loose fill

Battens fixed to joists support plywood

Plywood boarding supports insulation

Insulating from above

Wool quilts (*eg* mineral wool or sheep's wool)
Quilts are well known as a loft insulation material but are also widely used in timber floors, but being 'floppy' need to be supported. This is sometimes done using netting draped over the joist tops, but this method isn't recommended as the netting has a tendency to sag over time, dipping in the middle and pulling the insulation away from the joists. This results in tunnels of cold air running along the sides of the joists and under the floorboards with consequent thermal bridging.

Insulating a suspended floor from above

Photos courtesy: Kingspan Insulation

Various materials can be used to insulate between joists. This shows high performance rigid PIR insulation boards being fitted.

1. Clear out the room and strip floorboards
2. Measure down from top of joists and mark the point equivalent to thickness of insulation boards
3. Nail support battens along sides of joists
4. Measure the space between joists
5. Measure and mark insulation boards to match
6. Accurately cut the insulation boards
7. Place boards between joists resting on the batten rails
8 & 9 Push boards down until level with tops of joists
10. Stagger the layout of insulation boards
11. Place a perimeter strip of upstand insulation around the edge of the floor
12. Place a strip of DPC around the perimeter and ends of joists
13. There should be no air gaps anywhere in the insulation (seal any gaps with expanding foam)
14. Once all insulation boards are in place the floorboards can be re-laid.

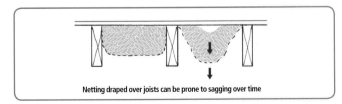

A better method is to support the quilt from wire hangers which are hung from each joist to cradle a layer of roofing lath/battens or fit plywood sheets supported on battens. Alternatively, netting or breather membrane can be stapled across the bottom of the joists, and fully filled up to the floorboards.

Netting draped over joists can be prone to sagging over time

Netting slung over joists to cradle mineral wool

2 layers of sheepswool laid between new joists

Photo: Thermafleece

Insulation batts (eg mineral wool, cellulose or sheep's wool)
Being compressible, batts can be friction-fitted between joists. But so they don't all slip out should you decide to hold a Zumba class in the room above, some form of restraint should be provided, such as battens fixed to the lower joists, or as described above for quilt insulation.

Rigid boards (eg PIR/PUR)
Boards can be cut to size and tightly wedged between joists, supported on battens fixed to the sides or at the base of each joist. Alternatively, boards can be slightly undersized so that polyurethane foam can be applied around the edges to ensure an airtight seal.

Loose-fill (eg cellulose or sheep's wool)
Can be poured on to sheets of breather membrane supported by battens fixed to the underside of the floor joists. However, this is the least best option because any gaps in the sheeting could allow air to blow through the floor void and disperse the insulation.

Breather membrane lapped tightly over and between joists to support loosefill or quilt insulation

Photo: ECD Architects

There are some other important considerations to bear in mind when insulating from above:

Airtightness

In addition to draughtproofing measures, it's a good idea to lay sheets of breather membrane over the tops of the newly insulated joists before replacing the floorboards. These should be sealed at the edges to the wall or skirting boards. The layer of breather membrane will help prevent cold draughts coming in and warm air from the room escaping into the floor (although underfloor ventilation should disperse any moisture so condensation is less of a problem).

Boarding out

To further enhance performance, an additional layer of rigid boarding (such as 12mm plywood) can be laid across the top of the joists prior to reinstating floorboards. This will minimise any risk of thermal bridging from the joists. But of course, raising the

An additional layer of insulation board is laid over a plywood deck to completely eliminate thermal bridging from joists

height of the floor – even a little – is likely to have knock-on effects with regard to skirting and doors etc.

Re-laying floorboards

Floorboards should be re-laid in their original positions, either nailed in place using traditional 'brads' (or brass screws where old plasterwork to basement ceilings might be disturbed by vibration from nailing). Chipboard panels may need to be replaced as they're notoriously prone to disintegrating when lifted. Additional battens screwed to joists may be needed for improved support. Above all, great care should be taken not to puncture any nearby pipes or cables.

However, it's not unusual for some old boards to have split in the process of lifting. New boards sold in DIY stores rarely match traditional styles, so historic boards should always be repaired where possible. These can normally be reinstated by being glued and cramped. Otherwise salvage yards can be a useful source of replacements.

Insulating from below

Traditional sub-floor voids can be surprisingly deep, so it's normally possible to insulate from below. All you need to do is lift a few boards and persuade a small agile person with no fear of spiders to crawl in and fit the insulation whilst crouching or lying on their back.

Working from underneath (assuming standard 200mm deep joists) mineral wool quilt can be pushed up between the joists. Alternatively, compressible batts or rigid boards cut to size can be squashed between the joists and pushed up to the floorboards

Mineral wool quilt between joists can accommodate pipe runs

above. However it's important not to compress the insulation too tightly, because the air between the fibres is key to maintaining its thermal performance. The insulation can be secured for example with plywood straps nailed across the undersides of the joists every 300mm. Ideally sheets of breather membrane should first be applied to limit air movement around it and through the floor, thus enhancing performance. Where space permits, a second layer of insulation can be fixed to the underside of joists, such as interlocking wood-fibre boards.

Where there's a cellar or basement under your floor,

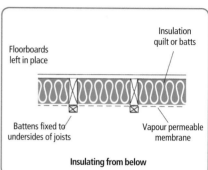

Floorboards left in place · Insulation quilt or batts · Battens fixed to undersides of joists · Vapour permeable membrane

Insulating from below

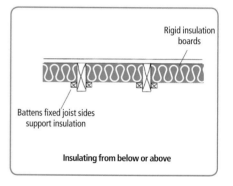

Rigid insulation boards · Battens fixed joist sides support insulation

Insulating from below or above

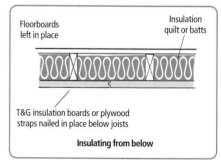

Floorboards left in place · Insulation quilt or batts · T&G insulation boards or plywood straps nailed in place below joists

Insulating from below

you have the luxury of being able to install insulation from below with minimum disturbance. But basements sometimes have historic ceilings that need to be retained. If this is the case, a layer of new insulation can be added directly beneath the ceiling, if headroom permits. The insulation should be returned down the cellar walls by about 400mm to reduce thermal bridging. Adding an insulated ceiling in this way can significantly enhance thermal performance (excellent U-values as low as 0.16 are possible).

Basements are, of course, well known for their 'dank and festering' ambience, so where there are damp walls immediately adjacent the insulation should be separated from them with a layer of breather membrane. It may also be advisable to improve ventilation by fitting additional air vents to the lower walls.

FITTING UNDERFLOOR INSULATION

(Courtesy SURE Insulation)

Health and safety
- Mask
- Hard hat
- Goggles
- Torch
- Gloves

SEALING AROUND THE EDGES OF A GROUND FLOOR ROOM

Tools and materials
- Sealant gun (ideally powered type)
- Plastic mesh
- Low expansion foam (one can will seal about 5m of edging)
- Silicon sealant (one tube will seal about 2m)

There are normally significant gaps around the edges of floors where the timber boards (or chipboard panels) don't quite meet the wall. These are usually concealed beneath skirting boards. Once any carpets etc have been removed, the gaps underneath the skirting boards (and at the top of the skirting with the walls) will be accessible.

Thin gaps around the edges of floorboards, and spaces between boards (0–10mm), can be sealed by applying silicon sealant. Low expansion foam is ideal for larger edge gaps (10–30mm). With very wide gaps (30–75mm) insert a length of stiff plastic mesh first and squirt regular lengths of expanding foam through the mesh to completely fill it up.

1 Large gaps between floorboards and wall.

2 Daylight visible from below.

3 A bead of low expansion foam.

4 A bead of silicone sealant in gaps.

5 Keep the can upside down.

6 For wide gaps apply mesh before sealing.

SEALING GAPS TO FLOORBOARDS AND AROUND PIPES AND CABLES

In many houses there are number of damaged floorboards, casualties of old installation works for pipes and cables. Tongued and grooved floorboards are especially vulnerable. Gaps and holes will allow cold air to blow into the living space, so it's important to seal them before fitting the insulation.

Tools and materials
- Sealant gun (ideally powered type)
- Silicone sealant
- Construction-grade adhesive
- Expanding foam
- Wood strips

Smaller gaps around cables and pipes can be filled with silicon sealant. Clear sealant will be less noticeable in areas where it's likely to be visible. Use expanding foam for larger gaps.

Where access is possible, inspect the whole under-surface of the floor being insulated. It can be useful to have a strong light in the room above to highlight the gaps. For small gaps run a bead of silicon sealant to completely fill the opening. For larger gaps use a suitably sized piece of wood glued into place.

1 Large gap in floorboards under kitchen unit.

2 Gap around central heating pipe entering a living space.

3 Old hole for pipe sealed with wood strip glued in place.

4 Silicone sealant around pipe.

5 Large hole cut for pipe and cable.

6 Large hole closed with wood panel and sealed.

PROTECTING THE ELECTRICS

Cellars and underfloor voids are commonly used for electric cable runs. To avoid having cables tightly surrounded by insulation they can either be moved or sheathed with a suitable conduit.

Tools and materials

- Sharp knife
- Pincers
- Hammer
- Lengths of flexible conduit (25mm diameter for individual cables, 100mm diameter where groups of cables can't be separated)
- Cable clips

Identify any cables located where insulation is to be fitted. Cables that run along the sides of joists should be unclipped and relocated on the lower face. Individual cables that cannot be moved should be fitted with conduit. Any junction boxes must also be moved away from the area being insulated. It should be possible to fit conduit without disconnecting the cables by making a slit down the length of the conduit.

1 Typical tangle of cables.

2 Trailing wires clipped up.

3 Thin conduit on a ring main cable.

4 Wide conduit fitted to a group of cables passing through floor joists.

5 Mains sockets to be moved.

6 Cable and junction box moved to bottom of joist.

INSULATING UNDERFLOOR PIPEWORK

Cellars and voids under ground floors are cold, with similar temperatures to outdoors. So any un-insulated hot water and central heating pipes will lose a lot of heat and waste energy. Cold water pipes also need to be insulated for frost protection. See Chapter 8.

Tools

- Sharp knife
- Scissors
- Screwdriver
- Hammer

Materials

- Pipe insulation for 15mm and 22mm diameter pipes
- Coloured tape – red, blue and green/yellow (eg electrical insulation tape)
- Radiator foil
- Metal strapping
- Clout nails
- Duct tape

Warning: Some types of old lagging may contain asbestos.

Remove any existing lagging. Try to identify pipes by tracing the pipe runs, and apply marker tape as follows:

- Domestic hot water and central heating pipes – red tape.
- Cold water pipes – blue tape.
- Gas pipes – green and yellow tape. These pipes don't need insulating.

It's important to ensure that no bare copper pipe is visible (other than gas pipes). Carefully cut each corner of the pipe insulation to ensure continuous insulation. When fitting long runs of insulation, slightly compress each piece against the next to allow for shrinkage over time. Seal all joints securely with duct tape.

If required, unclip hot water pipes from their mounts on joists and walls to allow the pipe insulation to be fitted. Strap hangers can be useful to support the newly insulated pipe runs.

In tight corners and where pipes are located very close to joists or walls there may not be enough space to fit thicker insulation. Instead strips of radiator foil can be inserted or expanding foam applied.

3 Typical array of un-insulated pipes.

4 Central heating and domestic hot water pipes now insulated with 25mm wall pipe insulation, cold water with 15mm. Gas pipe remains un-insulated.

1 Poorly insulated pipe.

2 Partially insulated central heating pipes.

5 Use of radiator foil for difficult sections.

6 Metal strap hanger.

FITTING THE INSULATION

The underfloor insulation needs to be fitted without any gaps. If just 5% of the insulated area contains gaps it can reduce the overall effectiveness of the insulation by as much as 50%. Care must also be taken to ensure that vents in the lower walls supplying underfloor ventilation aren't blocked.

Tools and materials
- Hammer and nails or a powered nail gun
- Mineral wool quilt (calculate the total amount from the underfloor area to be insulated)
- Plywood straps (or similar) approx 480mm x 40 mm x 4 mm, around 10 per square metre

Working from below, fill the space between joists with mineral wool quilt to the full depth of the joist (typically 200mm in older houses). Select rolls in widths suited to the joist spacing (commonly 400mm). Cut suitable lengths of quilt and insert them between the joists, making sure they touch the floorboards but aren't compressed too much. At the ends of each run the mineral wool can be 'bunched up' horizontally to ensure a complete fill with no gaps. Friction with the sides of the joists should hold the mineral wool temporarily in place. Then fix the plywood straps across the joists at intervals of around 300mm. Additional straps may be needed at the end of a run. The mineral wool should fill the entire space between the joists. Where the outer joist runs alongside a wall and is fairly close to it, offcuts of mineral wool can be used to fill this space.

1 Typical underfloor before insulation.

2 Mineral wool in place prior to fitting of wood straps. Note conduit around cable through joists.

3 Insulation in place with straps fitted. Note un-insulated gas pipe.

4 Showing insulation, expanding foam behind outer joist and insulated pipe.

5 A complete underfloor insulated.

6 Plastic barrier removed to allow free airflow.

7 Remove a section of floorboard near the external wall and pack the space between the wall and the joist with mineral wool.

SOLID GROUND FLOORS

Unless you're a TV property guru with quirky tastes, the idea of bare concrete floors gracing your home probably isn't hugely appealing. Unlike their timber cousins, solid floors are rarely left exposed for all to admire. Instead we conceal their harshness beneath carpets, vinyl, lino or some form of wood flooring or tiling. Nonetheless, solid ground floors score low in terms of comfort levels. Even if they don't immediately give your feet chillblains they can feel painfully cold, particularly in the winter. This is because the warmth is sucked out of them via direct conduction, often made worse by low-level draughts rampaging across the surface.

However, when you analyse this subject in the clear light of day the actual amount of heat lost through solid ground floors is actually far less than through walls, roofs and windows. As a result, energy savings from insulating them can sometimes be of marginal benefit. And when you take into account the disruption involved it may be more cost-effective to concentrate on the parts of the building (*eg* roofs and walls) that generate more tangible rewards. However, where an existing floor needs to be taken up, replaced or repaired for another reason it's worth taking advantage of the opportunity to upgrade its thermal efficiency.

Solid ground floor construction

Ground floors in early houses often comprised little more than compacted earth sprinkled with a few rushes. From the Tudor period many floors were embellished with flagstones, bricks or tiles laid directly on the earth or upon a bed of sand or lime mortar. Fast forward to the Victorian era and decorative floor tiles or clay quarry tiles had become commonplace, although suspended timber remained predominant until gradually superseded in the 20th century by solid concrete. However, insulation has only really started to be taken seriously for new floor construction in the last 15 years or so.

A typical solid floor comprises a layer of compacted hardcore rubble

Traditional solid concrete floor (but older floors were not insulated when built)

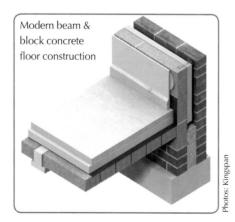

Modern beam & block concrete floor construction

Photos: Kingspan

about 100mm thick, on top of which another 150mm or so of concrete has been poured to form the slab which, if you're very lucky, may even contain a smattering of insulation. There should also be some form of damp-proof membrane, located either above or below the slab, such as plastic sheet (or in older houses a couple of coats of bitumen). The surface layer normally comprises sand/cement screed at least 65mm thick.

THERMAL PERFORMANCE

Most solid floors were built with very little insulation and are in direct contact with the ground. Despite this inauspicious

Big job: Excavation for new insulated floor with UFH

combination of negative factors, such floors aren't the enormous heat-sucking vampires you might have predicted. It's well known that if you dig down a few feet the ground harbours a certain amount of warmth (hence the wonders of ground source heat pumps). In fact the ground beneath the floor maintains a surprisingly stable temperature all year round of about 10°C. This means that the amount of heat you stand to lose isn't that much. Which makes sense when you consider that walls, roofs and windows are all directly facing the cold outside air, whereas the floor is relatively sheltered by the earth. So the temperature difference between indoor rooms and the ground under our feet is quite a bit less than for other parts of the building's envelope.

But solid ground floors have another trick up their thermal sleeves – the ability to store warmth and self-regulate their temperature over the course of the year. Because they have high 'thermal mass' it means they absorb heat over the warm summer months, but as the year progresses and the surroundings later cool down they start to release it very slowly, helping to maintain a steady temperature in the house.

This same ability to regulate temperature also works over a typical 24-hour period. For example, a solid floor next to south-facing windows can absorb a surprising amount of warmth in the form of 'solar gain' during the day that would otherwise have contributed to overheating of the indoor air. Then during the colder night-time it slowly releases the warmth. It should be possible to retain some of the benefits of thermal mass once a floor is insulated if you apply a conventional screed finish.

CONDENSATION RISK

If floors are damp this can sometimes be down to condensation, especially in steamy kitchens and bathrooms. The risk of moist indoor air hitting cold surfaces and condensing into damp is potentially more of an issue at times of greatest temperature difference between the floor and the air – which you'd imagine would be in the midst of cold winters. But because the ground maintains a fairly constant temperature throughout the year it'll be relatively warm in winter and cold in summer. So, strange as it may sound, you're more likely to encounter moist floor surfaces in spring and summer (although condensation can still run down cold walls depositing small puddles that soak into floors).

Before you start

There are a number of issues to consider before installing solid floor insulation:

Construction

Over the years many buildings will have been extended, and by now may have a mixture of floor types. In older properties the floors can be a significant part of the history and character, so it's important not to damage old tiles and flagstones etc. Instead they can be protected by a sheet of breather membrane and a suitable breathable insulation board such as wood fibre laid

Retain original floor tiles in period house where posssible

on top, with an appropriate finish of tiling or floorboarding.

Condition

Damp-proof membranes (DPMs) of one type or another have been installed in solid floors for the last 80 years or so. But even without DPMs, the concrete itself should form a barrier to water, so damp rising from below is rarely an issue.

Older historic properties work in a different way, by allowing any moisture percolating up from the ground to harmlessly evaporate away through the surface or via joints to tiles or flagstones; but as soon as you smother the floor with impermeable artificial coverings such as vinyl flooring or rubber-backed carpets it blocks evaporation, causing unpleasant clamminess. So this breathing performance in old floors should be maintained by using natural insulation materials and natural fibre floor coverings such as wool, seagrass, jute, sisal and coir. By the same token, unsealed natural wood flooring is preferable to laminate, and traditional lime mortar should be used to bed tiles or flagstones.

Where there are high levels of moisture the cause of the problem must be identified and solved, and the floor allowed to dry out before insulating. Common causes of dampness include water leaks, marshy ground, high external ground levels and condensation.

Floor levels

This would be a reasonably straightforward project if it wasn't for the fact that raising floor levels by more than a centimetre or two

is likely to involve enormous upheaval elsewhere. In properties with very low ceilings the effective reduction in headroom can be a serious issue. And in all cases careful planning is needed at the outset to get all the detailing right to skirting boards, doors, stairs etc – see 'Installation' below. To minimise disruption the works can be carried out on a room-by-room basis when the opportunity arises, ideally combined with other scheduled works.

Underfloor heating (UFH)

Right: Cut-away display of timber floor surface showing UFH system run above insulation boards

Photo: Kingspan Therma

If you're looking to upgrade your room heating, installing UFH will also involve insulating the ground floor. Having a heated floor inevitably increases the temperature difference between the floor and the ground beneath – by as much as 15°C. You don't need an MSc to work out the importance of insulating between the two, so that you're not paying to keep the earth warm. Normally purpose-made rigid insulation boards are laid on the floor and the UFH pipes slotted into pre-formed channels. To keep any raising of floor levels to a minimum, it may be possible to break up the old screed down to the surface of the concrete slab and replace it with a similar depth of insulation which can be finished with wood flooring, flagstones or tiles. Specialist installers can specify the appropriate type and depth of insulation.

Materials

Any insulation that's going to be walked upon obviously needs to be pretty tough, with a high compressive strength. Ready-made insulated floorboards are also available with the insulation pre-bonded to a timber deck. A typical choice of products might include:

- Rigid plastic foam boards (*eg* PIR/PUR or PF)
- Rigid polystyrene (EPS or XPS)
- Foamed glass
- Rigid natural materials (*eg* wood fibre and hemp-lime boards)

100mm thick rigid PF insulation boards placed over the original floor slab (with a plastic sheet DPM) after removing old cement screed. Timber floorboards are laid on top

Natural wood-fibre batts laid on the existing floor surface (over a breather membrane) between timber battens to support floor boards

Photo: NBT

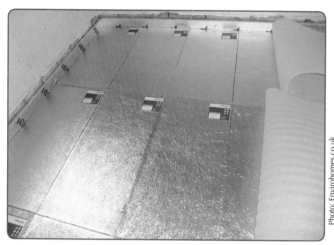

Photo: Envirohomes.co.uk

High performance vacuum panels (only 20mm thick) are ideal where there are restrictions on raising floor levels (can achieve excellent U-values of 0.17Wm2/K)

Installing insulation

Photos: Dow Building Solutions

Styrofoam EPS boards (left) and PUR insulation (right) are popular materials for insulating floors

One recently developed solution for historic buildings is to excavate the old floor and replace it with limecrete – a natural lime-based concrete. This is mixed with special Leca insulation aggregates comprising small clay balls to create a breathable insulated floor, which if required can incorporate plastic UFH pipes.

LIMECRETE

U-values

It's possible to exceed the 0.25W/m²K target by overlaying the existing floor with 70mm of PU polyurethane foam insulation. Together with a new screed and floor finish this can achieve a U-value of 0.21W/m²K. But in practice the available depth is often very limited. So as a rough guide:

- 25mm of EPS polystyrene should improve the U-value to 0.45W/m²K.
- 40mm of PIR should achieve 0.31W/m²K.
- 50mm of PIR should meet the target 0.25W/m²K.
- Exceptional performance 0.14W/m²K can be gained by excavating and building a completely new concrete floor laid on 200mm of EPS or PIR insulation.

Solid floors can be insulated very simply by laying insulation boards above the existing surface to form a new 'floating' floor. It's common practice to lay a sheet of damp-proof membrane beneath the insulation except in historic properties, where a breather membrane may be preferable. A suitable 'deck' can then be laid over the top with the desired floor covering.

Alternatively, instead of laying insulation on top of the existing floor it may be possible to break up the cement screed (typically about 65mm deep) and replace it with insulation boards laid over the existing concrete slab (as when installing UFH). This of course can be enormously disruptive.

Normally, the biggest challenge is in adapting the internal joinery to accommodate the raised floor thickness (allowing for your choice of covering). So the bottom of each door will need to be cut, as will the architraves and door stops, plus the skirtings will need to be re-fixed. In the worst-case scenario, the top of the door frame would need to be raised and lintels repositioned to maintain sufficient headroom.

By far the trickiest area is at the bottom of the stairs, because raising the floor level means the height of the lowest riser will have effectively decreased. Risers are typically 200–220mm high and the Building Regulations require that all risers are consistent to reduce the risk of accidents. One solution can be to build up the floor at the bottom of the stairs so it's level with the lowest step. This will

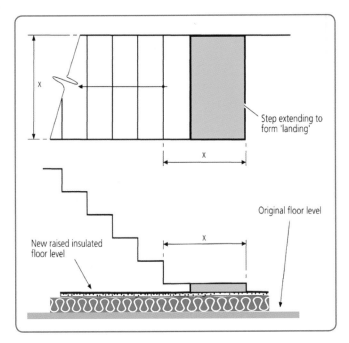

Step extending to form 'landing'

Original floor level

New raised insulated floor level

form a new 'landing' that's roughly 100mm higher than the newly insulated ground floor level adjoining it. The landing must be at least as wide as the staircase and extend by a similar or greater length. Alternatively, to maintain the height at the first step you could leave an un-insulated area of floor at the foot of the stairs (about 2m²). But in both cases an unexpected step, albeit small, will need to be very carefully designed.

The final job is to lay a suitable floor surface over the insulation, such as a conventional sand/cement screed or timber floorboards. Heavier finishes like tiles or thick interlocking boards should be self-supporting, otherwise insulated timber bearers are sometimes fitted between insulation boards as a base for fixing coverings.

New landing constructed at the bottom of stairs level with lowest tread, with subsidiary smaller step to insulated main floor

Insulating a solid floor

Photos courtesy: Kingspan Insulation

1

2

3

4

1 Lay a damp roof membrane (DPM) on a prepared surface with joints well lapped, folded and taped
2 Lay insulation in a staggered pattern to prevent gaps
3 Loose-lay insulation board with joints slightly butted
4 A perimeter strip of upstand insulation is required and should be level with the top of the concrete

5 Lay a thick polythene sheet on top of the insulation with 150mm overlaps, taped at the joints and turned up 10mm at the walls
6 Now the concrete slab and screed can be laid
7 Trim off any membrane around the edges. The floor is now ready for your choice of flooring

5

6

7

7 WINDOWS AND DOORS

Photo: SURE Insulation

Neatly applied secondary glazing boosts thermal efficiency whilst preserving original glass

In many properties the windows and doors are one of the largest sources of heat loss, accounting for as much as a quarter of the total leakage. So upgrading them can have a dramatic impact on comfort levels and energy bills. However, in some older buildings the windows and doors form a major part of the character of both the house and the local neighbourhood, and are best retained. Fortunately there's a range of solutions to suit properties of all shapes and sizes.

Photo: Greenhouseproject.co.uk

INSULATING DOORS AND WINDOWS

Easy options

Draughtproofing alone can reap major performance dividends. Another effective DIY option is the traditional approach favoured by Victorians – fitting robust curtains with thick linings to windows and doors. This can make a significant improvement to heat retention in the room. There are also some budget DIY improvements that may be worth considering. One simple temporary measure involves spreading large sheets of polythene over the window and then applying heat from a hair dryer to tighten and seal the film. A better option is to fit large sheets of Perspex as DIY secondary glazing – see page 121.

Golden opportunities

When internal or external wall insulation work is due to be carried out, coordinating it with replacement windows or doors will help minimise thermal bridging.

WINDOWS

It's a surprising fact that less than a quarter of the heat lost through a typical window actually escapes by conduction through the glass. The vast majority is lost by draughts and air leakage through gaps in frames and at wall junctions. So a few simple draughtproofing measures can be remarkably effective. But there's another problem with large expanses of glass. The cold surfaces make them very prone to condensation in cooler weather, something that draughtproofing alone won't solve. And purely in terms of comfort, the 'cool radiant effect' – where your body feels cold when sat next to a single-glazed window – can only be alleviated by the installation of more effective glazing (or warmer weather!).

However, simply ripping out your old single-glazed windows and replacing them with double-glazed units isn't always the best solution.

Payback

Although in overcast Britain we're wedded to the idea that fitting double glazing is an essential improvement, it can be a false economy to fit cheap replacements. Whereas many Victorian windows have lasted well over a century, thanks largely to their use of high-quality timber, many modern replacements are lucky to last more than 20 years. It's surprisingly common to find double-glazed units that have failed within the first few years of installation, with condensation penetrating the cavities causing 'misting', rendering the units useless. Even tough UPVC frames have a tendency to become brittle and discoloured over time. But

Building Regulations

New windows and doors are defined as 'controlled fittings' under Part L1B of the Building Regulations. However, in most cases installation work will be carried out by FENSA-registered installers (Fenestration Self-Assessment), who can self-certify the installation. So an application to Building Control only needs to be made when windows are replaced by an installer not registered as a 'competent person'. For more detailed information on compliance see the Code of Practice for window installation BS8213-4.

Replacement windows must meet a minimum performance standard based on either a 'C' Window Energy Rating (WER) or a minimum whole-window U-value of 1.6W/m²K.

Replacement windows also need to comply with the requirement for ventilation (both background and 'purge') unless mechanical ventilation systems are installed – see Chapter 3.

good quality new windows should last up to 50 years, so it makes sense to choose the best you can afford.

However, payback periods for double glazing are lengthier than you might imagine. Recouping the cost of installation from direct savings in energy bills can take up to 90 years – two or three times their likely lifespan, and significantly longer than some renewables such as PV solar.

Approximate U-values and g-values for timber framed windows and doors from SAP 2009

Opening type	U-value (W/m²K)	g-value
Single glazed window	4.8	0.85
Single glazed window with secondary glazing	2.4	0.76
Double glazed window	2.7–3.1	0.76
Double glazed window with low-e coating	2.1–2.7	0.63–0.72
Double glazed window with low-e and argon fill	2.0–2.5	0.62–0.72
Triple glazed window with low-e and argon fill	1.5–1.9	0.68
Modern high performance window	0.7	0.55
Solid timber external door	3.0	–
Modern insulated external door	1.0	–

Performance

A double-glazed sealed unit consists of two sheets of glass separated by an air gap. The sheets are kept apart by spacers and the edges are sealed. The air gap provides the insulating layer that slows down heat loss. However, the performance of a window depends on many factors. As well as heat seeping through the glass there's the question of how good the frame is at resisting conduction, plus the presence of any leaky cracks or gaps around the frame. Another variable that needs to be taken into account is the amount of warmth entering the home through the glass as 'solar gain'. To assess the effect of all these factors, a Window Energy Rating has been developed (administered by the BFRC –

British Fenestration Rating Council). Here windows are rated A to G depending on the U-value, solar transmission (g-value) and the level of air leakage – see panel.

Such has been the advance in technology over the past few years that it's now possible to upgrade older double-glazed units with new high-performance windows and achieve a similar increase in performance to that traditionally gained by replacing single panes with double glazing. The best performing triple-glazed windows can now achieve exceptional U-values of around 0.70W/m²K. A number of innovations have led to this dramatically improved performance:

■ Low-E (emissivity) coatings reduce radiative heat loss across the glazing cavity. Soft coatings can achieve very low-E ratings (below 0.05) with much-improved insulation levels compared to older hard coatings. Low-E glass also tends to have a lower g-value, which can help where south-oriented windows produce 'solar gain'.

Slim sealed units designed to fit period sash windows

■ Gas filling reduces conductive and convective heat transfer across the glazing cavity. Argon gas is most common but krypton can achieve better U-values – eg a thin 10mm krypton-filled gap can give the same performance as 16mm argon-filled glazing. Modern inert gas-filled triple glazing can be as slim as 40mm, little more than standard air-filled double glazing.

■ Super-insulated frames now incorporate 'warm edge' spacers to significantly reduce thermal bridging.

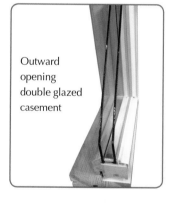

Outward opening double glazed casement

High performance 'energy gaining' triple glazed windows

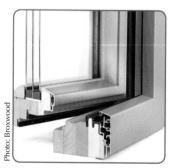

'Cold attracts mould' - aluminium frames without a 'thermal break'

Frames

When it comes to selecting frames there's a choice of materials, each with pros and cons:

■ Timber frames offer economy, but require periodic maintenance for continued robustness, although they're relatively adaptable and easy to adjust over the longer term.

Recent improvements have been made in the detailing of capillary grooves and drips to restrict the ingress of moisture and ensure that any water that does get in can safely drain away to the outside.

Standard UPVC double glazing (UPVC stands for *Unplasticised PolyVinylChloride* - ie plastic)

- UPVC offers economy and good performance plus minimal maintenance, but has higher environmental impacts associated with disposal and manufacturing.
- Aluminium-framed windows tend to be more costly but potentially offer long life and low maintenance. However, because metal-based materials have relatively high conductivity it's especially important they incorporate an effective thermal break between the glass and the metal.

Discreet sliding secondary glazing to sash windows

Photo: City Sound

The Great Escape

How windows leak heat

The way heat is lost through windows is surprisingly complex, but there are three main ways it can happen:

- By convection and conduction of warm room air through colder glass (normally the most conductive part of the window) and through the frame.
- By infrared radiation of warm air from the room being absorbed by the colder surface of the window.
- By air leakage allowing cold air in from outdoors (air infiltration) or letting warm room air escape out of the house.

Single glazing is a poor thermal insulator and readily conducts heat. A typical 4mm-thick glass panel has a very poor U-value of 5.4W/m²K. However, the loss of heat through the whole window will depend not only on how large the total area of glass is, but also on the conductivity of the frame material (metal being especially poor) and the quality of fit of the frame and glazing. So a typical U-value for the full single-glazed window (timber-framed) may still only achieve a relatively poor 4.8W/m²K.

With standard air-filled double glazing, for the best thermal performance the optimum airspace between the two panes is 16–20mm. Any larger and the air space would allow convection currents to develop within the cavity, causing more heat to be lost. For argon-filled units optimum width is 14–16mm.

Retro-fit options

There are three main options when it comes to improving the thermal efficiency of windows:

Overhaul the existing windows

Refurbishing and draughtproofing the existing windows is normally the least expensive option. Many older timber windows (*ie* pre-WW2) were of very high quality and with a thorough overhaul should provide many years more service. There are lots of specialist firms who offer this service, particularly for traditional sashes, including full draughtproofing of the windows. Performance can also be significantly boosted by fitting good quality secondary glazing, at an overall cost about half that of replacement windows. Although secondary glazing can traditionally achieve only about

Photo: Timberrepairs.co.uk

Restoration of period windows is often the best option

60% of the performance of replacements, with potentially less convenience in terms of opening, high-performance systems are now available – see page 119.

But you don't need to spend a king's ransom to keep cold breezes at bay; the traditional low-tech approach of fitting heavy curtains or blinds can be surprisingly effective at reducing draughts and heat loss – as can shutters, particularly when installed French-style on the outside of the building.

Photo: Excel Insulation

Shutters can significantly improve heat retention and draught-proofing

Replace just the glazing

Where windows need to be retained (*eg* in Conservation Areas) one option is to leave the frames intact and replace the old glazing with higher-performance units fitting into the existing rebates. Combined with a spot of draughtproofing around the frames and opening lights this should achieve significant energy efficiency improvements. This is also a good option where sealed double glazed units have failed but the frames are still sound (although many UPVC and aluminium windows can't be disassembled). If you're just replacing the glazing it doesn't count as a 'controlled fitting' and therefore isn't covered by Building Regulations.

However, with old single-glazed windows the rebates will be relatively small, restricting the thickness of the replacement double glazing. One solution is to specify super-slim (but more expensive) vacuum insulation units which combine high performance with minimum thickness. However, not all old frames can accept even super-thin glazing, for example metal windows, in which case secondary glazing is probably more effective (especially for period properties).

Precise new replicas of original windows incorporate high performance glazing

Complete replacement windows

Around two million windows are replaced in the UK each year. As noted earlier, window installation work must comply with the Building Regulations and ideally should be coordinated with any scheduled wall insulation works. Specifying wider frames or repositioning the new windows can permit a greater depth of insulation at the reveals to minimise thermal bridging.

Refurbished original sash window with slimline double glazing and trickle vent inserted to base (Kingspan 'Camden House' Project).

Thermal bridging

When new high-performance windows or doors are installed in existing homes there's a danger of excessive heat loss around the edges of the openings – at the heads, sills and reveals. In most properties there'll be virtually zero insulation at these points, with a consequent risk of cold bridging across. To make matters worse, lintels are commonly of cold steel or concrete, and until quite recently reveals in new construction were simply 'closed off' around openings using brick or blockwork.

Even where the ideal scenario of combining window installation with new wall insulation doesn't apply, significant improvements can still be made. For example, where existing windows or doorframes are being replaced, their removal will require hacking out plasterwork around the reveals. And where cavities are exposed, the open ends should be sealed (as in new construction) with strips of insulated cavity closers, squashed into the open ends of the cavities and lining the opening. Once the new units are in place, with the reveals insulated with an airtight surface, it should significantly reduce the extent of cold bridging and condensation.

When installing new window frames it's important to ensure that joints with the walls are airtight. Junctions can be sealed using expanding foam and special tapes. Externally the pointing to masonry jambs should be sound. Before installing timber-framed windows they should be protected with a strip of damp-proof membrane placed around the opening. It's also important to ensure that the sills project well clear of the walls below so that rainwater is dispersed rather than dribbling down and soaking into the wall.

One thing that's sometimes botched when fitting replacement windows is the need for support to the wall above. In houses built from the 1940s to 1970s it was common practice for lintels to be omitted, with the masonry resting on robust steel window frames. If installers fail to anticipate this, and the walls are insufficiently propped during the works, stepped cracking can develop as the brickwork above sags. More seriously, bay windows to many 1930s houses were constructed with discreet integral structural posts to support heavy loadings from roofs. This is something that UPVC replacements often fail to replicate, with the potential for serious structural problems developing in the future.

Lifestyles

If you have teenagers in the family, the following scenario may not be entirely unfamiliar: bedroom windows left casually open and the heating turned up to max. As occupants, our activities can vastly reduce the benefits of insulation. The fact is, most of us could profitably improve our bad habits, especially during the colder months, for example by only opening windows for short periods to allow occasional rapid fresh air 'purge' ventilation.

Secondary glazing

Above: Side hinged, inward opening.
Centre: Vertical sliding secondary glazing

Above right: Original coloured leaded lights retained with neat fixed double glazed units applied internally

Below: 'Eco-ease' DIY secondary panels are easy to fit (left) and almost invisible once fitted (right)

Secondary glazing is an ingeniously simple concept; fitting an extra layer of glass to the room-side of your existing windows provides a relatively inexpensive method of reducing heat loss and controlling air leakage. It can also be extraordinarily effective as a barrier to noise transmission. Because it works independently, the original windows can remain in place and needn't be altered, so there's little or no change to a building's appearance.

This can provide an excellent solution to insulating windows, particularly where replacing them may not be an option, such as in flats or to historic buildings (it has the added benefit of protecting fragile old glass).

There are various types of secondary glazing, either hinged, sliding or fixed, designed to integrate with existing windows. It should be virtually maintenance-free apart from occasional dusting, and the operation of curtains and blinds should be unaffected.

The type of glazing varies from standard 4mm float glass (plain or obscure) to toughened safety glass, and the latest high-performance low-E glazing or sound-deadening acoustic glass.

Thermal performance

There are no specific requirements for secondary glazing in the Building Regulations. However, the performance target for replacement windows fitted to existing homes is 1.6 W/m²K. Secondary glazing can achieve or even exceed this in combination with the existing window if low-E coated glass is used. This should reduce heat loss through the window by more than 60%. Performance can be boosted further with super-insulated frames and double-glazed units. Krypton-filled cavities can be as thin as 6mm, so combined with both panes of 4mm glass this makes a pleasingly slim total width of only 14mm.

Heat loss

As we have seen, a typical existing window leaks a considerable amount of heat through draughty gaps. So when installing 'secondary windows' it's essential they form an effective seal over the whole of the opening or existing window frame.

Unlike double glazing, secondary systems derive thermal benefit from the fact that the frame is physically separated from the primary window. However, the positioning of the secondary unit is usually dictated by the dimensions of the reveals, but a space of about 100mm from the primary window is fairly typical.

Solar gain

When you live in a climate like ours it's easy to overlook the fact that during hot summers large amounts of solar energy can be admitted through windows, leading to overheating. Traditionally curtains or blinds were used to help make rooms cooler during the day. Most secondary systems can be opened to alleviate summer heat, or fixed units can be taken down in the warmer months and stored. So the main windows can still be accessed and opened to ventilate rooms.

Condensation and ventilation

Anyone brought up in a house with single-glazed windows will be familiar with the pools of water that collect on the inside window ledges in the chilly winter months. Secondary glazing can overcome this problem by preventing warm, humid indoor air from reaching the cold windows and condensing. However, efficient perimeter-sealing is essential to achieve maximum airtightness.

Discreet custom-designed secondary glazing

To prevent any build-up of condensation it's best to maintain a small amount of ventilation to the air cavity between the main window and the secondary glazing, by, for example, not fully draughtproofing the original windows.

To provide adequate room ventilation, new double-glazed windows incorporate small trickle vents, so a similar arrangement may be advisable with secondary glazing, depending on the quality of existing ventilation. But effective air extraction is also important to remove water vapour at source, particularly from kitchens and wet rooms.

Sound insulation

Windows are one of the most vulnerable parts of a building to noise transmission due to their relatively lightweight construction. A single-glazed window may only achieve a noise reduction between outdoors and indoors of 18 to 25 decibels. The performance of double-glazed units in this respect is less impressive than you might expect, because both panes of glass are connected with a relatively thin cavity so they both resonate together.

Secondary glazing is a much better sound insulator than double glazing thanks to the much larger gap between the panes. A secondary window with an air gap of 100mm or more will de-couple the movement of the panes of glass, reducing the resonance between them. Sound insulation of up to 45 decibels can typically be achieved, with even better levels as the gap becomes wider (up to about 200mm), particularly if the reveals are lined with an acoustic material.

Reductions in external noise of around 75% are possible where laminated glass (typically 6.4mm thick) or acoustic glass (6.8mm thick) are specified. These are thicker and heavier than ordinary glass, which also aids thermal performance. Noise pollution can be further reduced, by as much as 90%, if the secondary windows are double glazed. Traditional shutters and heavy curtains can also make a significant contribution to the abatement of noise.

Full height period sash window with 'invisible' secondary hinged casement

Secondary glazing systems

Secondary glazing systems are custom-made to integrate with the existing windows, and it's normally possible to match the shape and style of the originals. They can be produced in a wide range of styles, including curved or arched designs, colour-matched to blend in. Most designs are either hinged or sliding (vertical or horizontal), although removable lift-outs or fixed units are sometimes used. For more complex windows, such as bays, a combination can work best.

Most systems use painted lightweight aluminium frames. Their slim profile means they can be designed to fit, for example, within the beading of a typical sash window, so features like ledges and shutters can be retained. More sophisticated systems comprise timber subframes into which opening casements or sliding sashes are fixed.

Specialist firms can design and install sophisticated high performance systems. At the other end of the spectrum there are budget DIY kits available, for example lightweight Perspex sheets can be cut to size and secured with magnetic strips. It's claimed that these can achieve U-values as low as 2.7 W/m²K, but large panels of Perspex can be prone to 'creaking' when wind blows through draughty windows.

Above: Not just for windows – secondary safety-glazing can also be applied to doors
Above right: Colour-matched, aluminium framed, hinged secondary double glazing
Below: Sliding frame to sloping roof window
Right: Sliding frame to period timber windows

Installing secondary glazing

Secondary glazing can have virtually zero visual impact if carefully planned. Frames can be discreetly concealed when viewed from the outside whilst remaining remarkably unobtrusive internally. When installed in combination with internal wall insulation they can be tied in almost seamlessly. However, this tends to be a specialist job as it involves complex joinery and glass cutting. And whilst

the framing material may be relatively lightweight, the glass itself is deceptively heavy – 10Kg/m^2 for 4mm thick panes and 15Kg/m^2 for 6mm.

When choosing secondary glazing there are a number of points to consider:

Existing windows

The design of the original window is key to determining the style of the secondary glazing. Although the dimensions of the primary window are fixed, the secondary glazing can comprise smaller, more manageable units. Note how the existing window opens and if there are bars running vertically or horizontally through the window. Also check the opening to see whether there's sufficient depth in the reveal to locate the new units.

Photo: SelectaGlaze.co.uk

Visual impact

To minimise the visual effect externally, the secondary glazing shouldn't be smaller than the glazed area of the primary window. Any divisions in the new system should be concealed behind the glazing bars in the existing window. For example, with sash windows, matching vertically sliding secondary panes can be made to invisibly blend in by aligning the horizontal bars.

Maintenance

Easy access should be maintained to the original windows and cavities for cleaning. The secondary window itself will only require the occasional squirt of *Windowlene*.

Safety and security

Part N1 of the Building Regulations requires safety glass to be used in critical locations, including any window where the lower edge is 880mm or less above floor level.

From a security perspective, secondary glazing incorporating window locks provides a significant additional barrier to deter break-ins.

New sliding frames over stone reveals in period house

Photo: City Sound

Magnetic secondary glazing systems

Magnetic DIY secondary glazing systems are self-adhesive. The glazing can be removed and taken down easily at any time. The main limitation is the maximum size of the 2mm acrylic panels of about 20sq ft. Larger areas will need additional support or thicker 3mm acrylic.

Photos: NigelsEcostore.com

■ Sheets of 2mm thick acrylic sheet are cut to suit the dimensions of the window, plus a little extra so it overlaps about 25mm with the frame. The surround of the window needs to be flat and at least 15mm wide.

■ Magnetic strips are attached to the edges of the acrylic.

■ A matching metal strip is firmly glued to the window frame surround so the strips align with the magnetic frame of the acrylic. Also apply to any additional frames in the middle of the window.

■ Align the strips and the magnetism pulls the sheet into place.

EXTERNAL DOORS

One part of the building that's frequently overlooked when upgrading insulation is the one that we use the most. Yet the average ill-fitting external door is a prime source of heat loss. All too commonly, breezy gaps around poorly sealed frames and thresholds compete with naked keyholes to allow gusts of cold air into the home. So substantial improvements can often be made with some well-targeted draughtproofing.

The options for boosting the thermal efficiency of doors are broadly the same as for windows – either overhaul the existing door and frame, replace just the door itself, or do the full monty and fit a combined replacement door and frame. The best option will inevitably depend on the available budget as well as the condition of the existing door and the type of property.

From a purely technical perspective, completely replacing draughty doors can be highly effective. But sticking a shiny new UPVC front door on the front of a period house is one of the quickest ways to wreck its character. It may also have planning implications. So for historic homes – especially Listed buildings and those in Conservation Areas – upgrading the originals is normally the best bet. Where this isn't practical, replacement with an exact replica is the next best option.

Whether you opt for upgrading the existing doors or fitting new replacements, the issue of cold bridging around the frame will need to be tackled. The reveals can be upgraded as described for windows, but there's the additional challenge of achieving an effective seal at the threshold – see page 127.

Thermal performance of doors can be significantly improved with pre-bonded aerogel boards (or vacuum panels) from a poor U-value of 3.16 W/m2K to an excellent 0.91 without affecting the exterior.

Right: Existing timber front door with 2 large recessed panels
Below left: Special composite insulation boards are inserted into both recessed panels on the internal face of the door. The boards comprise a thin layer of aerogel bonded to 9mm marine grade plywood.
Below centre: Sealant is applied around perimeter and timber beading mitred and fitted over it.
Below right: Thermal imaging shows significantly reduced cold ingress and heat loss

Upgrading existing doors

Ill-fitting doors need to be carefully assessed to identify gaps and reduce unwanted air leakage. Although it's not uncommon for doors to have warped, in most cases applying a flexible sealant or draught-stripping can accommodate irregularities – see 'Draughtproofing'. The use of multi-point locks can help ensure that doors close firmly so that seals are compressed. With timber doors it's also possible to make small adjustments with a spot of judicious planing (after first removing the door).

Keyholes can be closed off with escutcheon covers, and letterboxes can be sealed so that they close firmly, fitted with draughtproof brushes, or a small receptor box constructed on the inside. The time-honoured tradition of fitting thick curtains to the main doors can also be surprisingly effective.

To reduce heat losses it may be possible to refurbish door panels by adding insulation such as polyurethane or ideally high performance aerogel or vacuum panel cores. New panelling can be retrofitted to the inner face over the existing stiles, mullions and rails to create a new appearance whilst conserving the old. The simplest approach is to glue sheets of rigid insulation board over the thinner panelled areas concealed within a plywood sheet finish. Glazed areas can be over-clad with secondary glazing and the doorframe draughtproofed.

Fitting new doors

Where the combined door and frame are being replaced together they're defined as 'controlled fittings' – for which an energy rating scheme is currently being developed. Where a new replacement door is installed, the target U-value is 1.8W/m^{2}K or better for the whole door. Some new doors can achieve thermal efficiency as high as the best performing windows with U-values as low as 0.7W/m^{2}K, incorporating triple-glazed lights, pre-insulated cores and double seals. When specifying new doors those certified to PAS 23/PAS 24 should provide optimum security.

Cut-away of new door showing fully insulated inner core

This thermally-efficient new front door (left) contains high performance vacuum panels sandwiched inside (right)

Of all the possible energy-saving measures you can carry out, draughtproofing will normally give the fastest payback. This is a fairly straightforward DIY project with a low initial outlay and, hence, is one of the most cost-effective ways of improving the comfort of your home.

Gaps around doorframes are a significant source of draughts

Although draughts can emanate from many different parts of a building (see 'Airtightness', page 30), sealing the windows and doors normally pays the greatest dividends. A few simple measures can reduce air leakage from windows by as much as 50%, significantly cutting the amount of energy needed to heat the room. It also has the advantage of minimising the amount of noise and dust entering the house, plus the works can be done with barely any disturbance.

One fact that the double glazing industry doesn't go out of its way to advertise is that much of the benefit gained from replacement sealed units is actually down to the reduction of draughts by fitting new window frames. But these same benefits can be achieved at a fraction of the cost simply by sealing up gaps in the existing windows. However, there's no point carefully draughtproofing windows or doors that are falling apart or jammed, so it's important to first give them a thorough health-check.

When it comes to wind whistling through gaps in the fabric, doors tend to be worse offenders than windows (despite comprising a smaller total area). A typical unsealed external door has a gap of about 2mm to the frame, but at the threshold underneath there's often a super-sized void of 6mm or more (and no water bar). If you calculate the amount of air leakage this allows in it's equivalent to knocking a gaping hole nearly 125mm (5in) square in your door, or having a cat flap permanently jammed open. Worse, many doors are misaligned and therefore have even larger gaps. Yet despite the valuable savings

Below left: Traditional thick curtains can be surprisingly effective at draught-proofing
Below right: Secondary glazing to windows works in harmony with restored period shutters

that can be gained by draughtproofing, the Building Regulations are uncharacteristically silent on this subject. So the name of the game is simply to eliminate gaps by all means necessary. And if you've got a porch or conservatory, you're off to a head start since they act as 'airlocks', helping to reduce cold draughts.

Scouting for draughts

There are powerful forces at work creating draughts in our homes. One key driver is the fact that warm air in a house naturally rises, drawing in fresh air in its wake through the lower parts of the building. This is known as the 'stack effect'. Strong winds can also create 'pressure drops' where the air pressure difference between inside and outside can literally suck cold air into the building or force warm air to leak out. But of course, none of this would matter if there weren't gaps and cracks in the fabric. So the first job is to pinpoint the source of the problem.

The best time to check for draughts is when there's a bit of a gale blowing outside. Some gaps are only too obvious, such as a door or window that doesn't close properly. Others require a bit more detective work. According to folklore one clue to the location of leakage paths is where spiders have built webs, since there's a better chance of catching flies where air comes through. But a more reliable technique involves using specially designed smoke puffers or smoke pens to show how big the draughts are and where they go. Bubble blowers can perform a similar function (plus you can entertain the kids at the same time!). Or, if funds permit, it might be worth investing in a thermal-imaging camera to highlight any cold and draughty parts of the house. If the tests are repeated after improvement works have been carried out it should highlight any areas missed.

Photos: Retrotec.com

Smoke pens and smoke matches are useful for locating the sources of draughts

- Make sure any damage to windows and doors is first repaired.
- Seal gaps internally and externally with silicone mastic at junctions between the frames and wall reveals and to window ledges etc.
- Check that all the opening casements, sashes and top-lights close firmly before applying draught-stripping to gaps. Replace defective closing mechanisms.
- Ensure letterboxes seal shut.
- Cover exposed keyholes.
The performance standard for fitting draught strips is BS 7368.

Photo: Storm

DRAUGHTPROOFING FRAMES

Cracks often occur where dissimilar materials meet, due to different rates of expansion. But doors and windows suffer enormous wear and tear, especially if they've been binding or sticking and hence subjected to brute force. Casements left carelessly unsecured may have been smashed into their frames by powerful gusts of wind. Doors may suffer even worse maltreatment as devices for punctuating domestic disputes with bad-tempered slamming. So it's no surprise that cracks are fairly common – indeed it's often possible to feel blasts of air passing through them.

A good quality sealant can be used to fill cracks, but where frames have worked loose they may first need re-anchoring. Any sticking doors or windows will need to be eased and adjusted.

MIND THE GAP

Once a draught has been detected the gap needs to be investigated so that it can be treated with the correct material. With the door/window closed, check whether there's a uniform gap between the frame and the opening part. If the gap is consistent then strips of compressible foam tape can be used (see below). But if it varies in depth, the door or window may be warped, requiring some form of wiper seal or gel treatment. Where wooden doors or casements are severely warped the services of a joiner will be required. By skilfully adjusting the shape of the frame to match the warp it should become possible to fit standard draught strips.

Metal windows don't warp like wooden ones, but often develop small gaps on the hinge side that can be filled with a silicone gel or specialist draught strips. Epoxy resin car body filler can also be used to fill dips in frames. However, UPVC windows and doors usually have integral seals that are difficult to repair or replace.

A thin strip of non-stick solution is painted around the inner face of the door (or opening casement window). Silicone gel is then applied to the frame. When the door or window is closed the gel should mould into a perfect fit, forming a very effective compression seal once set.

Products

Many houses bear testament to half-hearted past attempts at banishing draughts with old foam strips dangling sadly where the glue never quite held. To do the job properly means picking the right material for the task. Many products can only deal with smaller gaps and won't work effectively where windows and doors are distorted, which is quite a common problem. So when choosing draughtproofing products there are some key considerations:

- How big are the gaps to be sealed?
- Do the gaps vary in width, and by how much?
- Do you need to allow for seasonal expansion and contraction of the door or window?
- Is it important that the draught-strip isn't seen?
- Does the draught-strip need to match the colour of the frame? (Painting the flexible part of some seals can damage their performance.)

The two main types of seals are 'compression strips' and 'wiper seals'.

COMPRESSION STRIPS

Compression strips are used where the moving part of the door or window closes against the frame. As the name suggests, they require a certain amount of compression to form an effective seal (but shouldn't be compressed too much). They're relatively cheap, easy to install and ideal for sealing narrow gaps of an even width. But they're not so well suited to warped surfaces with gaps of varying thickness.

Plastic 'spring seals' can be fitted to horizontal centre rails where 2 sash windows meet. When compressed they form a seal. Can be self-adhesive (right) or set into a cut groove (left).

Photo: Reddiseals.com

Because compression seals are mounted on the face of opening casements or doors (near the edges) it means they're not particularly affected by seasonal expansion and contraction of the window or door. Typical applications are around the entire perimeter of a door or opening casement window where it meets the frame, or to the top and bottom rails of sashes where they butt up against the top or bottom of the frame. Compression strips are produced in a range of materials, although silicone is the material of choice, and are available in a range of colours. There are several types in common use:

- Self-adhesive foam strips are the simplest option but cheapo ones have a short life. These are stuck to the frame rather than the door or opening casement. Once fitted the door or window will tend to close slightly further out than before, so the latch and lock may need slight adjustment.
- Self-adhesive silicone strips or EPDM polymerised artificial rubber are also straightforward to install, and more robust than foam seals. They're available in a variety of profiles and thicknesses catering for different gap widths.
- Synthetic rubber or silicone 'O' tubes are available in a variety of diameters. Some attach to the frame using an adhesive, others have an integral carrier strip that's either attached to or cut into the frame. V-shaped seals are an alternative design that can bridge a greater range of gap sizes and withstand larger amounts of compression.
- Silicone gels (or polymerised rubber gels) can be used to create a compression seal. These are ideal for metal windows, particularly where there are irregular gaps. The gel is applied to the frame from a tube. Non-stick tape or grease is applied to the meeting surfaces of the window, which is then closed to squeeze the sealant into a perfect fit. When the sealant is dry (after a few minutes), the window is opened, the seal trimmed, and the release tape or grease removed.
- Brush pile seals (typically used as wiper seals, described below) can also be used as compression seals to warped surfaces.

WIPER SEALS

These are used to seal moving parts that slide past each other. Wiper seals are the only way of sealing the sides of sash windows

Photo: Reddiseals.com

Carrier with pile

and sliding doors. They can also be applied to surfaces that are moderately warped. Brush-strip draught excluders follow the shape of the door or window, compressing slightly in the closed position, forming a seal. Some are supplied with a simple backing strip for gluing or pinning to a window frame. Others require a narrow groove cut into the wood into which the base of the seal is pushed.

Brush pile seals are the most common type. These are capable of sealing a range of gap sizes, or filling uneven gaps. Some include thin plastic fins in the centre to form a better seal. Where a heavy-duty seal is needed, silicone or thermoplastic strips are best.

Draughtproofing Products

		Wooden external doors	Wooden casement windows	Metal casement windows	Sliding sash windows	Pivot windows	Louvre windows	Loft hatches
Class 1								
	Q-Lon Retro 21B	✔						
	Q-Lon Retro 21L	✔						
Door Products								
	Q-Lon FS	✔						
	Door bottom brush	✔						
Class 2								
	Q-Lon Retro B		✔		✔	✔	✔	✔
	Q-Lon PS		✔		✔	✔	✔	✔
	Q-Lon FS				✔	✔		
	Q-Lon PSS		✔		✔	✔	✔	✔
	Q-Lon PSL		✔		✔	✔	✔	✔
	Sharkseal SBS				✔			
Miscellaneous								
	Silicone O Tube			✔				
	Silicone Mastic Bead			✔				
	Louvre Seal						✔	
	Zero Gap	✔	✔		✔	✔	✔	✔
	P Strip	✔	✔		✔	✔		✔
	E Strip	✔	✔		✔	✔		✔
	V Strip	✔	✔		✔	✔		✔

Photo: Firstinsulation.co.uk

Sash windows

Sash windows in older buildings are normally worth preserving. However, they're relatively complex, requiring the installation of compression seals to the tops and bottoms, and wiper seals to the sliding sides. Special V-strip seals are designed for use between the stiles and boxes of sliding sashes. There are several products available for DIY draughtproofing.

Highly effective results can be achieved by professional firms specialising in the overhaul and draughtproofing of period sash windows.

Sash repair kit

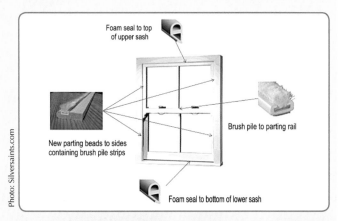

Foam seal to top
of upper sash

Brush pile to parting rail

New parting beads to sides
containing brush pile strips

Foam seal to bottom of lower sash

Photo: Silversaints.com

Photos: Timberrepairs.co.uk

Professional draughtproofing can transform draughty old sashes for a fraction of the cost of replacement

Photos: Core sash windows

Timber parting beads (left) and staff beads (right) with inset carriers for brushes

Photos: Reddiseals.com

Sealing doors

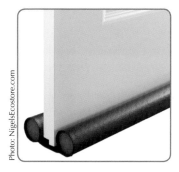

Photo: NigelsEcostore.com

The main entrance doors of your home have a much harder life than the windows. Having to endure heavy foot traffic on a daily basis means that they often need to withstand extreme levels of wear and tear.

Lengths of 'wiper blade' seals screwed to the outer frame form a tight seal when the door is closed. A very effective DIY draught-proofing measure - but requires accurate measuring and cutting

Notch for corner joint.

Photos: Nigel Griffiths

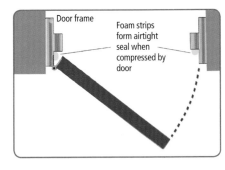

Door frame

Foam strips form airtight seal when compressed by door

Photo: Exitex.xom

Photo: Post-carbon-living.com

Thankfully technology has moved on a bit since the days when draught exclusion involved placing woolly 'door snakes' or stuffed 'sausage dogs' at the foot of a door – which, depending on your perspective, are either a useful temporary measure or a lethal tripping hazard! Although the armoury of materials for draughtproofing doors is similar to those used to upgrade windows, there's an additional range of specialist seals.

WEATHER STRIPS
Simple compression seals fixed into plastic or aluminium holders are screwed to the side jambs and heads of doorframes.

FLEXIBLE TUBE SEALS
Small diameter synthetic rubber tubes are set within a plastic or aluminium holder that's fixed to the doorframe. When the door's closed the tube compresses to close the gap between door and frame.

FLEXIBLE BLADE STRIPS
Used to seal irregular gaps, these consist of a flat strip of synthetic rubber, shaped like a car windscreen wiper fitted in a metal or plastic holder that's fixed to the doorframe. Also suitable for sliding patio doors.

BRUSH STRIPS
These can also be used where gaps are irregular. Lighter types consist of strips of siliconised nylon pile with a self-adhesive backing. More robust types comprise strips of nylon or polypropylene bristles fitted into a metal or plastic holder that's fixed to the doorframe. Also suitable for sliding patio doors.

THRESHOLD SEALS
Thresholds are probably the most difficult area to seal, as they need to withstand foot traffic and are sometimes exposed to extreme wind and water ingress.

The simplest threshold seals can be fixed into a groove on the underside of the door, or to the threshold beneath the door. These require a relatively even gap and a smooth surface to make a good seal.

A more sophisticated arrangement consists of two parts working in combination – a shallow aluminium threshold bar fitted in the threshold beneath the door, and a protruding weather bar fixed to the lower front of the door. The threshold bar contains a compressed synthetic rubber tube that, when the door's closed, presses against the underside of the door, sealing it from draughts and water ingress. Meanwhile, the overhanging weather bar diverts rain away from the threshold.

Brush seals

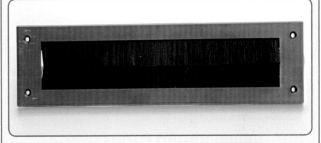

Photo: EcoFlap.co.uk

Photo: alternative-energy.co.uk

Draughty letterboxes can be sealed simply by fixing a cover over the inner opening. Before screwing in place position the cover and check that letters/papers can be posted easily and that the main flap doesn't stick in the brushes. Secure with screws through each of the corner screw-holes.

Alternatively you can make a 'gravity flap' by cutting a thick piece of timber boarding shaped to fit the opening, and gluing it to the inner face of the flap; the added weight will help it close firmly.

'Ecoflaps' are a recent development in letterbox technology. These cleverly harness the power of the wind to blow the letterbox shut, and are claimed to be totally draughtproof.

Gaps under doors can be draughtproofed with door brushes.

- First cut the plastic carrier so it fits the width of the door, starting at the end that doesn't have a screw hole in it.
- Then cut the brush strip to length and insert it into the carrier (using pliers to crimp the leading end).
- Drill a screw hole at the cut end to match the other end.
- Screw the strip and brush to the door.

Photo: FirstInsulation.co.uk

UPVC angle brush

DRAUGHTPROOFING

(Courtesy Hyde Farm CAN)

Materials

- Insulation strips – see product table
- Rigid high impact UPVC carrier with pre-punched holes at 150mm centres
- Silver tape
- Nails 20/25mm

Tools

- Small hammer
- Pruning secateurs
- Scissors
- Tape measure
- Screwdriver
- Junior hacksaw
- Nail punch
- Pliers
- Fine sandpaper
- Mitre block for 45° cuts
- Pieces of stiff thick cardboard to protect windows when hammering

SEALING CASEMENT WINDOWS WITH 'RETRO B STRIPS'

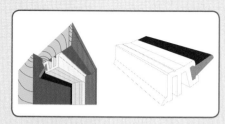

In this example they're used for sealing casement windows.

- Cut each strip to size using a hacksaw (or pruning secateurs). It's a good idea to initially leave a little extra so it's a bit too long, then trim to the exact size after checking it in position. Fit each strip before cutting the next one.
- Hammer in the nails via the preformed holes. Use 20/25mm stainless steel nails which have small heads and are rustproof. Initially only drive them in about halfway to allow slight adjustment later. At the ends where strips have been cut you may need to make an additional hole about 25mm from the end of the strip.
- The plastic flexible trim should push up against the closed window or door with gentle pressure to seal any gap – but not so hard that it prevents the window/door closing (or causes too much friction on a sliding sash).
- With each strip in place the nails can be driven home (don't overdo it or the nails can disappear through the PVC carrier).

SEALING DOORS AND SASH WINDOWS WITH 'RETRO B STRIPS'

Draughtproofing strips known as 'Retro B strips' are easy to fit and unobtrusive. They are very versatile and are widely used for doors, sash windows and loft hatches. This example shows the sides and top of a sash window being sealed.

- First measure and cut the strips for the sides of each sliding sash. Then nail them in place so they cover the vertical joint between the sliding sash and the frame.
- Once the sides are in place, measure and cut the bottom horizontal strip and apply to the bottom sash window.
- Repeat for the upper sash at the top, if possible applying the strip around the top sash from the outside. If access is difficult the strip can be attached instead to the frame where it meets the upper sash, rather than the opening sash window itself.

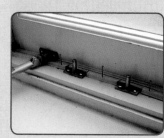

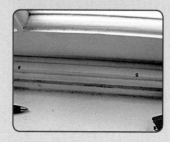

FILLING LARGER GAPS WITH '21 RETRO B STRIPS'

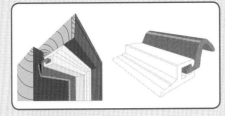

To seal larger gaps '21 retro B strips' can be fitted in the same way as 'retro B' strips shown above. These have more expansion capability and can cover larger gaps making them ideal for gaps around doors which expand and contract with the seasons. Because they're relatively easy to compress, once sealed the doors shouldn't be too difficult to close.

- ■ With the door shut and locked, apply the strips to the top of the door frame first, and then to the vertical sides.
- ■ Check that the seal is compressed (about 3mm) when the door is closed.
- ■ At the corners the strips can be mitred where they join at a 45° angle.

SEALING GAPS TO FRENCH DOORS AND SASH WINDOW MEETING RAILS WITH 'FS STRIPS'

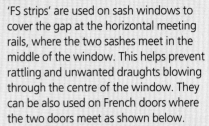

'FS strips' are used on sash windows to cover the gap at the horizontal meeting rails, where the two sashes meet in the middle of the window. This helps prevent rattling and unwanted draughts blowing through the centre of the window. They can be also used on French doors where the two doors meet as shown below.

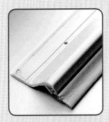

If the FS strip cannot cover the gap because the two sashes don't meet on the same level then try using a self-adhesive P-strip or 'Zero gap' strip stuck on the back of the meeting rail of the bottom of the sash.

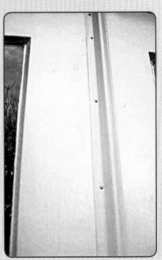

'P strip'

'Zero gap'

8 PIPEWORK AND WATER TANKS

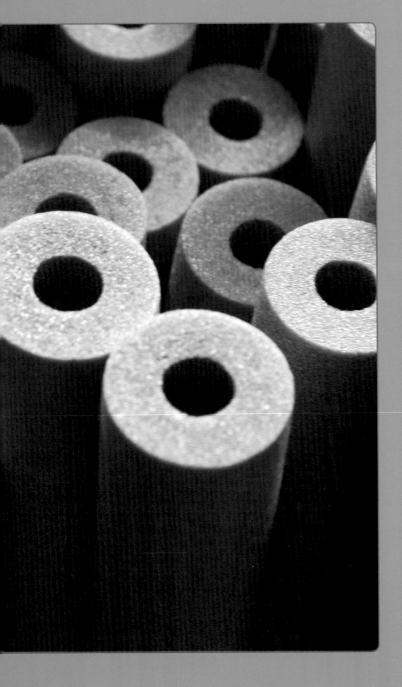

Until fairly recently, no one paid much attention to thermal efficiency and the running costs of our homes. Few people stopped to worry that long lengths of pipework ferrying hot water through cold lofts and floor voids was equivalent to paying to heat the sky or run a radiator outdoors. Worse, there was little understanding of dangers of leaving pipework unprotected. Periodic freezing and bursting of naked cold water pipes and tanks was regarded as something akin to an Act of God. But in recent years the shock of ever-rising fuel bills has spurred *Homo Domesticus* (with the possible exception of *Homo Hot-tubus*) to adapt to the changing environment. There is a new awareness that, out of all the delights on display at your local DIY store, few give a better return on investment than pipe lagging and insulation jackets.

Pipework

Fortunately this is a very rare sight– asbestos pipe lagging

Anywhere pipework is consistently exposed to a cold atmosphere it will be at risk of haemorrhaging heat or freezing solid. Either way the consequences are likely to be messy or expensive, and quite possibly both. Although here we focus on the part of the house most at risk – the loft space – the same advice applies equally to other neglected cubbyholes such as garages, cupboards adjoining outer walls and voids under timber ground floors.

One of the side effects of making your home nice and snug with lots of thick insulation is that these outlying spaces become extremely cold in winter, because you're no longer wasting money heating them with warmth seeping in from living spaces. Which means there's a much greater chance of tanks and pipes freezing, bursting and generally raining on your parade.

In many homes the loft is a treasure trove of plumbing. Most will contain some hot or cold water supply pipes and one or more water storage tanks. More rarely boilers, central heating pipes, and hot water cylinders find themselves parked up in roof voids (not the most accessible location). But during a prolonged cold spell the loft can become so cold that the water in the pipes starts to freeze, the consequent expansion causing them to burst and split.

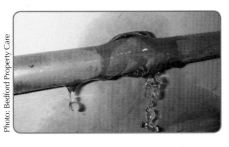

These calamitous events occurring just above your bedroom ceiling may not be immediately obvious, because as long as ice stays frozen it can't make things soggy down below. But when the freezing weather eventually comes to an end, thaw will suddenly turn to flood. There are two ways to stop this. Either don't bother to insulate your loft, and get used to paying sky-high energy bills; or – the cheaper and more sensible option – lag all the pipework.

What type of lagging?
A number of materials can be used to lag pipes:

HESSIAN ROLL
This traditional material comes in large rolls that you wind around existing pipe runs (or thread over new pipework as it's installed). It's a natural product (apart from the plastic sleeve it's adhered to) and has the advantage that rodents don't seem to enjoy the wholesome, fibrous taste. The downside is that it takes ages to apply and it's difficult to fit evenly around the pipes.

FOIL-BACKED INSULATION
This high-performance insulation is also the most expensive, which is why it's more widely used in commercial buildings. It's unnecessary for home use unless pipes are highly exposed to the cold.

FOAM INSULATION
This is the material of choice for most home insulation projects. It has the advantages of low cost and ease of use as it's manufactured pre-slit, ready to slide over pipes. The downside is it's not particularly eco-friendly, and rodents sometimes develop a taste for it.

More sophisticated foamed nitrile rubber lagging materials, such as Armaflex, can offer improved performance, and the lengthways slit allows self-sealing, but they cost a bit more.

Pest alert

It's not unknown for mice and squirrels to wreak havoc in lofts. As well as occasionally electrocuting themselves by nibbling PVC cables, they're very partial to foam pipe lagging. In an extreme case you might find that the insulation you applied last year is now little more than a pile of tiny offcuts, rendering it useless.

SELECTING FOAM INSULATION

There are three key points to consider when buying foam lagging for pipes:

- The diameter of the pipe to be insulated (normally 15mm or 22mm but occasionally 28mm).
- How thick the insulation needs to be (foam insulant has a thermal conductivity of $0.035W/m^2K$).
- How much you need.

Bear in mind that it's the *internal* diameter of the pipe that's quoted, so a 15mm pipe will actually be a little over 15mm when measured from the outside. Foam lagging is sold in two sizes – thick or thin. In an ideal world you'd always opt for thick, simply because no pipe has ever burst as a result of being over-insulated. But in practice thick insulation can be difficult to apply where two or more pipes are run close together or butted tightly against a wall. It's rare to find solitary pipes running across loft spaces, and even then it'll normally be clipped to a joist or wall. In areas with very limited access a useful alternative can be to insert multiple strips of radiator foil into small gaps, or if all else fails a squirt or two of expanding foam can come to the rescue.

Pipe insulation is usually sold in 1m or 2m lengths, so before ordering measure the rough total of all the pipe runs in your loft. It's better to buy too much than not enough as you can always take it back and get a refund.

Other pipes

A quick wander around your loft may reveal other pipes, such as plastic overflows or (very rarely) gas supply pipes. Although these don't need insulating, the general rule is 'if in doubt, insulate it', as there's no harm in overdoing things. Similarly, modern plastic water supply pipes are more flexible than metal pipes and are unlikely to split or burst when water freezes. But they should still be lagged, because, at best, a pipe blocked with frozen water won't be able to deliver the goods, and naked hot water pipes still waste energy whatever they're made of.

However, when it comes to waste pipes lagging isn't necessary. This is because they're of a considerably wider bore and are mostly made of plastic, so a spot of expansion shouldn't bother them unduly, plus they spend most of their time empty, bar the occasional gush or trickle. The exception to this rule is some condensate pipes serving modern condensing boilers. These are a relatively narrow bore and where run externally can suffer from freezing blockages in very cold weather, causing boilers to cut out. Ideally they should be re-routed internally.

INSULATING PIPEWORK

Tools and materials

- Mitre saw
- Tenon saw
- Tape measure
- Marker pen
- Pipe insulation
- Duct tape

Health and safety

- Knee pads

INSULATING STRAIGHT PIPE RUNS

1 Start by measuring the length of pipe you're going to insulate. Then cut the insulation to size. Foam insulation comes in 1m or 2m lengths, and here we have a 3m length of straight pipe.

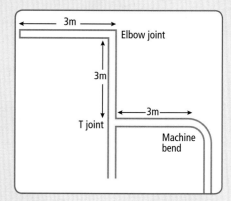

2 To apply the insulation look for the preformed split along its length – note that the cut doesn't penetrate all the way through the foam. Pull the lagging open at one end until you've freed up a short length. Then, holding one end, slowly run a finger down the foam to open it further.

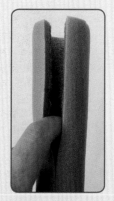

3 Once you've opened up about 1m you can put the opened end on the pipe and start pushing it along the pipework, opening up more of the foam as you go.

4 The foam wraps itself around the pipe but bulges out every time it goes over a pipe-clip. To help it fit take a utility knife and carefully cut a small slit either side of the clip.

5 Take a piece of duct tape and wrap it around the insulation to both sides of the clip to hold everything in place and ensure no bare copper is left exposed.

INSULATING CORNERS

1 Here we have a distance of 1m from the end of the insulation to the middle of the 90° bend (an elbow joint). So you first need to measure a 1m length of insulation and put it in the mitre block.

2 Use the 45° angle in the mitre block and make sure the tenon saw cuts across your mark in the middle of the insulation.

3 Now split the insulation as before and slide it on to the pipe until the bend is nestled in the middle of the cut.

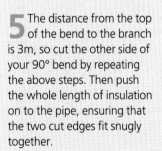

4 You now have two flat ends of insulation butted hard against each other. Use duct tape to stick these together.

5 The distance from the top of the bend to the branch is 3m, so cut the other side of your 90° bend by repeating the above steps. Then push the whole length of insulation on to the pipe, ensuring that the two cut edges fit snugly together.

6 Tape them together to stop the joints opening.

INSULATING A BRANCH

The next stage is to insulate a branch or 'tee'.

1 Measure the distance between the end of the existing insulation and the middle of the branch (distance A in the diagram). Mark this distance on the tube of insulation and put it in the mitre block.

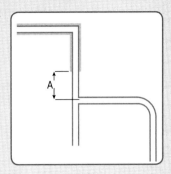

2 Make the first cut exactly the same as for a 90° bend, then make a second cut straight across the insulation, chopping off the end of the wedge to give you the shape shown.

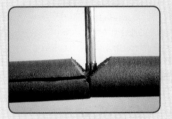

3 Fit this length of insulation and repeat the process for the other side of the branch.

4 To fit the insulation for the branch itself make the standard 45° cut then turn the foam over and make a second reverse cut. The result should be a perfect V shape, which now fits snugly into the gap to form a neat foam joint. Use the duct tape to secure it all in place.

INSULATING BENDS

The pipe runs a further 3m before bending down 90° in what's known as a 'machine bend' (*ie* the pipe's bent by machine, as opposed to the sharper elbow joint we just looked at).

Because these bends are relatively smooth you can get away without cutting the insulation, provided you use a decent amount of tape to ensure it stays fully wrapped around the pipe. As you split the insulation and push it over the pipe it starts to open up slightly as it goes around the bend. The amount to which it opens will increase or decrease as you give the foam a slight twist. To reduce any gaps, twist it accordingly and apply tape to the start, middle and end of the bend to ensure that no bare pipework shows.

Finally, repeat the above steps for any other un-insulated pipework, bearing in mind that you must cover the full length of pipework – even small gaps

in the insulation will be vulnerable to freezing and subsequent pipe bursts. Any stopcocks/valves should also be fully insulated, bearing in mind that the 'tap handle' must remain visible to be of any use.

Water tanks

A lot of homes have two tanks hidden away in the loft. The smaller one serves the central heating system and the larger is usually a reserve of cold water for both the hot and some of the cold water down below at the taps. Only where your home has a mains-supplied system such as a combination boiler or modern pressurised unvented cylinder will lofts normally be free of tanks.

Hot water cylinders normally reside in airing cupboards, except in homes where they've been made redundant by combination boilers. If you have a modern pressurised cylinder (typically of a large white steel type) it won't need insulating. However, most homes have a conventional copper hot water cylinder that's ready-insulated, encased in a greeny-yellow foam finish. Older cylinders (dating back 25 years or more) tend to have an insulation jacket (usually red) with parts of the copper body visible. Fitting an extra jacket on top is a worthwhile exercise. Try two 60mm or 80mm jackets on top of each other. Even foam-insulated tanks can benefit from being decked out with additional insulation.

As with pipework, if cold water storage tanks in lofts are left naked, they can be prone to freezing in winter. And preventing the consequent risk of 230 litres or more of water cascading through your ceiling is a pretty good reason for spending a few quid on lagging. But there's another worthwhile benefit – water in un-insulated tanks can reach 30° in summer, which is an ideal temperature for bacteria to start growing. Most of these will be

harmless but it's not generally a good idea to bathe in or drink bacteria-ridden water. However, the main reason why kids are admonished with parental warnings not to drink out of the hot water tap can be seen by taking a look inside the water storage tank. Accumulated limescale, dust and grime – even decomposing pigeons aren't unknown, hence the importance of tanks having firmly fitted lids.

Most storage tanks do have a certain amount of 'lagging' draped over them, usually comprising anything that happened to be at hand last time someone was up in the loft, such as offcuts of carpets, bin bags full of old clothes and assorted bits of polystyrene packaging. This isn't a particularly efficient way of insulating the tank's contents – the stored water that you want to keep cool and clean. The best advice is to strip this away and insulate it properly. If it turns out your tank is made of galvanised steel or asbestos cement it's probably at least 50 years old and the best advice is to replace it.

Fortunately, the vast majority of tanks are of standard-issue black plastic (some older tanks are of grey fibreglass), for which you can buy purpose-made kits.

These kits are called the 'Byelaw 30 kit' (aka 'Regulation 16 kit') and comprise an insulation jacket, a rubber seal and insect-proof

filters. Importantly, a close-fitting lid is also included, but you need to specify one of the right size to fit your tank, so before ordering check the label on the tank or measure its length, height and width.

Eagle-eyed readers will recall that back in Chapter 5 we questioned the conventional wisdom of leaving the area beneath tanks un-insulated, preferring instead to insulate the underside of the tank or deck. This a golden opportunity to make such improvements. And while you're at it, unless the deck is of robust plywood (minimum 19mm thick) and well supported on at least three chunky-looking bearers, it's likely to need some improvement.

Once your tank's been fully insulated with a firmly fitted lid, the water within should be safely protected from the twin hazards of contamination and freezing weather.

Thanks to Andy Blackwell for contributing key information and many of the photos for this chapter.

Detailed professional advice on all aspects of plumbing can be found in The Haynes Home Plumbing Manual.

INSULATING STORAGE TANKS

Tools and materials

- Adjustable spanner
- Drill
- Hole-sawing kit
- Craft knife
- Duct tape
- Marker pen

FITTING A TANK INSULATION KIT

1 First clear away any clutter until you have a lidless and insulation-free tank. Check the tank is stable and leak-free and check the condition of the ball valve and overflow pipe. If the water is dirty and the tank is filled with sediment, drain down the tank and give it a good clean with fresh water and a sponge. Before refilling it with clean water check the condition of the deck and insulate underneath as described earlier.

2 Before fitting the new lid you need to cut two small holes in it – one for the vent pipe to poke through and another to let air in and out of the tank. The vent pipe can be found dipping down into the storage tank. It's usually copper and allows air to escape from the hot water system (in an emergency water gushes out). Mark this position on the new lid.

3 The vent pipe should pass through the lid into the tank, but not into the water. If it's too short it can be extended with a 22mm push-fit connector and a short length of extra pipe (plastic or copper). Once extended it should pass through the lid.

4 Your kit should include a rubber bung with a hole in it. This fits on the vent pipe as it passes through the lid and ensures an insect-proof seal. Measure the size of this bung

and select an appropriately sized drill-saw. Drill the hole for the vent pipe where you marked the lid.

5 Avoid getting any plastic shards and debris in the tank or it could block the pipework. Fit the bung by sliding it on to the vent pipe first with a dab of silicone grease, and then push it down into position when the lid's been fitted.

6 Now fit the air vent, which can go anywhere in the lid. Measure the base of the vent and drill a suitably sized hole. Push the vent into position. The lid can now be fitted to the tank. The vent pipe mustn't touch the water. Push down all the lid edges to ensure it's firmly in place.

7 Wrap the insulation jacket around the tank. Use a piece of duct tape to stick one end of the insulation to the tank, then pass the insulation around

the tank and use another piece of tape to secure it in place, like wrapping a parcel. Holes should be cut in the insulation to accommodate any pipes entering the tank, then use a bit of duct tape around the holes to keep everything in place.

8 Finally, insulation can be applied to the lid. Cut a small hole to accommodate the air vent and wrap the insulation around the vent pipe, secured with duct tape. Then seal the insulation on the lid to the insulation around the tank with duct tape.

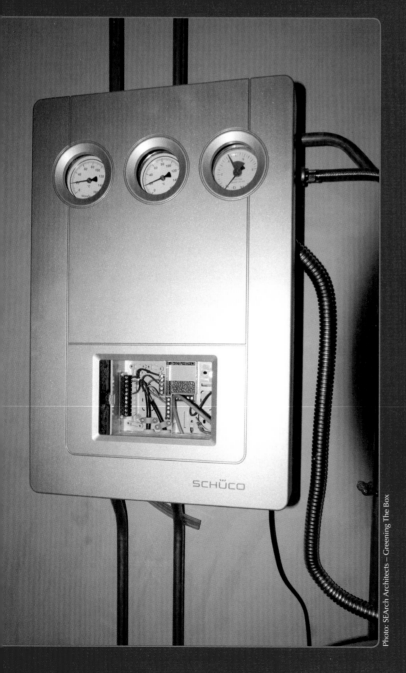

Home Insulation Manual

9 WHAT TO DO NEXT

Photo: SEArch Architects – Greening The Box

Warning: this is the stage when people can actually start to look forward to energy bills plopping through the letterbox. Sad though it may sound, as the benefit of all that hard graft in the preceding chapters starts to kick in, there's a certain pleasure in gloating over how much money you're denying the multinational power companies. But even with every nook and cranny in your home

GU10 – LED

Exterior LED –blue

LED downlighter

Sealed waterproof shower ceiling light

Photo: Uklightingdirect

Photo: wholesaleLEDlights

Photo: ightingstyles.co.uk

generously insulated, there are still a couple more 'easy wins' that nearly all households can take advantage of to reduce bills even further.

Although this book is primarily concerned with how best to insulate your home, the benefits of upgrading lighting and heating can be so substantial that it wouldn't be complete without showing how to go the extra mile to save energy.

Lighting

The lighting in your home can account for as much as a quarter of the total electricity used. So significant reductions in consumption can be achieved simply by swapping old-style bulbs for energy efficient replacements which use only about a quarter of the power. Conventional light bulbs actually generate more heat than light. In most cases high performance bulbs can be fitted straight into standard fittings without the need to replace the bulb holder, although some types of holder are designed to only accept low energy bulbs.

New bulbs and light fittings

It makes sense to install the most energy-efficient replacement bulbs possible. LED bulbs are the best option. Although relatively expensive to buy, they consume less energy than even compact

fluorescent (CF) bulbs and a fraction of the amount gobbled up by older halogen or incandescent bulbs. Although some types of eco-lighting are incompatible with dimmer switches, there are dimmable LED and compact fluorescent bulbs available.

Most CF bulbs take a couple of seconds to light and up to three minutes to attain full brightness, so they may not be suitable for locations such as staircases, where immediate full illumination is needed. They work best in areas where lights are left on for long periods.

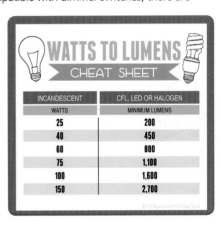

WATTS TO LUMENS CHEAT SHEET	
INCANDESCENT	CFL, LED OR HALOGEN
WATTS	MINIMUM LUMENS
25	200
40	450
60	800
75	1,100
100	1,600
150	2,700

2012 Apartment Therapy Tech

At the present time LED technology is advancing fast. The criticisms of some earlier bulbs have now been overcome, such as the light being 'too blue' or inconsistent in colour, or not being 're-lampable'. LEDs produce a negligible amount of heat and last much longer than other types, with lifespans of up to 50,000 hours – about 20 times longer than most conventional lights.

To achieve the maximum increase in the efficiency of your lighting, choose replacement bulbs rated at 55 lumens per Watt or higher. This is three times more efficient than conventional halogen or incandescent lighting, and on average should last at least three times as long, which helps justify the higher price.

BATHROOMS
When fitting new lighting to bathrooms or wet rooms, there are special safety provisions that need to be observed to prevent

possible electrical shock. Installing shower-proof fittings is recommended, since these are draughtproof and with LED lights installed consume minimal energy.

If you have an older electrical system then bear in mind that current Building Regulations require that no electrical fitting of any type should be touchable from where a person could be in contact with water at the same time, and should be located well away from any risk of shower spray. For obvious reasons no power sockets are permitted (other than shavers). Only specially protected, low voltage fittings can be installed and light switches should be of the pull cord type, or located to the landing/hall wall outside the bathroom door.

Old-style bulbs to replace
These are inefficient, with a short life, and should be replaced with LEDs or compact fluorescent units.

Type of bulb	Efficiency (lumens/Watt)	Typical bulb life/ hours
Incandescent	12–18	2,000
Halogen	12–19	3,000

New-style replacement bulbs

Type of bulb	Efficiency (lumens/ Watt)	Typical bulb life/ hours	Warm-up time	Dimmable?
LED	20–100	50,000	0 seconds	Yes
Select ones with at least 55 lumens, bulb life close to 50k hours and colour temperature of 3,000k.				
CFL compact fluorescent	50–75	10,000	Up to 3 minutes	Yes to 10%
Widely available in a range of sizes and styles, from spotlights to floodlights to chandeliers.				

(Source: SURE Insulation)

Heating

It obviously makes sense to invest in heating appliances that consume less power, but spending a lot of money on generating heat in a property that's leaky and poorly insulated is putting the cart before the horse. You can only reap the full benefit once your home is well insulated. To reduce the amount of energy consumed for space heating and for hot water you need to consider not just the boiler but also the hot water cylinder, the effectiveness of the controls, and even the optimum type of taps to minimise hot water usage.

A modern unvented hot water system with advanced programmable controls

Boilers

In recent years the efficiency of boilers has progressed enormously. All new domestic boilers are now of a 'condensing' type, which means they achieve efficiencies of around 90%. They're designed to extract as much heat as they can from the hot flue gases by using more than one heat exchanger. As a result, some of the water vapour in the exhaust gases condenses back into water before it can leave the end of the flue. This water runs back along the flue and down into the boiler before draining away via a little plastic pipe. Where there's no room to connect these to an indoor waste pipe they're sometimes run through an external wall into an outdoor drain. As we saw earlier, the risk of them freezing causing the boiler to shut down means condensate pipes should be insulated along with your hot and cold water supply pipework (see Chapter 8).

When selecting a new boiler, bear in mind that an oversized one will run less efficiently, so it's important to take into account improvements made insulating the property. Most new boilers are now of a relatively efficient 'A'-rated standard. To check your existing boiler visit **www.sedbuk.com**.

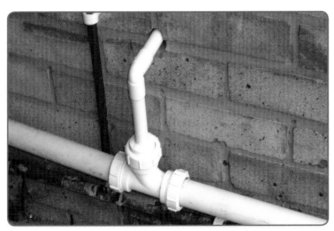

Condensate pipes to boilers are best run internally to prevent freezing – external runs must be lagged

Hot water cylinders

Tucked away in the airing cupboards of many homes there's a traditional copper hot water cylinder, concealed behind an insulation jacket or foam coating. In the last chapter we looked at how to boost insulation to such existing systems, but, if your budget can stretch to it, it may be worth replacing an old cylinder with a more efficient modern unvented one.

Either way, savings can be made simply by setting the hot water cylinder thermostat to 55°C, which should be sufficient if hot taps and shower are close enough to the cylinder. It also makes sense to fit more sophisticated controls with a seven-day programmer which will provide hot water at suitable times.

Heating controls

The aim of any heating system is to provide heat where there's a demand for it and avoid wasting money and energy where there isn't. For a household that's unoccupied during the day a simple timer or programmer which sets the heating to come on in the morning and again in the evening is essential to save energy. But more sophisticated programmable room thermostats and zoning controls allow different temperatures to be set depending on the level of occupation over a 24-hour period.

Intelligent weather compensators measure the temperature outside and learn how the heating system functions and self-adjust for greater efficiency. By predicting when the external temperature's likely to rise sufficiently to warm up the building it should be possible to shut off the boiler earlier with consequent savings.

The simplest and cheapest way to set different temperatures for each room is to fit thermostatic radiator valves (TRVs) to radiators. These can sense and deliver the correct amount of heat on a room-by-room basis. This is now standard practice for new systems.

After insulating and draughtproofing your home the heat demand should be much lower, so existing radiators may now be oversized, and fitting TRVs will help resolve this. But you need to be aware that if there's already a wall-mounted thermostat in a room a TRV shouldn't be installed in the same room. Also, if a TRV is fitted to every radiator it'll be necessary to fit an automatic bypass valve at the boiler (unless it already has one internally).

Underfloor heating (UFH)

Warm air rises, so the most efficient means of delivering heat to a room is from the floor upwards. Whereas radiators need to be at a high temperature to radiate and convect heat to all corners of a room, underfloor heating can be run at lower temperatures for the same degree of thermal comfort. This means the boiler can operate more efficiently, saving money and energy. Warm water systems are normally run through plastic pipes laid in floor screeds or in special insulation boards, and are compatible with solar hot water systems. Alternatively, electric UFH systems can be installed. These take the form of very thin fabric mats containing electrical elements. Although these are easier to retro-fit they're more expensive to run and best suited to smaller areas such as cloakrooms.

Future generation

With your home now a snug bastion of thermal efficiency, hopefully this Haynes Manual will have paid for itself several times over. It may even have played a part in alerting you to potentially dubious, sales-driven advice, or preventing rogue installers carrying out inappropriate works. Either way, as the proud owner of a 'superhome' you may now be wondering whether there are any

worthwhile projects left to tackle. If so, one thing that might appeal is the idea of energy companies paying you large sums of money for generating your own renewable energy. This is where the Haynes' *Eco House Manual* can come in useful, even showing you how to harvest rainwater and amaze your friends with composting toilets and eco-friendly reed bed waste systems.

Glossary

BBA	British Board of Agreement.
BFRC	British Fenestration Rating Council.
BISF	British Iron & Steel Federation.
BRE	Building Research Establishment
CIGA	Cavity Insulation Guarantee Agency.
CWGA	Cavity Wall Guarantee Agency.
CWI	Cavity wall insulation.
DPC	Damp-proof course.
DPM	Damp-proof membrane.
ECO	Energy Company Obligation.
EPC	Energy Performance Certificate.
EPDM	Ethylene propylene diene monomer.
EPS	Expanded polystyrene.
EWI	External wall insulation.
FENSA	Fenestration Self-Assessment.
g-value	Measurement of solar transmission through glass.
HRV	Heat recovery ventilation.
INCA	Insulated Render and Cladding Association.
IWI	Internal wall insulation.
LESA	Landlords' Energy Saving Allowance.
MEV	Mechanical extract ventilation.
OSB	Oriented strand board.
PF	Phenolic foam.

PIR	Polyisocyanurate.
PMCR	Polymer-modified cement render.
PRC	Pre-reinforced concrete.
PSV	Passive stack ventilation.
PUR	Polyurethane foam.
R-value	Measure of a material's ability to resist the transfer of heat.
SAP	Standard Assessment Procedure.
SWIGA	Solid Wall Insulation Guarantee Agency.
UF	Urea-formaldehyde foam.
UFH	Underfloor heating.
U-value	Measure of the rate at which heat is transmitted through $1m^2$ of a structure, where the temperature difference between the inner and outer face is 1°C.
VIP	Vacuum insulation panel.
WER	Window Energy Rating.
W/(l/s)	Measurement of fan power: Watts per litre per second of extracted air.
W/m²K	Measurement of insulation: Watts per square metre of surface area assuming a temperature difference of 1°C per metre of thickness.
XPE	Extruded polyethylene.
XPS	Extruded polystyrene.